# ברכון מסורת הרב

The Mesorat HaRav Birkon

קורן ירושלים

OUPRESS

## Note on the Cover Design

Adorning the back cover is the image of a small nightingale, one of the most musical of all songbirds. This artistic motif is an allusion to the Soloveitchik family name, which in Russian means "little nightingale." The Soloveitchik family are Levites, and legend has it that the origin of the name harks back to the family's sacred role as Levites in the Beit HaMikdash, gracing the service with song that accompanied the *korbanot*.

THE WINTMAN EDITION

# ברכון מסורת הרב
# THE MESORAT HARAV BIRKON

WITH COMMENTARY
BASED ON THE TEACHINGS
OF

Rabbi Joseph B. Soloveitchik

EDITED BY

Rabbi David Hellman

MATERIAL FOR COMMENTARY COMPILED BY

Rabbi Daniel Besser

•

OU PRESS
KOREN PUBLISHERS JERUSALEM

The Mesorat HaRav Birkon
The Wintman Edition, 2016

OU Press, an imprint of the Orthodox Union (hereafter "OU")
11 Broadway, New York, NY 10004
www.oupress.org



Koren Publishers Jerusalem Ltd.
POB 4044, Jerusalem 9104001, ISRAEL
POB 8531, New Milford, CT 06776, USA

www.korenpub.com



Printed in the United States of America

Standard Size, Hardcover, ISBN 978-965-301-856-3

BMHR1

*This Birkon*
*is lovingly dedicated*
*to the memory of our parents*

**Abraham and Sylvia Wintman**
**אברהם צבי בן יצחק חיים**
**שרה בלומא בת קלמן מרדכי הכהן**

*Our parents' lives together*
*devoted to family, community, and Klal Yisrael,*
*and the especially close relationship*
*our parents maintained with the Rav,*
*have been a wellspring of inspiration*
*to our entire family*

**Kenny Wintman and Sandy Welkes**

## THE WINTMAN FAMILY AND THE RAV: A UNIQUE RELATIONSHIP

Abraham and Sylvia Wintman had a unique relationship with Rabbi Joseph B. Soloveitchik, the Rav. The Wintmans' friendship with the Rav was well known, a friendship demonstrated by the numerous family photographs of the Rav together with the Wintmans – the Rav holding their daughter Sandy on his lap, relaxing with Abe and Sylvia in Onset, Massachusetts, and attending their son Kenny's high school graduation from the Maimonides School. The Wintman family's warm relationship with the Rav dates back to the 1940s, when Abe took it upon himself to serve as the Rav's personal driver. Coming from his home in Malden, Massachusetts, Abe would drive the Rav each week from his residence in Brookline to the Boston airport for the Rav's trip to Yeshiva University in New York, and Abe would pick the Rav up from the airport upon his return to Boston. Abe referred to his car as his "yeshiva on wheels," because of the education he received while driving the Rav. This service earned Abe Wintman the Rav's enduring friendship, and both Abe and Sylvia entered the small circle of the Rav's trusted confidants.

When their son Kenny was a student in Yeshiva University, he continued this tradition of personal service to the Rav, acting as the Rav's "*shammash*," or personal assistant, which meant shopping and running errands for the Rav, as well as arranging the Rav's schedule of appointments. This position enabled Kenny to encounter many of the dignitaries who sought to meet with the Rav, including Israel's then Chief Rabbi Shlomo Goren. Yeshiva University's student newspaper, *The Commentator*, aptly characterized Kenny's relationship with the Rav: "Of the many who say they know Rabbi Joseph Soloveitchik, Kenny is one of the few who can say that the Rav is a life-long friend."

Abe and Sylvia Wintman, staunch members of the Jewish community in the greater Boston area, served in a multitude of Jewish communal positions over the course of their lives. Abe served as president of the Young Israel of Mattapan, of the New England Council of Young Israel, and of the summer shul at Old Orchard Beach, Maine. He was a director of Congregation Beth Israel in Malden, the Malden Hebrew School and the former Beth Jacob Academy/North Shore Hebrew Day School, and was

◂ an active

an active member of the American Jewish Congress Administrative Committee. Sylvia served as a volunteer library assistant at the Maimonides School, and was a life member and National Board member of the UOJCA Women's Branch, and a life member of Amit Women, Yeshiva University Women, the Malden Hebrew School, and Congregation Beth Israel, where she served as Sisterhood president. She often polished the silver for the Sifrei Torah at the Young Israel of Malden and worked on the sanctuary tapestries with the women of the Young Israel of Brookline.

But this partial list of communal activities and involvements, while historically accurate, does not come close to capturing the kind of people Abe and Sylvia Wintman were. Their sensitivity in dealing with others, the depth of their commitment to Yiddishkeit, their boundless dedication to family, friends, and community, were clear to all. Abe, the perennial gabbai at Congregation Beth Israel of Malden, was known for his ability to handle the most difficult situations with tact, diplomacy, and consideration, while making it look so easy. He had an uncanny ability to relate to each Jew at his own level. Sylvia, a gracious and elegant homemaker, was the selfless caretaker of her family.

The Rav had a feel for people and their genuine worth and could tell what they were like beneath the surface. His warm relationship with the Wintmans undoubtedly stemmed from the Rav's sense of their true nature. They were modest and unassuming to all who knew them, model communal servants and solid family people to be sure. But there are many among us who fit that description. There must have been some other dimension to Abe and Sylvia that made the Rav feel so comfortable with them. The Rav must have perceived another quality hidden beneath the surface that may not have been apparent to other people but which the Rav saw very clearly – an extraordinary nobility of character and saintliness of spirit so rare, so outstanding, and so remarkable that led the Rav, the towering intellectual and religious giant, to seek their friendship, camaraderie, and company. How appropriate it is that this *Birkon*, a book of blessings combined with the Rav's profound commentary, graces the memory of Abe and Sylvia Wintman.

# CONTENTS



**Note to the Reader**

For essays on Rabbi Soloveitchik's conceptual understanding of Birkat HaMazon, Zimmun, and Kiddush, turn to the other end of this volume.

## PREFACE

OU Press is proud to present, together with Koren Publishers Jerusalem, the *Mesorat HaRav Birkon*. The Birkon is a unique book. After all, what is it about eating a meal that requires a book of its own? Is not eating a biological necessity shared by man and animal alike? To eat, according to the ancient Greeks, was to engage in a shameful necessity, and as such it is best performed privately, in seclusion. Yet Judaism takes a different view of the meal – eating a meal embodies not mere necessity, but the possibility of achieving holiness. "In the eyes of the *halakha*," the Rav explained in his work *Festival of Freedom*, "the meal is not something incidental, meaningless, and completely mechanical … The meal is more than this – it is a halakhic institution."

The Jewish perspective, as the Rav noted, is rooted in the Ḥumash: "And Aaron came and all the elders of Israel to eat bread with Moses' father-in-law before God" (Ex. 18:12). "There you shall eat before the Lord your God" (Deut. 12:7). In these and other verses, eating is elevated from a mere biological function to an experience which takes place "before God." But how does this transformation occur?

*Halakha*, in the Rav's analysis, transforms eating by means of "a new institution, the *se'uda*. It is neither an ordinary meal nor a feast; it is more than that … The realization of the idea of *se'uda* can occur only when man eats differently than the animal, when he displays uniqueness even with regard to the physiological processes in which he must engage in order to satisfy the demands of his body." Through the *se'uda*, a new community is formed with a collective and elevated purpose. "The *halakha* is aware of the fact that a meal partaken together unites people, fosters friendship, and fashions a company of eaters that may, in the long run, become a community of God-seekers and the God-committed."

For the Rav, the concept of *zimmun*, in which three people eating together form a *ḥabura*, or unit, for the collective recitation of *Birkat HaMazon*, represents the ideal of community formed through the *se'uda*. In the *zimmun*, we find a halakhic illustration of the *ḥabura*'s attainment of a unified goal. (See the essay "The *Zimmun*: Eating Together, Blessing God as a Community" in this volume.) But another manifestation of this concept relates to Torah study, as found in the Mishna (*Avot* 3:4):

◂ Rabbi Shimon

> Rabbi Shimon says: Three who ate at one table and did not recite upon it words of Torah, it is as if they ate from the offerings to the dead [i.e., idolatrous sacrifice] … But three who ate at one table and recited upon it words of Torah, it is as if they have eaten from the table of God, as it says, "This is the table that is before the LORD." (Ez. 41:22)

Just as three people who eat together form a *ḥabura* for the purpose of reciting *Birkat HaMazon* collectively, they likewise form a *ḥabura* for the purpose of collective Torah study (see Rabbenu Yona on *Avot, ibid.*). This creates an obligation to transform their meal into a *se'uda,* to endow the meal with a covenantal dimension through Torah study. In the absence of *divrei Torah,* the meal remains an unredeemed and hedonistic exercise. Conversely, the discussion of *divrei Torah* at a meal transforms the table upon which it is eaten to the table of God, and the meal to a *se'uda lifnei Hashem.*

This concept may also explain a perplexing passage in the Talmud Yerushalmi. The Yerushalmi (*Berakhot* 7:1) cites a dispute about whether two people can form an optional *zimmun,* and then equates it to the question of whether two people, instead of three, suffice to form a *beit din.* At first glance, it is difficult to discern any connection between these two disparate areas of *halakha.* (See the Rav's commentary, p. 131.)

However, in light of the above, we can explain the Yerushalmi's equation. The *ḥabura* formed by a meal of three also creates a forum for the discussion and clarification of *divrei Torah.* If two people can establish the *ḥabura* necessary for *zimmun,* then with regard to Torah study as well, two people can establish the forum for Torah discussion which is necessary for a *beit din.* Far from representing two remote areas, the laws of *se'uda* and of *beit din* are closely connected – both revolve around an exchange and debate of *divrei Torah.* The *se'uda,* like the *beit din,* is a community formed for the purpose of attaining greater Torah understanding.

Many individuals were involved in the production of this Birkon. My son-in-law Rabbi Daniel Besser initially compiled the material for the commentary. Rabbi David Hellman edited the commentary and compiled the essays in this volume. Dr. Joel B. Wolowelsky was a primary impetus for bringing this project into being, and has generously given his assistance and advice throughout its stages of development. Within

OU Press I would like to acknowledge the capable work of my colleagues Rabbi Simon Posner, Rabbi David Bashevkin, Yocheved Goldberg, Eliyahu Krakowski, and Rivki Rosenblatt. I would also like to acknowledge the work of Koren Publishers Jerusalem, under the able leadership of Matthew Miller, and a special thanks to Dena Landowne Bailey, Tani Bayer, and Esther Be'er.

This Birkon with the Rav's profound commentary is a fitting tribute to the lives of Abraham and Sylvia Wintman, lovingly dedicated by their children, Kenny and Sandy. I remember Mr. and Mrs. Wintman's devotion to the Rav from the time I spent with the Rav in Boston, as well as the Rav's fondness and affection for Kenny and Sandy. The Rav explained that the meal allows us to enter into a dialogue with the generations:

> In Judaism, the covenant expresses the idea of historical comradeship and unity, of the metaphysical congregation of the members of our faith of all times: those living, those who have passed on, and those yet unborn. The covenant is always established through a meal. The latter symbolizes and celebrates the fellowship of generations, of past, present, and future, the relatedness of the single person to a community stretching beyond the boundaries of his transient existence.

May the Rav's *divrei Torah* contained in this Birkon serve to carry on the memory of Abraham and Sylvia Wintman for generations to come.

Menachem Dov Genack
General Editor, OU Press

The Rav remarked that his grandfather, Rav Ḥayyim Soloveitchik, revolutionized the halakhic realm of *Yoreh De'ah,* transforming it from a collection of laws governing pots and pans into a sophisticated world of halakhic concepts and principles. In a similar vein, the Rav took our corpus of prayers and blessings and breathed life into them, taking what many see as nothing more than formulas to be recited at various occasions, and demonstrating their precise halakhic definitions and the profound religious beliefs that they express. For example, the Rav uncovered within the single blessing of Kiddush three distinct purposes: the sanctification of Shabbat, praise of the day, and establishing the meals as fulfillments of *oneg Shabbat.* He uncovered, and brought into sharp focus, the distinction between the individual's recitation of *Birkat HaMazon* and the performance of the group, the *ḥabura,* which offers a single, unified blessing. In these cases and in so many more, the Rav explained which concepts are derived from the Torah and which were instituted by the Rabbis; he demonstrated what ideas are common to all blessings and what distinguishes different categories. Moreover, he went beyond conceptual analysis and expounded upon the language of the blessings, their philosophical meaning, and their relevance to our religious lives. After studying the Rav's analysis of *Birkat HaMazon,* Kiddush, Havdala, and other blessings, it is impossible not to recite them with greater intensity, inspiration, and appreciation of their meaning.

In preparing the commentary for this Birkon and its accompanying essays, I read the lectures of the Rav that examine these blessings and prayers in all of their halakhic and hashkafic aspects. I had never studied so intensely the powerful and profound ideas of the Rav, and as I delved into them, those published by the Rav himself and those recorded by his students, I started to perceive patterns in his thought, central ideas appearing and reappearing in different contexts, and even phrases and formulations that he would often employ. I became absorbed in the world of the Rav's interrelated ideas and I began to feel his approach becoming integrated into my own thinking. I started to see myself as, dare I say, a *talmid* of the Rav, and not merely a student of his students. I experienced

◀ a "merging

a "merging of generations," to use a phrase of the Rav, and even after I would finish listening to a recording of the Rav delivering a lecture, I would continue to hear the voice of the Rav in my head, both literally and figuratively. Now, when I read one of his works, I am not merely reading words printed on a page, but I can imagine the Rav speaking those words. I am now able to detect the Rav's voice, one of his ideas, or a turn of phrase that he would use, echoing in the words of my own illustrious teachers even when they are not directly quoting or referencing him. Through absorbing his ideas, I feel connected and indebted to the Rav, and in that way linked to his teachers and to the entire *mesorah* that he magnificently transmitted. I humbly hope that this Birkon will allow many others to hear the majestic, soaring voice of the Rav teaching and explaining the ideas contained in these pages, even if they did not, as I did not, hear the Rav speak in his lifetime.

While most of the commentary and essays are sourced to published material, they are not necessarily exact quotes. Hebrew sources were obviously translated, but even English works sometimes had to be condensed or modified to fit the format of this commentary. The Rav developed his thoughts at great length to flesh out their full import; it was not always possible, however, to reproduce his ideas in full in a work like this that requires shorter presentations. Thus, I encourage anyone who finds a particular idea intriguing to look up the original source to see it in context and in its full presentation. For the essays, I combined several sources where the Rav explained related ideas in different contexts, and I organized the material into its present form. It is a very serious responsibility to present the Torah ideas of a giant such as the Rav. I have endeavored to be as accurate as possible, but if there are any mistakes or inaccuracies the fault is entirely mine.

I must express my sincere appreciation to Rabbi Menachem Genack, General Editor of OU Press, for inviting me to work on this project and granting me the opportunity to study and disseminate the ideas of the Rav. I similarly thank Rabbi Simon Posner and Eliyahu Krakowski and the entire team at OU Press as well as Mathew Miller and Koren Publishers Jerusalem for their work on this project. It is especially meaningful to me that this Birkon is being sponsored by my good friend, Kenny Wintman, and his sister, Sandy Welkes, in memory of their parents, Abraham and

◂ Sylvia Wintman

Sylvia Wintman, who were close friends of the Rav. Kenny has shared with me so many stories of his own interactions with the Rav and I have learned greatly from them.

I take this opportunity to thank my parents and parents-in-law for their constant love and for everything that they do for us. We know that your greatest joy is to see us happy. Finally, I express my unending gratitude to my wife, Ariella, who always places our family's needs before her own. Any success or accomplishment that I have is due to her encouragement, support, and advice. I pray that Hashem should grant us the ability to raise all of our children to have *yirat shamayim* and *midot tovot* and find joy in the service of Hashem and the study of His Torah.

David Hellman
Brookline, Massachusetts
May, 2016

# ברכון מסורת הרב

# THE MESORAT HARAV BIRKON

# ליל שבת
# SHABBAT EVENING

## THE ESSENCE OF SHABBAT EVE

There are times when we can sense the Almighty's presence residing within this world. We see the Creator in the twinkling star, the rush of the tide, in every phenomenon which has been explained to us or which science does not understand and will never understand. However, sometimes God reveals himself from beyond the universe, from his transcendental abode. According to Naḥmanides, the verse "לְשִׁכְנוֹ תִדְרְשׁוּ וּבָאתָ שָּׁמָּה, and you shall seek out His dwelling place and there you shall go" (Deut. 12:5), alludes to discovering God in both of His modes of revelation. First, man must seek out God in this world; he must see God in every sip of water and every bite of fruit. God's presence within all natural phenomena is what the Rabbis call the *Shekhina*, and, Naḥmanides explains, the term is based on the wording of this verse. However, if a person will come to the realization that God is present in every experience within this world, he will not stop there. As the verse continues, "and there you shall go" – the one in search of God will go "there," a little further, and he will confront the Almighty who reveals His transcendental glory from outside and beyond this world.

Shabbat evening is dedicated to the first stage in the revelation of God, to the *Shekhina*, to finding the Divine Presence which is manifest in nature. The Amida of Shabbat eve revolves around creation ("You sanctified the seventh day for Your name's sake, as the culmination of the creation of heaven and earth"), and we also include the passage describing Shabbat Bereishit, "וַיְכֻלּוּ הַשָּׁמַיִם וְהָאָרֶץ, The heavens and the earth were completed," in both the evening Amida and Kiddush. At this time, we focus upon Shabbat as *zekher lema'aseh bereishit*, a commemoration of creation, and in creation we see traces of the Creator. However, this leads to the experience of seeing God from beyond the universe, which, in turn, is the theme of Shabbat day. The Amida of Shabbat morning is not focused on Shabbat Bereishit, but rather evokes the revelation of Sinai in which God's transcendental existence was made manifest in this world. (*Derashot HaRav*, pp. 38–39)

### PREPARING FOR SHABBAT

In defining the concept of *kevod Shabbat*, Maimonides (*Hilkhot Shabbat* 30:2) presents as the primary obligation that one should "wash his face, hands and feet in hot water… wrap himself in *tzitzit*, and solemnly anticipate greeting

# Candle Lighting

*On Erev Shabbat that is not a Yom Tov, cover the eyes with the hands after lighting the candles, and say:*

בָּרוּךְ Blessed are You, Lord our God, King of the Universe,
who has made us holy through His commandments,
and has commanded us to light the Sabbath light.

*On Erev Yom Tov, say the following blessing and then light the candles from an existing flame. If also Shabbat, cover the eyes with the hands after lighting the candles and say the following blessing, adding the words in parentheses.*

בָּרוּךְ Blessed are You, Lord our God, King of the Universe,
who has made us holy through His commandments,
and has commanded us to light (the Sabbath light and)
the festival light.

*The blessing "Sheheḥeyanu" ("Who has given life") is said on Yom Tov evenings, except on the last two evenings of Pesaḥ. (In Israel, it is not said on the last evening of Pesaḥ.)*

בָּרוּךְ Blessed are You, Lord our God, King of the Universe,
who has given us life, sustained us, and brought us to this time.

*On Erev Yom Kippur, cover the eyes with the hands after lighting the candles, and say (on Shabbat add the words in parentheses):*

בָּרוּךְ Blessed are You, Lord our God, King of the Universe,
who has made us holy through His commandments,
and has commanded us to light (the Sabbath light and)
the light of the Day of Atonement.

בָּרוּךְ Blessed are You, Lord our God, King of the Universe,
who has given us life, sustained us, and brought us to this time.

---

to prepare ourselves to greet the divine presence just as we would prepare for prayer. The essence of *kevod Shabbat* is to ready ourselves for an encounter with the Divine, to await with awe the coming of the King of Kings. (*Shiurim LeZekher Abba Mari*, vol. 1, pp. 76–77)

CANDLE LIGHTING ON SHABBAT AND YOM TOV
Based on the verse in Isaiah (58:13), "וְקָרָאתָ לַשַּׁבָּת עֹנֶג לִקְדוֹשׁ יהוה מְכֻבָּד, Call the Sabbath a delight, honored, holy for the Lord," *Ḥazal* delineated two

# הדלקת נרות

*On* ערב שבת *that is not a* יום טוב*, cover the eyes with the hands after lighting the candles, and say:*

בָּרוּךְ אַתָּה יהוה אֱלֹהֵינוּ מֶלֶךְ הָעוֹלָם
אֲשֶׁר קִדְּשָׁנוּ בְּמִצְוֹתָיו וְצִוָּנוּ לְהַדְלִיק נֵר שֶׁל שַׁבָּת.

*On* ערב יום טוב*, say the following blessing and then light the candles from an existing flame. If also* שבת*, cover the eyes with the hands after lighting the candles and say the following blessing, adding the words in parentheses.*

בָּרוּךְ אַתָּה יהוה אֱלֹהֵינוּ מֶלֶךְ הָעוֹלָם
אֲשֶׁר קִדְּשָׁנוּ בְּמִצְוֹתָיו
וְצִוָּנוּ לְהַדְלִיק נֵר שֶׁל (שַׁבָּת וְשֶׁל) יוֹם טוֹב.

*The blessing* שֶׁהֶחֱיָנוּ *is said on* יום טוב *evenings, except on the last two evenings of* פסח*. (In* ארץ ישראל*, it is not said on the last evening of* פסח*.)*

בָּרוּךְ אַתָּה יהוה אֱלֹהֵינוּ מֶלֶךְ הָעוֹלָם
שֶׁהֶחֱיָנוּ וְקִיְּמָנוּ, וְהִגִּיעָנוּ לַזְּמַן הַזֶּה.

*On* ערב יום כיפור*, cover the eyes with the hands after lighting the candles, and say (on* שבת *add the words in parentheses):*

בָּרוּךְ אַתָּה יהוה אֱלֹהֵינוּ מֶלֶךְ הָעוֹלָם
אֲשֶׁר קִדְּשָׁנוּ בְּמִצְוֹתָיו
וְצִוָּנוּ לְהַדְלִיק נֵר שֶׁל (שַׁבָּת וְשֶׁל) יוֹם הַכִּפּוּרִים.

בָּרוּךְ אַתָּה יהוה אֱלֹהֵינוּ מֶלֶךְ הָעוֹלָם
שֶׁהֶחֱיָנוּ וְקִיְּמָנוּ, וְהִגִּיעָנוּ לַזְּמַן הַזֶּה.

---

the presence of Shabbat, as one goes out to greet the king." Strikingly, this group of preparations parallels exactly the preparations that Maimonides requires before prayer (see *Hilkhot Tefilla* 3:3, 4:17, and *Hilkhot Tzitzit* 3:11). Both Shabbat and prayer are encounters with God, both are moments when we stand before the Almighty. Thus the primary *mitzva* of *kevod Shabbat* is

*Some add:*

יְהִי May it be Your will, LORD our God and God of our ancestors, that the Temple be speedily rebuilt in our days, and grant us our share in Your Torah. And may we serve You there in reverence, as in the days of old and as in former years. *Mal. 3*

*Prayer after candlelighting (add the words in parentheses as appropriate):*

יְהִי May it be Your will, LORD my God and God of my forebears, that You give me grace – me (and my husband/and my father/and my mother/and my sons and my daughters) and all those close to me, and give us and all Israel good and long lives. And remember us with a memory that brings goodness and blessing; come to us with compassion and bless us with great blessings. Build our homes until they are complete, and allow Your Presence to live among us. And may I merit to raise children and grandchildren, each one wise and understanding, loving the LORD and in awe of God, people of truth, holy children, who will cling on to the LORD and light up the world with Torah and with good actions, and with all the kinds of work that serve the Creator. Please, hear my pleading at this time, by the merit of Sarah and Rebecca, Rachel and Leah our mothers, and light our candle that it should never go out, and light up Your face, so that we shall be saved, Amen.

---

includes that which we do and enjoy on Shabbat itself to distinguish it from the rest of the week. In accordance with the Vilna Gaon's definition, the *Beit HaLevi* (*Teshuvot* 1:11) explains that lighting the Shabbat candles is a double fulfillment, an expression of both *kavod* and *oneg Shabbat*. Lighting the candles on Friday afternoon in preparation and expectation for the onset of Shabbat is an act of *kevod Shabbat*, while enjoying the illumination of the candles which fills the home on Shabbat evening is a form of *oneg Shabbat*. Accordingly, it is preferable to light candles before sunset on the eve of Yom Tov, even though it would be permissible to light them on Yom Tov from a preexisting flame, because lighting the candles after sunset would fulfill only the element of *oneg*, by providing light for the Yom Tov meal. However, by lighting the candles before Yom Tov we also demonstrate our anticipation for the day, which is the essence of the *mitzva* of *kavod*. (*MiPeninei HaRav*, p. 76; *Divrei HaRav*, p. 173; *Noraos HaRav*, vol. 2, p. 76)

*Some add:*

יְהִי רָצוֹן מִלְּפָנֶיךָ יהוה אֱלֹהֵינוּ וֵאלֹהֵי אֲבוֹתֵינוּ, שֶׁיִּבָּנֶה בֵּית הַמִּקְדָּשׁ בִּמְהֵרָה בְיָמֵינוּ, וְתֵן חֶלְקֵנוּ בְּתוֹרָתֶךָ, וְשָׁם נַעֲבָדְךָ בְּיִרְאָה כִּימֵי עוֹלָם וּכְשָׁנִים קַדְמֹנִיּוֹת. וְעָרְבָה לַיהוה מִנְחַת יְהוּדָה וִירוּשָׁלָםִ כִּימֵי עוֹלָם וּכְשָׁנִים קַדְמֹנִיּוֹת: מלאכי ג

*Prayer after candlelighting (add the words in parentheses as appropriate):*

יְהִי רָצוֹן מִלְּפָנֶיךָ יהוה אֱלֹהַי וֵאלֹהֵי אֲבוֹתַי, שֶׁתְּחוֹנֵן אוֹתִי (וְאֶת אִישִׁי/ וְאֶת אָבִי/ וְאֶת אִמִּי/ וְאֶת בָּנַי וְאֶת בְּנוֹתַי) וְאֶת כָּל קְרוֹבַי, וְתִתֶּן לָנוּ וּלְכָל יִשְׂרָאֵל חַיִּים טוֹבִים וַאֲרֻכִּים, וְתִזְכְּרֵנוּ בְּזִכְרוֹן טוֹבָה וּבְרָכָה, וְתִפְקְדֵנוּ בִּפְקֻדַּת יְשׁוּעָה וְרַחֲמִים, וּתְבָרְכֵנוּ בְּרָכוֹת גְּדוֹלוֹת, וְתַשְׁלִים בָּתֵּינוּ וְתַשְׁכֵּן שְׁכִינָתְךָ בֵּינֵינוּ. וְזַכֵּנִי לְגַדֵּל בָּנִים וּבְנֵי בָנִים חֲכָמִים וּנְבוֹנִים, אוֹהֲבֵי יהוה יִרְאֵי אֱלֹהִים, אַנְשֵׁי אֱמֶת זֶרַע קֹדֶשׁ, בַּיהוה דְּבֵקִים וּמְאִירִים אֶת הָעוֹלָם בַּתּוֹרָה וּבְמַעֲשִׂים טוֹבִים וּבְכָל מְלֶאכֶת עֲבוֹדַת הַבּוֹרֵא. אָנָּא שְׁמַע אֶת תְּחִנָּתִי בָּעֵת הַזֹּאת בִּזְכוּת שָׂרָה וְרִבְקָה וְרָחֵל וְלֵאָה אִמּוֹתֵינוּ, וְהָאֵר נֵרֵנוּ שֶׁלֹּא יִכְבֶּה לְעוֹלָם וָעֶד, וְהָאֵר פָּנֶיךָ וְנִוָּשֵׁעָה. אָמֵן.

---

distinct obligations: *kevod Shabbat,* to honor the day of the Sabbath, and *oneg Shabbat,* to fill the day with pleasure and delight. Specifically, Maimonides writes (*Hilkhot Shabbat* 30:2–3, 7) that the *mitzva* of *kevod Shabbat* includes the obligation to bathe on Friday, put on special clothing in honor of the day, and to prepare the house and set the table. The *mitzva* of *oneg Shabbat,* he writes, is to indulge in delicacies that one does not regularly indulge in during the week. Some (see, e.g., *Arukh HaShulḥan, Oraḥ Ḥayyim* 263:4) understand that the fundamental distinction between *kavod* and *oneg* is that *kavod* incorporates the ways in which we honor Shabbat that don't provide bodily pleasure, while *oneg* incorporates the Shabbat activities that bring us physical contentment. The Vilna Gaon (*Biur HaGra, Oraḥ Ḥayyim* 529:5), however, distinguishes between these two obligations differently, based on when they are performed: *kavod* includes all actions done before the onset of Shabbat through which we demonstrate our eagerness for it to begin, while *oneg*

# Blessing the Children

*On the evenings of Shabbat and Yom Tov, many have the custom to bless their children.*

*To sons, say:*

יְשִׂמְךָ May God make you like Ephraim and Manasseh. *Gen. 48*

*To daughters, say:*

יְשִׂימֵךְ May God make you like Sarah, Rebecca, Rachel and Leah.

יְבָרֶכְךָ May the Lord bless you and protect you. *Num. 6*
May the Lord make His face shine on you
and be gracious to you.
May the Lord turn His face toward you
and grant you peace.

---

man's act of creation has not ended; on the contrary, it has just begun. The three-fold community of father, mother, and child, of I, thou, and he, is complete only through bringing up the child, providing him with moral values, and befriending him to his Maker. In the *aggada,* God Himself appears in the role of teacher, spending time every day instructing young children. Physical creation and sustenance of being are not enough. Only by helping children find themselves, by taking hold of their inherent aptitudes and acquainting them with the eternal verities which give man a sense of rootedness, is the creative gesture complete. Father and mother are not meant to be merely a procreative, natural community, but a creative, teaching fellowship that forms the child's spiritual personality, fosters his good qualities and sublimates his primitive desires. Parents find their existential fulfillment only through the creative act of teaching and educating a child. (*Family Redeemed,* pp. 39, 57–59)

# ברכת הבנים

*On* ליל שבת *and* ליל יום טוב*, many have the custom to bless their children.*

*To sons, say:*

בראשית מח
יְשִׂמְךָ אֱלֹהִים כְּאֶפְרַיִם וְכִמְנַשֶּׁה:

*To daughters, say:*

יְשִׂימֵךְ אֱלֹהִים כְּשָׂרָה רִבְקָה רָחֵל וְלֵאָה.

במדבר ו
יְבָרֶכְךָ יהוה וְיִשְׁמְרֶךָ:
יָאֵר יהוה פָּנָיו אֵלֶיךָ וִיחֻנֶּךָּ:
יִשָּׂא יהוה פָּנָיו אֵלֶיךָ וְיָשֵׂם לְךָ שָׁלוֹם:

---

BLESSING CHILDREN

The central Judaic ethical norm to walk in the footsteps of God obligates man to become a creator and bear a child. Just as God created a world in order to care, to sustain, and to love, so too must man. However, the Jewish mystics equated creation with a movement of recoil on the part of God; the Almighty, they said, sacrificed His all-inclusiveness, His all-consuming infinity, and retreated into transcendence in order to let a world emerge outside of Himself. Creation, accordingly, is sacrificial divine action. God retreated and left a void for the universe to fill. Similarly, the two lonely human beings who are driven to creativity by their yearning for giving and bestowing love engage in sacrificial action and offer everything they cherish for the sake of the new member; they fulfill Imitatio Dei by withdrawing from self-centered romanticism into a *ḥessed*-oriented community which binds man to a life yet unborn.

However, if man imitates God by creating life, this happens primarily in the field of spiritual, and not natural, life. With the physical birth of the child,

*Many people sing each of the four verses of the following song three times:*

שָׁלוֹם עֲלֵיכֶם Welcome, ministering angels, angels of the Most High,
from the Supreme King of kings,
the Holy One, blessed be He.

Enter in peace, angels of peace, angels of the Most High,
from the Supreme King of kings,
the Holy One, blessed be He.

Bless me with peace, angels of peace, angels of the Most High,
from the Supreme King of kings,
the Holy One, blessed be He.

Go in peace, angels of peace, angels of the Most High,
from the Supreme King of kings,
the Holy One, blessed be He.

כִּי מַלְאָכָיו He will command His angels about you, *Ps. 91*
to guard you in all your ways.
May the Lord guard your going out and your return, *Ps. 121*
from now and for all time.

---

the other direction: the *Shekhina* descends from heaven and comes to find us. Thus, the Kabbalists of Safed developed the concept of *kabbalat Shabbat*, the service in which we welcome and receive the *Shekhina*, the Shabbat Queen that enters the world of man. On Yom Tov, though, there is no such liturgical institution, for on Yom Tov it is man who leaves his regular life and places himself in the realm of God. Only on Shabbat does the divine presence pay us a visit in our world and becomes a guest in our home. Even before we usher in Shabbat with the recitation of Kiddush, we sing *Shalom Aleikhem* and welcome the *Shekhina* and angels who have come to join us. On Shabbat we celebrate the revelation of the *Shekhina* at our table; we sense the dwelling of the divine presence in our lives and within our families. Shabbat is to see God in this world, in every flower and every tree, in every drop of water and in every niche of the universe. (*Shiurim LeZekher Abba Mari*, vol. 1, pp. 81–83)

*Many people sing each of the four verses of the following song three times:*

שָׁלוֹם עֲלֵיכֶם מַלְאֲכֵי הַשָּׁרֵת, מַלְאֲכֵי עֶלְיוֹן
מִמֶּלֶךְ מַלְכֵי הַמְּלָכִים, הַקָּדוֹשׁ בָּרוּךְ הוּא.

בּוֹאֲכֶם לְשָׁלוֹם מַלְאֲכֵי הַשָּׁלוֹם, מַלְאֲכֵי עֶלְיוֹן
מִמֶּלֶךְ מַלְכֵי הַמְּלָכִים, הַקָּדוֹשׁ בָּרוּךְ הוּא.

בָּרְכוּנִי לְשָׁלוֹם מַלְאֲכֵי הַשָּׁלוֹם, מַלְאֲכֵי עֶלְיוֹן
מִמֶּלֶךְ מַלְכֵי הַמְּלָכִים, הַקָּדוֹשׁ בָּרוּךְ הוּא.

צֵאתְכֶם לְשָׁלוֹם מַלְאֲכֵי הַשָּׁלוֹם, מַלְאֲכֵי עֶלְיוֹן
מִמֶּלֶךְ מַלְכֵי הַמְּלָכִים, הַקָּדוֹשׁ בָּרוּךְ הוּא.

כִּי מַלְאָכָיו יְצַוֶּה־לָּךְ, לִשְׁמָרְךָ בְּכָל־דְּרָכֶיךָ: תהלים צא
יהוה יִשְׁמָר־צֵאתְךָ וּבוֹאֶךָ, מֵעַתָּה וְעַד־עוֹלָם: תהלים קכא

---

SHALOM ALEIKHEM

On both Shabbat and Yom Tov there is a rendezvous between Israel and the Almighty; however, there is a fundamental difference in the way we meet God on these days. On Yom Tov, the *Shekhina* does not leave her place; rather it is the Jew who must leave his home to encounter the Divine. In the days of the Temple, there was an obligation on the holidays to make the arduous journey, ascend to Jerusalem, and "appear before the LORD your God" (Deut. 16:16). Even today that is the religious experience of Yom Tov: we leave our regular lives behind and we enter the abode of the holy. This is why there is an obligation of *simḥa*, joy, on Yom Tov, for *simḥa* is associated with standing *lifnei Hashem*, in the presence of God, as the verse states, "And you shall rejoice before the LORD, your God." However, on Shabbat there is no obligation of *simḥa*, because on Shabbat we don't stand before God in His abode, rather the infinite chasm between us and our Creator is bridged from

*Some say:*

רִבּוֹן כָּל הָעוֹלָמִים Master of all worlds, LORD of all souls, LORD of peace, mighty, blessed and great King, King who speaks peace, King who is glorious, enduring and pure, King who gives life to worlds, King who is good and does good, King alone and unique, great King who robes Himself in compassion, King who reigns over all kings, who is exalted and supports those who fall, King who is Author of creation, who redeems and rescues, who is radiant and ruddy, King who is holy, high and exalted, King who hears prayer, King whose way is just: I thank You, LORD my God and God of my ancestors, for all the loving-kindness You have done and will do for me, and all the members of my household and all my fellow creatures. Blessed are Your angels, holy and pure, who do Your will. LORD of peace, King to whom peace belongs, bless me with peace, and grant me and the members of my household, and all Your people the house of Israel, a good and peaceful life. King exalted over all the heavenly array, who formed me and who formed creation, I entreat Your radiant presence, that You find me and all the members of my household worthy of grace and good favor in Your eyes and the eyes of all people and all who see us, that we may serve You. May we be worthy to receive Sabbaths amidst great joy, wealth and honor, and few sins. May You remove from me and all the members of my household and all Your people the house of Israel all sickness and disease, all poverty, hardship and destitution. Grant us a virtuous desire to serve You in truth, awe and love. May we find honor in Your eyes and the eyes of all who see us, for You are the King of honor: to You it belongs, to You it accords. Please, King who reigns over all kings, command Your angels, ministering angels who minister to the Most High, to act compassionately toward me when they enter my house on our holy day, for I have lit my lights, spread my couch and changed my clothes in honor of the Sabbath; I have come to Your House to lay my pleas before You that You remove my sighs; I have testified that in six days You created all things, and said it a second time, and will testify to it a third time over my cup, in joy, as You commanded me to remember it, delighting in the extra soul You have given me. On it [the Sabbath] I shall rest as You have commanded me, thereby to serve You. So too I will declare Your greatness in joyful song, for I have set the LORD before me, that You may have compassion upon me in my exile, redeeming me and awakening my heart to Your love. Then I will keep Your commands and statutes without sadness, praying correctly as is right and fitting. Angels of peace, come in peace and bless me with peace; declare blessed the table I have prepared, and go in peace, now and forever. Amen, Selah.

*Some say:*

רִבּוֹן כׇּל הָעוֹלָמִים, אֲדוֹן כׇּל הַנְּשָׁמוֹת, אֲדוֹן הַשָּׁלוֹם. מֶלֶךְ אַבִּיר, מֶלֶךְ בָּרוּךְ, מֶלֶךְ גָּדוֹל, מֶלֶךְ דּוֹבֵר שָׁלוֹם, מֶלֶךְ הָדוּר, מֶלֶךְ וָתִיק, מֶלֶךְ זַךְ, מֶלֶךְ חֵי הָעוֹלָמִים, מֶלֶךְ טוֹב וּמֵטִיב, מֶלֶךְ יָחִיד וּמְיֻחָד, מֶלֶךְ כַּבִּיר, מֶלֶךְ לוֹבֵשׁ רַחֲמִים, מֶלֶךְ מַלְכֵי הַמְּלָכִים, מֶלֶךְ נִשְׂגָּב, מֶלֶךְ סוֹמֵךְ נוֹפְלִים, מֶלֶךְ עֹשֶׂה מַעֲשֵׂה בְרֵאשִׁית, מֶלֶךְ פּוֹדֶה וּמַצִּיל, מֶלֶךְ צַח וְאָדֹם, מֶלֶךְ קָדוֹשׁ, מֶלֶךְ רָם וְנִשָּׂא, מֶלֶךְ שׁוֹמֵעַ תְּפִלָּה, מֶלֶךְ תָּמִים דַּרְכּוֹ. מוֹדֶה אֲנִי לְפָנֶיךָ, יהוה אֱלֹהַי וֵאלֹהֵי אֲבוֹתַי, עַל כׇּל הַחֶסֶד אֲשֶׁר עָשִׂיתָ עִמָּדִי וַאֲשֶׁר אַתָּה עָתִיד לַעֲשׂוֹת עִמִּי וְעִם כׇּל בְּנֵי בֵיתִי וְעִם כׇּל בְּרִיּוֹתֶיךָ, בְּנֵי בְרִיתִי. וּבְרוּכִים הֵם מַלְאָכֶיךָ הַקְּדוֹשִׁים וְהַטְּהוֹרִים שֶׁעוֹשִׂים רְצוֹנֶךָ. אֲדוֹן הַשָּׁלוֹם, מֶלֶךְ שֶׁהַשָּׁלוֹם שֶׁלּוֹ, בָּרְכֵנִי בַשָּׁלוֹם, וְתִפְקֹד אוֹתִי וְאֶת כׇּל בְּנֵי בֵיתִי וְכׇל עַמְּךָ בֵּית יִשְׂרָאֵל לְחַיִּים טוֹבִים וּלְשָׁלוֹם. מֶלֶךְ עֶלְיוֹן עַל כׇּל צְבָא מָרוֹם, יוֹצְרֵנוּ, יוֹצֵר בְּרֵאשִׁית, אֲחַלֶּה פָנֶיךָ הַמְּאִירִים, שֶׁתְּזַכֶּה אוֹתִי וְאֶת כׇּל בְּנֵי בֵיתִי לִמְצֹא חֵן וְשֵׂכֶל טוֹב בְּעֵינֶיךָ וּבְעֵינֵי כׇּל בְּנֵי אָדָם וּבְעֵינֵי כׇל רוֹאֵינוּ לַעֲבוֹדָתֶךָ. וְזַכֵּנוּ לְקַבֵּל שַׁבָּתוֹת מִתּוֹךְ רֹב שִׂמְחָה וּמִתּוֹךְ עֹשֶׁר וְכָבוֹד וּמִתּוֹךְ מִעוּט עֲוֹנוֹת. וְהָסֵר מִמֶּנִּי וּמִכׇּל בְּנֵי בֵיתִי וּמִכׇּל עַמְּךָ בֵּית יִשְׂרָאֵל כׇּל מִינֵי חֹלִי וְכׇל מִינֵי מַדְוֶה וְכׇל מִינֵי דַלּוּת וַעֲנִיּוּת וְאֶבְיוֹנוּת. וְתֵן בָּנוּ יֵצֶר טוֹב לְעׇבְדְּךָ בֶּאֱמֶת וּבְיִרְאָה וּבְאַהֲבָה. וְנִהְיֶה מְכֻבָּדִים בְּעֵינֶיךָ וּבְעֵינֵי כׇל רוֹאֵינוּ, כִּי אַתָּה הוּא מֶלֶךְ הַכָּבוֹד, כִּי לְךָ נָאֶה, כִּי לְךָ יָאֶה. אָנָּא, מֶלֶךְ מַלְכֵי הַמְּלָכִים, צַוֵּה לְמַלְאָכֶיךָ, מַלְאֲכֵי הַשָּׁרֵת, מְשָׁרְתֵי עֶלְיוֹן, שֶׁיִּפְקְדוּנִי בְּרַחֲמִים וִיבָרְכוּנִי בְּבוֹאָם לְבֵיתִי בְּיוֹם קׇדְשֵׁנוּ, כִּי הִדְלַקְתִּי נֵרוֹתַי וְהִצַּעְתִּי מִטָּתִי וְהֶחֱלַפְתִּי שִׂמְלוֹתַי לִכְבוֹד יוֹם הַשַּׁבָּת וּבָאתִי לְבֵיתְךָ לְהַפִּיל תְּחִנָּתִי לְפָנֶיךָ, שֶׁתַּעֲבִיר אַנְחָתִי, וָאָעִיד אֲשֶׁר בָּרָאתָ בְשִׁשָּׁה יָמִים כׇּל הַיְצוּר, וָאֶשְׁנֶה וַאֲשַׁלֵּשׁ עוֹד לְהָעִיד עַל כּוֹסִי בְּתוֹךְ שִׂמְחָתִי, כַּאֲשֶׁר צִוִּיתַנִי לְזׇכְרוֹ וּלְהִתְעַנֵּג בְּיֶתֶר נִשְׁמָתִי אֲשֶׁר נָתַתָּ בִּי. בּוֹ אֶשְׁבֹּת כַּאֲשֶׁר צִוִּיתַנִי לְשָׁרְתֶךָ, וְכֵן אַגִּיד גְּדֻלָּתְךָ בְּרִנָּה, וְשִׁוִּיתִי יהוה לִקְרָאתִי שֶׁתְּרַחֲמֵנִי עוֹד בְּגָלוּתִי לְגׇאֳלֵנִי לְעוֹרֵר לִבִּי לְאַהֲבָתֶךָ. וְאָז אֶשְׁמֹר פִּקּוּדֶיךָ וְחֻקֶּיךָ בְּלִי עֶצֶב, וְאֶתְפַּלֵּל כַּדָּת כָּרָאוּי וְכַנָּכוֹן. מַלְאֲכֵי הַשָּׁלוֹם, בּוֹאֲכֶם לְשָׁלוֹם, בָּרְכוּנִי לְשָׁלוֹם, וְאִמְרוּ בָּרוּךְ לְשֻׁלְחָנִי הֶעָרוּךְ, וְצֵאתְכֶם לְשָׁלוֹם מֵעַתָּה וְעַד עוֹלָם, אָמֵן סֶלָה.

אֵשֶׁת־חַיִל A woman of strength, who can find? *Prov. 31*
Her worth is far beyond pearls.
Her husband's heart trusts in her,
and he has no lack of gain.
She brings him good, not harm,
all the days of her life.
She seeks wool and linen,
and works with willing hands.
She is like a ship laden with merchandise,
bringing her food from afar.
She rises while it is still night,
providing food for her household, portions for her maids.
She considers a field and buys it;
from her earnings she plants a vineyard.
She girds herself with strength,
and braces her arms for her tasks.
She sees that her business goes well;
her lamp does not go out at night.
She holds the distaff in her hand,
and grasps the spindle with her palms.
She reaches out her palm to the poor,
and extends her hand to the needy.

---

standing his great intellectual prowess, finds himself entranced and is about to fail in the implementation of his fatherhood commitment, the mother rises heroically and assumes the role of her husband's keeper, his guardian and teacher. Man's mind roams about in a world of abstractions and twisted ideas. He is at times too critical, too skeptical to realize the simple truth which brooks no interference from the oversophisticated intellect. That is why the Bible has always portrayed the woman as the determining influence, saving the male from committing grave errors. In normal times, when routine decisions are reached, the man makes up his mind and the Biblical woman follows him. However, in times of upheaval and transition, when the covenantal community finds itself at crossroads and the choice of alternative courses of actions is about to be made, a choice that will shape destiny, it is then that the mother steps to the fore and takes command. The greatness of

משלי לא

אֵשֶׁת־חַיִל מִי יִמְצָא
וְרָחֹק מִפְּנִינִים מִכְרָהּ:
בָּטַח בָּהּ לֵב בַּעְלָהּ
וְשָׁלָל לֹא יֶחְסָר:
גְּמָלַתְהוּ טוֹב וְלֹא־רָע
כֹּל יְמֵי חַיֶּיהָ:
דָּרְשָׁה צֶמֶר וּפִשְׁתִּים
וַתַּעַשׂ בְּחֵפֶץ כַּפֶּיהָ:
הָיְתָה כָּאֳנִיּוֹת סוֹחֵר
מִמֶּרְחָק תָּבִיא לַחְמָהּ:
וַתָּקָם בְּעוֹד לַיְלָה
וַתִּתֵּן טֶרֶף לְבֵיתָהּ, וְחֹק לְנַעֲרֹתֶיהָ:
זָמְמָה שָׂדֶה וַתִּקָּחֵהוּ
מִפְּרִי כַפֶּיהָ נָטְעָה כָּרֶם:
חָגְרָה בְעוֹז מָתְנֶיהָ
וַתְּאַמֵּץ זְרוֹעֹתֶיהָ:
טָעֲמָה כִּי־טוֹב סַחְרָהּ
לֹא־יִכְבֶּה בַלַּיְלָה נֵרָהּ:
יָדֶיהָ שִׁלְּחָה בַכִּישׁוֹר
וְכַפֶּיהָ תָּמְכוּ פָלֶךְ:
כַּפָּהּ פָּרְשָׂה לֶעָנִי
וְיָדֶיהָ שִׁלְּחָה לָאֶבְיוֹן:

---

EISHET ḤAYIL

In the covenantal community, motherhood is a more powerful spiritual force than fatherhood. In moments of dismay and chaos, when man, notwith-

She has no fear for her family when it snows,
for all her household is clothed in crimson wool.
She makes elegant coverings;
her clothing is fine linen and purple wool.
Her husband is well known in the gates,
where he sits with the elders of the land.
She makes linen garments and sells them,
and supplies merchants with sashes.
She is clothed with strength and dignity;
she can laugh at the days to come.
She opens her mouth with wisdom,
and the law of kindness is on her tongue.
She watches over the ways of her household,
and never eats the bread of idleness.
Her children rise and call her happy;
her husband also praises her:
"Many women have excelled,
but you surpass them all."
Charm is deceptive and beauty vain:
it is the God-fearing woman who deserves praise.
Give her the reward she has earned;
let her deeds bring her praise in the gates.

---

sons, Ishmael and Isaac, but the covenant was confined to Isaac because his mother was Sarah. When she demanded the expulsion of Ishmael, Abraham was not eager to comply with her request. God tells him in terse terms, "In all that Sarah has said unto you, hearken to her voice." Similarly, Rebecca is responsible for the covenant being transmitted to Jacob instead of Esau. Isaac had contemplated entrusting the spiritual heritage to his oldest son, but at the hour of crisis Rebecca intervened and thereby determined the historical destiny of the covenantal community. The destiny of mankind and our people was shaped by the woman. The Book of Proverbs dedicated its last section to the woman of valor in whom the heart of her husband trusts. Valor as a trait of the feminine personality was born in the covenantal community where motherhood, instead of being a natural fact, became a spiritual challenge and ideal. (*Family Redeemed*, pp. 116–119)

לֹא־תִירָא לְבֵיתָהּ מִשָּׁלֶג
כִּי כָל־בֵּיתָהּ לָבֻשׁ שָׁנִים:
מַרְבַדִּים עָשְׂתָה־לָּהּ
שֵׁשׁ וְאַרְגָּמָן לְבוּשָׁהּ:
נוֹדָע בַּשְּׁעָרִים בַּעְלָהּ
בְּשִׁבְתּוֹ עִם־זִקְנֵי־אָרֶץ:
סָדִין עָשְׂתָה וַתִּמְכֹּר
וַחֲגוֹר נָתְנָה לַכְּנַעֲנִי:
עוֹז־וְהָדָר לְבוּשָׁהּ
וַתִּשְׂחַק לְיוֹם אַחֲרוֹן:
פִּיהָ פָּתְחָה בְחָכְמָה
וְתוֹרַת־חֶסֶד עַל־לְשׁוֹנָהּ:
צוֹפִיָּה הֲלִיכוֹת בֵּיתָהּ
וְלֶחֶם עַצְלוּת לֹא תֹאכֵל:
קָמוּ בָנֶיהָ וַיְאַשְּׁרוּהָ
בַּעְלָהּ וַיְהַלְלָהּ:
רַבּוֹת בָּנוֹת עָשׂוּ חָיִל
וְאַתְּ עָלִית עַל־כֻּלָּנָה:
שֶׁקֶר הַחֵן וְהֶבֶל הַיֹּפִי
אִשָּׁה יִרְאַת־יהוה הִיא תִתְהַלָּל:
תְּנוּ־לָהּ מִפְּרִי יָדֶיהָ
וִיהַלְלוּהָ בַשְּׁעָרִים מַעֲשֶׂיהָ:

---

the woman manifests itself at the hour of crisis, when the situation does not lend to piecemeal understanding, but requires instead instantaneous action that flows from the very depths of a sensitive personality. Abraham had two

# Kiddush for Shabbat Evening

*For Kiddush on Yom Tov see page 22,*
*and on Rosh HaShana, see page 28.*

*Quietly:* And it was evening, and it was morning – *Gen. 1*
יוֹם הַשִּׁשִּׁי the sixth day.

Then the heavens and the earth were completed, and all their array. *Gen. 2*
With the seventh day, God completed the work He had done.
He ceased on the seventh day from all the work He had done.
God blessed the seventh day and declared it holy,
because on it He ceased from all His work
He had created to do.

*When saying Kiddush for others, add:*
Please pay attention, my masters.

Blessed are You, LORD our God, King of the Universe,
who creates the fruit of the vine.

---

the Almighty in the act of creation, man as creator of worlds. The scriptural text, "Then the heavens and the earth were completed (וַיְכֻלּוּ), and all the host of them" (Gen. 2:1), which the Targum, the Aramaic translation of the Pentateuch, translates as "and the heaven and earth were perfected (וְאִשְׁתַּכְלָלוּ)," is both a profound expression of the soul of the people and the most fervent desire of the man of God. This lofty, ontological idea illuminates the path of the eternal people. When a Jew on the Sabbath eve recites this passage as part of the Kiddush, he testifies not only to the existence of a Creator but of man's obligation to become a partner with the Almighty in the continuation and perfection of the creation. Just as the Almighty constantly refined and improved the realm of existence during the six days of creation, so must man complete the creation and transform the domain of chaos and void into a perfect and beautiful reality. (*Halakhic Man*, pp. 99, 105)

# קידוש לליל שבת

*For* קידוש *on* יום טוב *see page 23,*
*and on* ראש השנה*, see page 29.*

*Quietly* וַיְהִי־עֶרֶב וַיְהִי־בֹקֶר בראשית א
יוֹם הַשִּׁשִּׁי:
וַיְכֻלּוּ הַשָּׁמַיִם וְהָאָרֶץ וְכָל־צְבָאָם: בראשית ב
וַיְכַל אֱלֹהִים בַּיּוֹם הַשְּׁבִיעִי מְלַאכְתּוֹ אֲשֶׁר עָשָׂה
וַיִּשְׁבֹּת בַּיּוֹם הַשְּׁבִיעִי מִכָּל־מְלַאכְתּוֹ אֲשֶׁר עָשָׂה:
וַיְבָרֶךְ אֱלֹהִים אֶת־יוֹם הַשְּׁבִיעִי, וַיְקַדֵּשׁ אֹתוֹ
כִּי בוֹ שָׁבַת מִכָּל־מְלַאכְתּוֹ, אֲשֶׁר־בָּרָא אֱלֹהִים, לַעֲשׂוֹת:

*When saying* קידוש *for others, add:*
סַבְרִי מָרָנָן

בָּרוּךְ אַתָּה יהוה אֱלֹהֵינוּ מֶלֶךְ הָעוֹלָם
בּוֹרֵא פְּרִי הַגָּפֶן.

---

KIDDUSH FOR SHABBAT EVENING

וַיְכֻלּוּ הַשָּׁמַיִם וְהָאָרֶץ *Then the heavens and the earth were completed.* Halakhic man is a man who longs to create, to bring into being something new, something original. The study of Torah, by definition, means gleaning new, creative insights from the Torah, *ḥiddushei Torah*. This notion of *ḥiddush*, of creative interpretation, is not limited solely to the theoretical domain, but extends as well into the practical domain, into the real world. The most fervent desire of halakhic man is to behold the replenishment of the deficiency in creation, when the real world will conform to the ideal world and the most exalted and glorious of creations, the ideal *halakha*, will be actualized in its midst. The dream of creation is the central idea in the halakhic consciousness – the idea of the importance of man as a partner of

Blessed are You, LORD our God, King of the Universe,
who has made us holy through His commandments,
who has favored us,
and in love and favor
gave us His holy Sabbath as a heritage,
a remembrance of the work of creation.
It is the first among the holy days of assembly,
a remembrance of the exodus from Egypt.
For You chose us and sanctified us from all the peoples,
and in love and favor
gave us Your holy Sabbath as a heritage.
Blessed are You, LORD, who sanctifies the Sabbath.

*On Shabbat Ḥol HaMo'ed Sukkot, if Kiddush is made in the sukka, add:*
Blessed are You, LORD our God, King of the Universe,
who has made us holy through his commandments
and has commanded us to dwell in the sukka.

*It is customary for all present to drink of the wine.*

---

sanctified the day at the time of creation: "And God blessed the seventh day and He hallowed it" (Gen. 2:3). For this reason, the Shabbat Kiddush concludes with the blessing, "Blessed are You, LORD, who sanctifies the Sabbath," as opposed to the Yom Tov Kiddush which closes with the phrase, "Blessed are You, LORD, who sanctifies Israel and the Festivals." The Talmud (*Pesaḥim* 117b; *Beitza* 17a) explains that since the people of Israel create the *kedusha* of Yom Tov, we refer to them in the Kiddush blessing, but we do not mention the people of Israel in the Shabbat Kiddush because the sanctity of Shabbat flows directly from the Creator Himself. (*Shiurim LeZekher Abba Mari*, vol. 2, p. 141)

בָּרוּךְ אַתָּה יהוה אֱלֹהֵינוּ מֶלֶךְ הָעוֹלָם
אֲשֶׁר קִדְּשָׁנוּ בְּמִצְוֹתָיו, וְרָצָה בָנוּ
וְשַׁבַּת קָדְשׁוֹ בְּאַהֲבָה וּבְרָצוֹן הִנְחִילָנוּ
זִכָּרוֹן לְמַעֲשֵׂה בְרֵאשִׁית
כִּי הוּא יוֹם תְּחִלָּה לְמִקְרָאֵי קֹדֶשׁ
זֵכֶר לִיצִיאַת מִצְרָיִם
כִּי בָנוּ בָחַרְתָּ וְאוֹתָנוּ קִדַּשְׁתָּ מִכָּל הָעַמִּים
וְשַׁבַּת קָדְשְׁךָ בְּאַהֲבָה וּבְרָצוֹן הִנְחַלְתָּנוּ.
בָּרוּךְ אַתָּה יהוה, מְקַדֵּשׁ הַשַּׁבָּת.

*On* שבת חול המועד סוכות*, if* קידוש *is made in the* סוכה*, add:*

בָּרוּךְ אַתָּה יהוה אֱלֹהֵינוּ מֶלֶךְ הָעוֹלָם
אֲשֶׁר קִדְּשָׁנוּ בְּמִצְוֹתָיו וְצִוָּנוּ לֵישֵׁב בַּסֻּכָּה.

*It is customary for all present to drink of the wine.*

---

**מְקַדֵּשׁ הַשַּׁבָּת** *Who sanctifies the Sabbath.* There is an enigmatic Midrash (*Yalkut Shimoni*, 830) which states that there are three sanctified entities in this world: the name of God, Shabbat and the people of Israel. Yet, we know of many other holy entities: the Land of Israel, the Temple, and Yom Tov, among other examples, which the Midrash seemingly ignores. The solution is that the Midrash lists only those sanctities created by God Himself, for all other manifestations of holiness in this world are, in fact, secondary, derived from the sanctity of Israel. For example, the Jewish people consecrated the Land of Israel and the Temple, and the High Court endows every Yom Tov with its *kedusha* through its jurisdiction over the calendar. But the sanctity of Shabbat preceded the election of the nation of Israel, as God Himself

# Kiddush for Festival Evening

*On Shabbat add:*

*quietly:* And it was evening, and it was morning – *Gen. 1*

יוֹם הַשִּׁשִּׁי the sixth day.

Then the heavens and the earth were completed, and all their array. *Gen. 2*
With the seventh day, God completed the work He had done.
He ceased on the seventh day from all the work He had done.
God blessed the seventh day and declared it holy,
because on it He ceased from all His work He had created to do.

*On other evenings Kiddush starts here:*

*When saying Kiddush for others, add:*
Please pay attention, my masters.

Blessed are You, Lord our God, King of the Universe,
who creates the fruit of the vine.

*On Shabbat, add the words in parentheses.*

בָּרוּךְ Blessed are You, Lord our God, King of the Universe,
who has chosen us from among all peoples,
raised us above all tongues,
and made us holy through His commandments.
You have given us, Lord our God, in love

---

providence in Aristotle's view, the love of the Prime Mover for the world is abolished. The Torah, though, which bases all of Judaism on the principle of creation and providence, and on the chosenness of the Jewish people, introduced into the center of our world the concept of loving-kindness and love as a reciprocal process. God's providence over His creatures in general, and His choice of the Congregation of Israel in particular, is a manifestation of His infinite love. Indeed, the books of the Torah and the prophets are replete with descriptions of God's love for Israel. "The Lord desired your fathers to love them and He chose their offspring after them" (Deut. 10:15). "I have loved you, says God… and I love Jacob" (Mal. 1:2). Anyone who claims that Judaism commands the individual to love God, but does not

# קידוש לליל שלוש רגלים

*On* שבת *add:*

*quietly* וַיְהִי־עֶרֶב וַיְהִי־בֹקֶר בראשית א

יוֹם הַשִּׁשִּׁי:

וַיְכֻלּוּ הַשָּׁמַיִם וְהָאָרֶץ וְכָל־צְבָאָם: בראשית ב

וַיְכַל אֱלֹהִים בַּיּוֹם הַשְּׁבִיעִי מְלַאכְתּוֹ אֲשֶׁר עָשָׂה

וַיִּשְׁבֹּת בַּיּוֹם הַשְּׁבִיעִי מִכָּל־מְלַאכְתּוֹ אֲשֶׁר עָשָׂה:

וַיְבָרֶךְ אֱלֹהִים אֶת־יוֹם הַשְּׁבִיעִי, וַיְקַדֵּשׁ אֹתוֹ

כִּי בוֹ שָׁבַת מִכָּל־מְלַאכְתּוֹ, אֲשֶׁר־בָּרָא אֱלֹהִים, לַעֲשׂוֹת:

*On other evenings the* קידוש *starts here:*

*When saying* קידוש *for others, add:*

סַבְרִי מָרָנָן

בָּרוּךְ אַתָּה יהוה אֱלֹהֵינוּ מֶלֶךְ הָעוֹלָם, בּוֹרֵא פְּרִי הַגָּפֶן.

*On* שבת*, add the words in parentheses.*

בָּרוּךְ אַתָּה יהוה אֱלֹהֵינוּ מֶלֶךְ הָעוֹלָם

אֲשֶׁר בָּחַר בָּנוּ מִכָּל עָם

וְרוֹמְמָנוּ מִכָּל לָשׁוֹן

וְקִדְּשָׁנוּ בְּמִצְוֹתָיו

וַתִּתֶּן לָנוּ יהוה אֱלֹהֵינוּ בְּאַהֲבָה

---

KIDDUSH FOR YOM TOV EVENING

וַתִּתֶּן לָנוּ יהוה אֱלֹהֵינוּ בְּאַהֲבָה *You have given us, Lord our God, in love.* Aristotelian philosophy maintains that love in the relationship between God and man moves in one direction only: man yearns for God, the Prime Mover, without experiencing love reciprocally. The Prime Mover is aloof from the world and does not long for it; his relationship to the world is that of a necessary cause, without desire or intention. Furthermore, since there is no directed

(Sabbaths for rest), festivals for rejoicing,
holy days and seasons for joy,
(this Sabbath day and) this day of:

| | |
|---|---|
| *On Pesaḥ:* | the festival of Matzot, the time of our freedom |
| *On Shavuot:* | the festival of Shavuot, the time of the giving of our Torah |
| *On Sukkot:* | the festival of Sukkot, our time of rejoicing |
| *On Shemini Atzeret & Simḥat Torah:* | the festival of the eighth day, Shemini Atzeret, our time of rejoicing |

(with love), a holy assembly in memory of the exodus from Egypt.
For You have chosen us and sanctified us above all peoples,
and given us as our heritage (Your holy Sabbath in love and favor and)
Your holy festivals for joy and gladness.

---

aspects of rejoicing that Maimonides cites for men, children, and women, respectively? One must conclude, rather, that the *kiyyum* of *simḥat Yom Tov* consists, in essence, of heartfelt inner rejoicing, which can be expressed in various ways: in Temple times, through the eating of sacrificial meat; nowadays, through bringing about happiness in the various ways likely to arouse it in the human heart. This is also how the *mitzva* of *simḥat Yom Tov* differs fundamentally from the obligations of *kavod* and *oneg* on Shabbat. Honor and delight require external action, but they do not demand an inner state or experience. Therefore, Shabbat also differs from Yom Tov in that it doesn't cancel the *shiva* period of mourning as does Yom Tov. While we do not allow public demonstrations of mourning on Shabbat, the day doesn't require an inner fulfillment of joy. Thus a person can outwardly honor Shabbat, while still mourning his deceased relative inwardly and through private actions. However, *simḥat Yom Tov* obligates us in both outer expressions of rejoicing and sincere inner happiness, and thus Yom Tov, unlike Shabbat, contradicts and annuls any fulfillment of mourning. (*Out of the Whirlwind*, pp. 65–66, 71–72)

(שַׁבָּתוֹת לִמְנוּחָה וּ) מוֹעֲדִים לְשִׂמְחָה
חַגִּים וּזְמַנִּים לְשָׂשׂוֹן
אֶת יוֹם (הַשַּׁבָּת הַזֶּה וְאֶת יוֹם)

בפסח: חַג הַמַּצּוֹת הַזֶּה, זְמַן חֵרוּתֵנוּ
בשבועות: חַג הַשָּׁבוּעוֹת הַזֶּה, זְמַן מַתַּן תּוֹרָתֵנוּ
בסוכות: חַג הַסֻּכּוֹת הַזֶּה, זְמַן שִׂמְחָתֵנוּ
בשמע״צ ובש״ת: הַשְּׁמִינִי חַג הָעֲצֶרֶת הַזֶּה, זְמַן שִׂמְחָתֵנוּ

(בְּאַהֲבָה) מִקְרָא קֹדֶשׁ, זֵכֶר לִיצִיאַת מִצְרָיִם
כִּי בָנוּ בָחַרְתָּ וְאוֹתָנוּ קִדַּשְׁתָּ מִכָּל הָעַמִּים
(וְשַׁבָּת) וּמוֹעֲדֵי קָדְשֶׁךָ (בְּאַהֲבָה וּבְרָצוֹן)
בְּשִׂמְחָה וּבְשָׂשׂוֹן הִנְחַלְתָּנוּ.

---

promise him reciprocal love is a heretic. How unfortunate it is that many scholars pursued folly and suspected that Maimonides, Heaven forbid, agreed with the teaching of Aristotelian philosophy that the yearnings of the world for God are one-way, without any reciprocal yearnings. On Yom Tov, the Kiddush as well as the central blessing in the Amida, which dwell upon Israel's chosenness, are coined in terms of love. (*And From There You Shall Seek*, pp. 153–155)

מוֹעֲדִים לְשִׂמְחָה *Festivals for rejoicing.* In the days of the Temple the *mitzva* of *simḥat Yom Tov* obligated a person to offer and partake in *shelamim* sacrifices. Maimonides maintains (in contrast to *Tosafot, Mo'ed Katan* 14b s.v. *aseh*) that the *mitzva* of *simḥa*, joy, on Yom Tov remains a Biblical imperative even today, and in the absence of *shelamim* offerings, it is fulfilled through other means of rejoicing, "each person in a manner appropriate for him" (*Hilkhot Yom Tov* 6:17–18). At first blush, it seems perplexing that the Biblical obligation to rejoice on the festival can be fulfilled nowadays. We can understand how the eating of sacrificial meat on the festival fulfills the obligation, but how can that purpose be achieved by the mere consumption of meat for pleasure, or the distribution of roasted nuts, or the purchase of colorful clothing – the

Blessed are you, Lord,
who sanctifies (the Sabbath,) Israel and the festivals.

*On Motza'ei Shabbat, the following Havdala is added:*

בָּרוּךְ Blessed are You, Lord our God, King of the Universe,
who creates the lights of fire.

Blessed are You, Lord our God, King of the Universe, who distinguishes between sacred and secular, between light and darkness, between Israel and the nations, between the seventh day and the six days of work. You have made a distinction between the holiness of the Sabbath and the holiness of festivals, and have sanctified the seventh day above the six days of work. You have distinguished and sanctified Your people Israel with Your holiness. Blessed are You, Lord, who distinguishes between sacred and sacred.

*On Sukkot, say the following blessing. On the first night it is said before the blessing "who has given us life"; on the second night, after it (some say it before on both nights).*

בָּרוּךְ Blessed are You, Lord our God, King of the Universe,
who has made us holy though His commandments,
and has commanded us to dwell in the sukka.

*The following blessing is omitted on the last two nights of Pesaḥ (in Israel, the last night).*

בָּרוּךְ Blessed are You, Lord our God, King of the Universe,
who has given us life, sustained us, and brought us to this time.

*It is customary for all present to drink of the wine.*

---

The three *regalim* – Pesaḥ, Shavu'ot and Sukkot – all share the same *kedushat hayom*. Moreover, they are not entirely independent festivals, but rather constitute an integrated series. We see this from the laws of delaying sacrifices, *bal te'aḥer*. According to one view, a person violates the prohibition against delaying a sacrifice after three festivals have passed and he still has not offered the sacrifice he had promised; another view maintains that the person violates the prohibition only after the three *regalim* have passed in their proper order: Pesaḥ, Shavu'ot, and then Sukkot. We see that the *halakha* recognizes the *regalim* not as three disparate holidays, but rather as a unit. Thus, at the conclusion of Kiddush, as well as the conclusion of the Yom Tov Amida, we don't refer to a particular festival. Instead, we offer our blessing to God for the three *regalim* which share the identical sanctity and together constitute our holy times. (*Nefesh HaRav*, p. 182; *Guide to Jewish Prayer*, pp. 170–171)

בָּרוּךְ אַתָּה יהוה
מְקַדֵּשׁ (הַשַּׁבָּת וְ) יִשְׂרָאֵל וְהַזְּמַנִּים.

*On* מוצאי שבת*, the following* הבדלה *is added:*

בָּרוּךְ אַתָּה יהוה אֱלֹהֵינוּ מֶלֶךְ הָעוֹלָם, בּוֹרֵא מְאוֹרֵי הָאֵשׁ.

בָּרוּךְ אַתָּה יהוה אֱלֹהֵינוּ מֶלֶךְ הָעוֹלָם, הַמַּבְדִּיל בֵּין קֹדֶשׁ לְחֹל, בֵּין אוֹר לְחֹשֶׁךְ, בֵּין יִשְׂרָאֵל לָעַמִּים, בֵּין יוֹם הַשְּׁבִיעִי לְשֵׁשֶׁת יְמֵי הַמַּעֲשֶׂה. בֵּין קְדֻשַּׁת שַׁבָּת לִקְדֻשַּׁת יוֹם טוֹב הִבְדַּלְתָּ, וְאֶת יוֹם הַשְּׁבִיעִי מִשֵּׁשֶׁת יְמֵי הַמַּעֲשֶׂה קִדַּשְׁתָּ, הִבְדַּלְתָּ וְקִדַּשְׁתָּ אֶת עַמְּךָ יִשְׂרָאֵל בִּקְדֻשָּׁתֶךָ. בָּרוּךְ אַתָּה יהוה, הַמַּבְדִּיל בֵּין קֹדֶשׁ לְקֹדֶשׁ.

*On* סוכות*, say the following blessing. On the first night it is said before the blessing* שֶׁהֶחֱיָנוּ*; on the second night, after it (some say it before on both nights).*

בָּרוּךְ אַתָּה יהוה אֱלֹהֵינוּ מֶלֶךְ הָעוֹלָם
אֲשֶׁר קִדְּשָׁנוּ בְּמִצְוֹתָיו וְצִוָּנוּ לֵישֵׁב בַּסֻּכָּה.

*The following blessing is omitted on the last two nights of* פסח *(in* ארץ ישראל*, the last night).*

בָּרוּךְ אַתָּה יהוה אֱלֹהֵינוּ מֶלֶךְ הָעוֹלָם
שֶׁהֶחֱיָנוּ וְקִיְּמָנוּ וְהִגִּיעָנוּ לַזְּמַן הַזֶּה.

*It is customary for all present to drink of the wine.*

---

**מְקַדֵּשׁ יִשְׂרָאֵל וְהַזְּמַנִּים** *Who sanctifies Israel and the festivals.* The Kiddush of Yom Tov ends with a generic blessing, "Blessed are You, Lord, who sanctifies Israel and the festivals," without specifying the name of the festival. Rabbi Barukh Epstein, author of the *Torah Temima* (in his commentary on the siddur, *Barukh SheAmar*), argued that the last word of this text is based on a copyist's error; rather than using the generic term, the blessing should conclude with the specific name of the holiday being celebrated (e.g., "who sanctifies Israel and the festival of Sukkot"). Rabbi Epstein suggested that in early printings of the siddur, the word "וְהַזְּמַנִּים" appeared in brackets, with the intent that the reader fill in the name of the specific holiday, and later editors misunderstood the meaning and included the word into the text of the blessing itself. This speculation, however, is unfounded; the reason that we don't specify the particular festival in the closing of the blessing is readily understandable.

# Kiddush for Rosh HaShana Evening

*On Shabbat add:*

*quietly:* And it was evening, and it was morning – *Gen. 1*

יוֹם הַשִּׁשִּׁי the sixth day.

Then the heavens and the earth were completed, and all their array. *Gen. 2*
With the seventh day, God completed the work He had done.
He ceased on the seventh day from all the work He had done.
God blessed the seventh day and declared it holy,
because on it He ceased from all His work He had created to do.

*On other evenings start Kiddush here:*

*When saying Kiddush for others:* Please pay attention, my masters.

Blessed are You, LORD our God, King of the Universe,
who creates the fruit of the vine.

*On Shabbat, add the words in parentheses.*

בָּרוּךְ Blessed are You, LORD our God, King of the Universe,
who has chosen us from among all peoples,
raised us above all tongues,
and made us holy through His commandments.
You have given us, LORD our God, in love,
this (Sabbath and this) Day of Remembrance,
a day of (remembering) blowing the shofar (in love),
a holy assembly in memory of the exodus from Egypt,

---

people mistakenly believe that somehow the mind is in conflict with emotion, that people endowed with great intelligence lack in passion. On the contrary, reason supports emotion and enriches it. Cognition bestows its glory upon emotionality, and elevates it from a passive compulsion to a free action. On the other hand, emotion unaccompanied by logic and perception is a transient sensation that quickly fades. Admittedly, it is true that feelings coupled with intellect are often not as loud as mindless emotions, which must be given vent by dancing, shouting, or singing. However, one who

# קידוש לליל ראש השנה

*On שבת add:*

בראשית א *quietly* וַיְהִי־עֶרֶב וַיְהִי־בֹקֶר

**יוֹם הַשִּׁשִּׁי:**

בראשית ב **וַיְכֻלּוּ הַשָּׁמַיִם וְהָאָרֶץ וְכָל־צְבָאָם:**

**וַיְכַל אֱלֹהִים בַּיּוֹם הַשְּׁבִיעִי מְלַאכְתּוֹ אֲשֶׁר עָשָׂה**

**וַיִּשְׁבֹּת בַּיּוֹם הַשְּׁבִיעִי מִכָּל־מְלַאכְתּוֹ אֲשֶׁר עָשָׂה:**

**וַיְבָרֶךְ אֱלֹהִים אֶת־יוֹם הַשְּׁבִיעִי, וַיְקַדֵּשׁ אֹתוֹ**

**כִּי בוֹ שָׁבַת מִכָּל־מְלַאכְתּוֹ, אֲשֶׁר־בָּרָא אֱלֹהִים, לַעֲשׂוֹת:**

*On other evenings start קידוש here:*

*When saying קידוש for others* סַבְרִי מָרָנָן

**בָּרוּךְ אַתָּה יהוה אֱלֹהֵינוּ מֶלֶךְ הָעוֹלָם, בּוֹרֵא פְּרִי הַגָּפֶן.**

*On שבת, add the words in parentheses.*

**בָּרוּךְ אַתָּה יהוה אֱלֹהֵינוּ מֶלֶךְ הָעוֹלָם**

**אֲשֶׁר בָּחַר בָּנוּ מִכָּל עָם**

**וְרוֹמְמָנוּ מִכָּל לָשׁוֹן**

**וְקִדְּשָׁנוּ בְּמִצְוֹתָיו**

**וַתִּתֶּן לָנוּ יהוה אֱלֹהֵינוּ בְּאַהֲבָה**

**אֶת יוֹם (הַשַּׁבָּת הַזֶּה וְאֶת יוֹם) הַזִּכָּרוֹן הַזֶּה, יוֹם (זִכְרוֹן) תְּרוּעָה**

**(בְּאַהֲבָה) מִקְרָא קֹדֶשׁ, זֵכֶר לִיצִיאַת מִצְרָיִם**

---

KIDDUSH FOR ROSH HASHANA EVENING

It is true that I come from a very sober, level headed, rational family. However, their emphasis upon precise logic and their unwillingness to surrender to any emotion when explaining and analyzing halakhic concepts didn't prevent my forebears from experiencing Judaism with all their hearts and souls. Some

for You have chosen us and sanctified us above all peoples,
and Your word is true and endures for ever.
Blessed are You, Lord, King over all the earth,
who sanctifies (the Sabbath,) Israel and the Day of Remembrance.

*On Motza'ei Shabbat, the following Havdala is added:*

בָּרוּךְ Blessed are You, Lord our God, King of the Universe,
who creates the lights of fire.

Blessed are You, Lord our God, King of the Universe, who distinguishes between sacred and secular, between light and darkness, between Israel and the nations, between the seventh day and the six days of work. You have made a distinction between the holiness of the Sabbath and the holiness of festivals, and have sanctified the seventh day above the six days of work. You have distinguished and sanctified Your people Israel with Your holiness. Blessed are You, Lord, who distinguishes between sacred and sacred.

*The following blessing is said on both nights of Rosh HaShana. On the second night, new fruit is placed on the table, and one should have in mind that the blessing is also on the new fruit.*

בָּרוּךְ Blessed are You, Lord our God, King of the Universe,
who has given us life, sustained us, and brought us to this time.

*It is customary for all present to drink of the wine.*

---

evening I reproduce in my mind and relive listening to Rav Ḥayyim's Kiddush. I can similarly remember, like it was yesterday, when I was a child listening to Rav Ḥayyim recite the *avodah* section of the Yom Kippur *mussaf*. He would read it calmly, without raising his voice, but watching him recount the steps of the Yom Kippur service, one felt that Rav Ḥayyim had been transported and was physically standing in the Temple, in the presence of the Almighty. Throughout millennia of persecution and abuse, in a myriad of hostile lands, it has been the Torah that has allowed us to survive. However, it was not just the Torah of our minds, but also the Torah of our hearts, of the great experiential tradition of being in the presence of our Maker, that has given us the strength to persevere. (*Noraos HaRav*, vol. 15, pp. 45–47)

כִּי בָנוּ בָחַרְתָּ וְאוֹתָנוּ קִדַּשְׁתָּ מִכָּל הָעַמִּים
וּדְבָרְךָ אֱמֶת וְקַיָּם לָעַד.
בָּרוּךְ אַתָּה יהוה, מֶלֶךְ עַל כָּל הָאָרֶץ
מְקַדֵּשׁ (הַשַּׁבָּת וְ) יִשְׂרָאֵל וְיוֹם הַזִּכָּרוֹן.

*On* מוצאי שבת*, the following* הבדלה *is added:*

בָּרוּךְ אַתָּה יהוה אֱלֹהֵינוּ מֶלֶךְ הָעוֹלָם, בּוֹרֵא מְאוֹרֵי הָאֵשׁ.

בָּרוּךְ אַתָּה יהוה אֱלֹהֵינוּ מֶלֶךְ הָעוֹלָם, הַמַּבְדִּיל בֵּין קֹדֶשׁ לְחֹל, בֵּין אוֹר לְחֹשֶׁךְ, בֵּין יִשְׂרָאֵל לָעַמִּים, בֵּין יוֹם הַשְּׁבִיעִי לְשֵׁשֶׁת יְמֵי הַמַּעֲשֶׂה. בֵּין קְדֻשַּׁת שַׁבָּת לִקְדֻשַּׁת יוֹם טוֹב הִבְדַּלְתָּ, וְאֶת יוֹם הַשְּׁבִיעִי מִשֵּׁשֶׁת יְמֵי הַמַּעֲשֶׂה קִדַּשְׁתָּ, הִבְדַּלְתָּ וְקִדַּשְׁתָּ אֶת עַמְּךָ יִשְׂרָאֵל בִּקְדֻשָּׁתֶךָ. בָּרוּךְ אַתָּה יהוה, הַמַּבְדִּיל בֵּין קֹדֶשׁ לְקֹדֶשׁ.

*The following blessing is said on both nights of* ראש השנה*.*
*On the second night, new fruit is placed on the table, and one should have in mind that the blessing is also on the new fruit.*

בָּרוּךְ אַתָּה יהוה אֱלֹהֵינוּ מֶלֶךְ הָעוֹלָם
שֶׁהֶחֱיָנוּ וְקִיְּמָנוּ וְהִגִּיעָנוּ לַזְּמַן הַזֶּה.

*It is customary for all present to drink of the wine.*

---

engages in Torah study is not precluded from the emotional experience. His inner feelings will be controlled, muted, and hidden, but they will be just as beautiful and splendid.

In particular, I can still vividly recall listening to my grandfather Rav Ḥayyim reciting the Kiddush on Rosh HaShana. One could detect a stormy sea of emotion raging under Rav Ḥayyim's cerebral mask of sobriety and indifference. For my grandfather, the *kedushat hayom* was not just an abstract concept; it was an experience, a reality of standing *lifnei Hashem*, man before his Creator. The scene left an indelible impression upon me, and many years later, when I feel unable to conjure the proper mood on Rosh HaShana

# Zemirot for Shabbat Evening

כָּל מְקַדֵּשׁ All who fittingly sanctify the seventh day,
All who protect the Sabbath properly from desecration,
Will have great reward in accord with their deed.
"Each in his own camp, each under his own banner." *Num. 1*

Lovers of the LORD, who await the building of the Temple,
Be glad and joyful on the Sabbath as if receiving the gift
of God's inheritance,
Raise your hands in holiness and say to God:
"Blessed is the LORD who has given rest to His people Israel." *I Kings 8*

Seekers of the LORD, offspring of His beloved Abraham,
Who are slow to leave the Sabbath but hasten to enter it,
Who rejoice to keep it and make its *eiruv* –
"This is the day the LORD has made; let us rejoice and be glad
in it." *Ps. 118*

Remember Moses' Torah, from which the laws of Sabbath
are learned,
Engraved is the seventh day like a bedecked bride between
her companions,
The pure inherit it and sanctify it with the words:
"All that He had made…
With the seventh day God completed the work He had done." *Gen. 2*

It is a sacred day from beginning to end,
All Jacob's offspring will honor it as the King's word
and decree,
Resting on it and rejoicing with delights of food and drink.
"All the congregation of Israel will observe it." *Ex. 12*

# זמירות לליל שבת

כָּל מְקַדֵּשׁ שְׁבִיעִי כָּרָאוּי לוֹ
כָּל שׁוֹמֵר שַׁבָּת כַּדָּת, מֵחַלְּלוֹ
שְׂכָרוֹ הַרְבֵּה מְאֹד עַל פִּי פָעֳלוֹ
אִישׁ עַל־מַחֲנֵהוּ וְאִישׁ עַל־דִּגְלוֹ: במדבר א

אוֹהֲבֵי יהוה הַמְחַכִּים לְבִנְיַן אֲרִיאֵל
בְּיוֹם הַשַּׁבָּת שִׂישׂוּ וְשִׂמְחוּ כִּמְקַבְּלֵי מַתַּן נַחֲלִיאֵל
גַּם שְׂאוּ יְדֵיכֶם קֹדֶשׁ וְאִמְרוּ לָאֵל
בָּרוּךְ יהוה אֲשֶׁר נָתַן מְנוּחָה לְעַמּוֹ יִשְׂרָאֵל: מלכים א, ח

דּוֹרְשֵׁי יהוה זֶרַע אַבְרָהָם אוֹהֲבוֹ
הַמְאַחֲרִים לָצֵאת מִן הַשַּׁבָּת וּמְמַהֲרִים לָבוֹא
וּשְׂמֵחִים לְשָׁמְרוֹ וּלְעָרֵב עֵרוּבוֹ
זֶה־הַיּוֹם עָשָׂה יהוה, נָגִילָה וְנִשְׂמְחָה בוֹ: תהלים קיח

זִכְרוּ תּוֹרַת מֹשֶׁה בְּמִצְוַת שַׁבָּת גְּרוּסָה
חֲרוּתָה לַיּוֹם הַשְּׁבִיעִי, כְּכַלָּה בֵּין רֵעוֹתֶיהָ מְשֻׁבָּצָה
טְהוֹרִים יִירָשׁוּהָ, וִיקַדְּשׁוּהָ בְּמַאֲמַר כָּל אֲשֶׁר עָשָׂה
וַיְכַל אֱלֹהִים בַּיּוֹם הַשְּׁבִיעִי מְלַאכְתּוֹ אֲשֶׁר עָשָׂה: בראשית ב

יוֹם קָדוֹשׁ הוּא, מִבּוֹאוֹ וְעַד צֵאתוֹ
כָּל זֶרַע יַעֲקֹב יְכַבְּדוּהוּ, כִּדְבַר הַמֶּלֶךְ וְדָתוֹ
לָנוּחַ בּוֹ וְלִשְׂמֹחַ בְּתַעֲנוּג אָכוֹל וְשָׁתֹה
כָּל־עֲדַת יִשְׂרָאֵל יַעֲשׂוּ אֹתוֹ: שמות יב

Extend Your loving-kindness to those who know You, zealous
and retributive God,
Those who keep the seventh day, fulfilling "Remember" and
"Observe,"
Grant them the joy of Jerusalem rebuilt, make them shine with
the light of Your face.
"Fill them with the rich plenty of Your House, give them drink *Ps. 36*
from Your river of delights."

Help those who, on the seventh day, rest from plow and harvest,
Who walk slowly, and eat three meals to bless You.
May their righteousness shine like the light of the seven days,
LORD God of Israel, grant completion. *I Sam. 14*

*Some add:*

LORD, God of Israel, Savior for all times.

*The following verse is often omitted:*

(Make them holy in Your commands,
and pure as the very sky is pure.
Bring them to rest with Your spirit,
as cattle descend from mountain to valley,
May their Sabbaths bring them to dwell in the moon [shaped]
inheritance [the Sanhedrin],
"Like streams stretched out, like gardens on the river side.") *Num. 24*

מְשֹׁךְ חַסְדְּךָ לְיוֹדְעֶיךָ, אֵל קַנּוֹא וְנוֹקֵם
נוֹטְרֵי יוֹם הַשְּׁבִיעִי זָכוֹר וְשָׁמוֹר לְהָקֵם
שַׂמְּחֵם בְּבִנְיַן שָׁלֵם, בְּאוֹר פָּנֶיךָ תַּבְהִיקֵם
יִרְוְיֻן מִדֶּשֶׁן בֵּיתֶךָ, וְנַחַל עֲדָנֶיךָ תַשְׁקֵם: תהלים לו

עֲזֹר לַשּׁוֹבְתִים בַּשְּׁבִיעִי, בֶּחָרִישׁ וּבַקָּצִיר עוֹלָמִים
פּוֹסְעִים בּוֹ פְּסִיעָה קְטַנָּה
סוֹעֲדִים בּוֹ, לְבָרֵךְ שָׁלֹשׁ פְּעָמִים
צִדְקָתָם תַּצְהִיר כְּאוֹר שִׁבְעַת הַיָּמִים
יהוה אֱלֹהֵי יִשְׂרָאֵל, הָבָה תָמִים: שמואל א, יד

*Some add:*

יהוה אֱלֹהֵי יִשְׂרָאֵל, תְּשׁוּעַת עוֹלָמִים.

*The following verse is often omitted:*

(קַדְּשֵׁם בְּמִצְוֹתֶיךָ, וְטַהֲרֵם כְּעֶצֶם הַשָּׁמַיִם לָטֹהַר
רוּחֲךָ תְּנִחֵמוֹ, כַּבְּהֵמָה תֵּרֵד בַּבִּקְעָה מִן הָהָר
שַׁבְּתֵיהֶם תַּשְׁכִּנֵם בְּנַחֲלַת הַסַּהַר
כִּנְחָלִים נִטָּיוּ, כְּגַנֹּת עֲלֵי נָהָר:) במדבר כד

מְנוּחָה וְשִׂמְחָה Rest and joy, light for all Jews,
Is the Sabbath day, day of delights;
Those who keep and recall it bear witness
That in six days all creation was made.

The highest heavens, land and seas,
The hosts of heaven, high and sublime;
Sea monsters, humans and all wild beasts,
Were created by God, the Lord,
who formed all worlds.

It was He who spoke to His treasured people:
"Keep it to make it holy from beginning to end."
The holy Sabbath is His day of delight,
For on it God rested from all His work.

Through the Sabbath commandment
God will give you strength,
Rise, pray to Him, and He will invigorate you.
Recite the Nishmat prayer, and the Kedusha,
Then eat with joy, for He is pleased with you.

With twin loaves, and wine for the Kiddush,
With many delicacies and a willing spirit;
Those who delight in it shall merit great reward:
The coming of the redeemer,
and life in the World to Come.

מְנוּחָה וְשִׂמְחָה אוֹר לַיְּהוּדִים
יוֹם שַׁבָּתוֹן, יוֹם מַחֲמַדִּים
שׁוֹמְרָיו וְזוֹכְרָיו הֵמָּה מְעִידִים
כִּי לְשִׁשָּׁה כֹּל בְּרוּאִים וְעוֹמְדִים.

שְׁמֵי שָׁמַיִם, אֶרֶץ וְיַמִּים
כָּל צְבָא מָרוֹם גְּבוֹהִים וְרָמִים
תַּנִּין וְאָדָם וְחַיַּת רְאֵמִים
כִּי בְּיָהּ יהוה צוּר עוֹלָמִים.

הוּא אֲשֶׁר דִּבֶּר לְעַם סְגֻלָּתוֹ
שָׁמוֹר לְקַדְּשׁוֹ מִבּוֹאוֹ עַד צֵאתוֹ
שַׁבַּת קֹדֶשׁ יוֹם חֶמְדָּתוֹ
כִּי בוֹ שָׁבַת אֵל מִכָּל מְלַאכְתּוֹ.

בְּמִצְוַת שַׁבָּת אֵל יַחֲלִיצָךְ
קוּם קְרָא אֵלָיו, יָחִישׁ לְאַמְּצָךְ
נִשְׁמַת כָּל חַי וְגַם נַעֲרִיצָךְ
אֱכֹל בְּשִׂמְחָה כִּי כְבָר רָצָךְ.

בְּמִשְׁנֶה לֶחֶם וְקִדּוּשׁ רַבָּה
בְּרֹב מַטְעַמִּים וְרוּחַ נְדִיבָה
יִזְכּוּ לְרַב טוּב הַמִּתְעַנְּגִים בָּהּ
בְּבִיאַת גּוֹאֵל לְחַיֵּי הָעוֹלָם הַבָּא.

מַה־יְּדִידוּת How beloved is your rest, Sabbath Queen,
We run to greet you: Come, royal bride,
Dressed in fine robes. We light the light with blessing.
All labors end [as is said:] "You shall do no work."
To savor the delights of fowl, quail and fish.

In advance all kinds of tasty food have been prepared,
Fattened chickens made ready while it was still day.
Varied dishes set out, and fragrant wines to drink,
And special delicacies all three times.
To savor the delights of fowl, quail and fish.

They shall inherit Jacob's heritage, a heritage unbounded,
Rich and poor will honor [the Sabbath] and be worthy of redemption,
If you keep the Sabbath day you will be My special treasure,
Six days shall you labor – and on the seventh let us rejoice.
To savor the delights of fowl, quail and fish.

---

weekday attire should not be the same as one's Shabbat attire, and if he does not have [clothing] to change, he should lower his *tallit* so that his attire is not the same as during the week." Maimonides doesn't stress that his Shabbat attire be more elegant; rather, the essential idea is that it be noticeably different than what he wears during the week. By setting aside garments to wear specifically on Shabbat, even if they are not necessarily superior to our weekday clothing, we demonstrate that Shabbat is singular and holy, set aside from the rest of the week. People mistakenly believe that we put on our best suits for the synagogue to honor the solemn prayers, but this is incorrect. We wear a distinctive dress in honor of the day itself, and whether we are in the synagogue, in our homes or on the street we must demonstrate that Shabbat is unique, and unlike any other day. (*Harerei Kedem*, vol. 3, pp. 232–233)

מֵעֶרֶב מַזְמִינִים כָּל מִינֵי מַטְעַמִּים *In advance all kinds of tasty food have been prepared.* Regarding the obligation to prepare for Shabbat, Maimonides (*Hilkhot*

מַה־יְּדִידוּת מְנוּחָתֵךְ, אַתְּ שַׁבָּת הַמַּלְכָּה
בְּכֵן נָרוּץ לִקְרָאתֵךְ, בּוֹאִי כַלָּה נְסוּכָה
לְבוּשׁ בִּגְדֵי חֲמוּדוֹת, לְהַדְלִיק נֵר בִּבְרָכָה
וַתֵּכֶל כָּל הָעֲבוֹדוֹת, לֹא תַעֲשׂוּ מְלָאכָה.
לְהִתְעַנֵּג בְּתַעֲנוּגִים בַּרְבּוּרִים וּשְׂלָו וְדָגִים.

מֵעֶרֶב מַזְמִינִים כָּל מִינֵי מַטְעַמִּים
מִבְּעוֹד יוֹם מוּכָנִים תַּרְנְגוֹלִים מְפֻטָּמִים
וְלַעֲרֹךְ כַּמָּה מִינִים, שְׁתוֹת יֵינוֹת מְבֻשָּׂמִים
וְתַפְנוּקֵי מַעֲדַנִּים בְּכָל שָׁלֹשׁ פְּעָמִים.
לְהִתְעַנֵּג בְּתַעֲנוּגִים בַּרְבּוּרִים וּשְׂלָו וְדָגִים.

נַחֲלַת יַעֲקֹב יִירָשׁ, בְּלִי מְצָרִים נַחֲלָה
וִיכַבְּדוּהוּ עָשִׁיר וָרָשׁ, וְתִזְכּוּ לִגְאֻלָּה
יוֹם שַׁבָּת אִם תְּכַבֵּדוּ וִהְיִיתֶם לִי סְגֻלָּה
שֵׁשֶׁת יָמִים תַּעֲבֹדוּ וּבַשְּׁבִיעִי נָגִילָה.
לְהִתְעַנֵּג בְּתַעֲנוּגִים בַּרְבּוּרִים וּשְׂלָו וְדָגִים.

---

MAH YEDIDUT

**לְבוּשׁ בִּגְדֵי חֲמוּדוֹת** *Dressed in fine robes.* The Talmud (*Shabbat* 113a) instructs that if one can afford to, he should have separate garments for Shabbat, and if not, he should "unroll his garments." Rashi (ad loc.) explains that by unrolling his garments, he is following the practice of the wealthy and leisurely, who wear long, flowing clothes, because they did not need to worry about dirtying their clothing in the fields. Rashi understands that a person's Shabbat attire should be more elegant than his weekday clothing. If one cannot afford different clothing, then on Shabbat he should wear his clothing in a more dignified manner. However, Maimonides (*Hilkhot Shabbat* 30:3) seemingly understands this obligation differently, writing that "one's

Your secular concerns are forbidden; so too are
calculations.
Reflections are permitted, and arranging matches for girls,
And teaching a child a book, and singing songs of praise,
And meditating on fine words at every place and gathering.
To savor the delights of fowl, quail and fish.

Your walk shall be unhurried; you shall call the Sabbath
a delight.
Sleep too is praiseworthy, for it refreshes the spirit.
Therefore my soul yearns for you, to rest in you in love,
As if within a fence of roses: on it son and daughter rest.
To savor the delights of fowl, quail and fish.

A foretaste of the World to Come is the day of Sabbath rest.
All who take delight in it will be worthy of great joy.
They will be delivered with relief from the birthpangs
of the Messiah,
May our redemption spring forth, and sadness and sighing
flee away.
To savor the delights of fowl, quail and fish.

---

with regard to Shabbat preparations, Maimonides does not write that it is preferable for the person to do it himself; he writes that it is a requirement, even for the most distinguished individuals. While personal involvement is only a *hiddur* for other *mitzvot*, for Shabbat preparations it is a requirement. This is because the *mitzva* of *kevod Shabbat* is not merely a means to ensure that we will have food and other necessities available on Shabbat. Instead, by preparing for Shabbat beforehand, a person demonstrates his personal love and anticipation for the day. Thus, if he delegates all of the necessary arrangements for Shabbat to others, he has not properly honored the day, because he has not shown his own anticipation and eagerness for Shabbat's arrival. (*Mesorah*, vol. 5, pp. 16–17)

חֲפָצֶיךָ אֲסוּרִים וְגַם לַחְשֹׁב חֶשְׁבּוֹנוֹת
הִרְהוּרִים מֻתָּרִים וּלְשַׁדֵּךְ הַבָּנוֹת
וְתִינוֹק לְלַמְּדוֹ סֵפֶר, לַמְנַצֵּחַ בִּנְגִינוֹת
וְלַהֲגוֹת בְּאִמְרֵי שֶׁפֶר בְּכָל פִּנּוֹת וּמַחֲנוֹת.
לְהִתְעַנֵּג בְּתַעֲנוּגִים בַּרְבּוּרִים וּשְׂלָו וְדָגִים.

הִלּוּכָךְ יְהֵא בְנַחַת, עֹנֶג קְרָא לַשַּׁבָּת
וְהַשֵּׁנָה מְשֻׁבַּחַת כְּדָת נֶפֶשׁ מְשִׁיבַת
בְּכֵן נַפְשִׁי לְךָ עָרְגָה וְלָנוּחַ בְּחִבַּת
כַּשּׁוֹשַׁנִּים סוּגָה, בּוֹ יָנוּחוּ בֵּן וּבַת.
לְהִתְעַנֵּג בְּתַעֲנוּגִים בַּרְבּוּרִים וּשְׂלָו וְדָגִים.

מֵעֵין עוֹלָם הַבָּא יוֹם שַׁבָּת מְנוּחָה
כָּל הַמִּתְעַנְּגִים בָּהּ יִזְכּוּ לְרֹב שִׂמְחָה
מֵחֶבְלֵי מָשִׁיחַ יֻצָּלוּ לִרְוָחָה
פְּדוּתֵנוּ תַצְמִיחַ, וְנָס יָגוֹן וַאֲנָחָה.
לְהִתְעַנֵּג בְּתַעֲנוּגִים בַּרְבּוּרִים וּשְׂלָו וְדָגִים.

---

*Shabbat* 30:6) writes that "even a very important person who is unaccustomed to buying items at the marketplace or to doing housework is required to perform, himself, tasks to prepare for the Sabbath, for that is its honor. Amongst the Sages of earlier generations, one would chop wood to use for cooking, one would salt meat, one would braid wicks…The more one does, the more praiseworthy it is." In general, even when it is possible to appoint an agent to fulfill a *mitzva*, it is preferable for the person to perform the *mitzva* himself. Although the person discharges his obligation either way, when he chooses to do it himself he demonstrates his devotion to the *mitzva*. It is a *hiddur mitzva*, an added enhancement of the *mitzva*. However,

יוֹם זֶה לְיִשְׂרָאֵל This day for Israel is light and joy,
a Sabbath of serenity.
At the assembly at Sinai You decreed the laws,
Sabbath and the festivals – to keep them all my years;
Setting a table before me with courses of fine food –
A Sabbath of serenity.

This day, for Israel, is light and joy, a Sabbath of serenity.

Heart's delight to a shattered people,
To suffering spirits, an extra soul.
From troubled hearts may it banish sighs –
A Sabbath of serenity.

This day, for Israel, is light and joy, a Sabbath of serenity.

You sanctified and blessed it above all other days.
In six days You finished the making of all worlds.
On it sad souls find quiet and safety –
A Sabbath of serenity.

This day, for Israel, is light and joy, a Sabbath of serenity.

All work is forbidden by the revered One's commandment,
I will merit royal glory if I keep the Sabbath day,
Bringing the awesome One a sweetly scented gift –
A Sabbath of serenity.

This day, for Israel, is light and joy, a Sabbath of serenity.

---

time. To Judaism, in contrast, time is a living entity. There is substance and quality to time, essence. Time is not a mere void but a real entity, and thus we can ascribe attributes such as joyous or sad to time just as one can ascribe these attributes to people. One can refer to a day as evil, meaning that the day itself is cursed. Similarly, when we refer to a day as holy, we do not merely signify that it is a day in which man somehow experiences holiness. The day itself has an inner endowment, a charisma hidden in its very substance. It has suddenly become a metaphysical entity. (*Halakhic Mind*, pp. 47–48)

יוֹם זֶה לְיִשְׂרָאֵל אוֹרָה וְשִׂמְחָה, שַׁבַּת מְנוּחָה.
צִוִּיתָ פִּקּוּדִים בְּמַעֲמַד סִינַי
שַׁבָּת וּמוֹעֲדִים לִשְׁמֹר בְּכָל שָׁנַי
לַעֲרֹךְ לְפָנַי מַשְׂאֵת וַאֲרוּחָה שַׁבַּת מְנוּחָה.
יוֹם זֶה לְיִשְׂרָאֵל אוֹרָה וְשִׂמְחָה, שַׁבַּת מְנוּחָה.

חֶמְדַּת הַלְּבָבוֹת לְאֻמָּה שְׁבוּרָה
לִנְפָשׁוֹת נִכְאָבוֹת נְשָׁמָה יְתֵרָה
לְנֶפֶשׁ מְצֵרָה יָסִיר אֲנָחָה שַׁבַּת מְנוּחָה.
יוֹם זֶה לְיִשְׂרָאֵל אוֹרָה וְשִׂמְחָה, שַׁבַּת מְנוּחָה.

קִדַּשְׁתָּ בֵּרַכְתָּ אוֹתוֹ מִכָּל יָמִים
בְּשֵׁשֶׁת כִּלִּיתָ מְלֶאכֶת עוֹלָמִים
בּוֹ מָצְאוּ עֲגוּמִים הַשְׁקֵט וּבִטְחָה שַׁבַּת מְנוּחָה.
יוֹם זֶה לְיִשְׂרָאֵל אוֹרָה וְשִׂמְחָה, שַׁבַּת מְנוּחָה.

לְאִסּוּר מְלָאכָה צִוִּיתָנוּ נוֹרָא
אֶזְכֶּה הוֹד מְלוּכָה אִם שַׁבָּת אֶשְׁמְרָה
אַקְרִיב שַׁי לַמּוֹרָא, מִנְחָה מֶרְקָחָה שַׁבַּת מְנוּחָה.
יוֹם זֶה לְיִשְׂרָאֵל אוֹרָה וְשִׂמְחָה, שַׁבַּת מְנוּחָה.

---

YOM ZEH L'YISRAEL
To modern man, a day is not a living entity. We do not understand time as something to which we can ascribe attributes or attach character traits. To modern man, time is a mathematical concept. Modern physics has combined time with space, rendering time as empty as space, merely one coordinate of a system within which we try to model the universe. The seasons of the year or the astronomical events of sunrise and sunset do not, in the least, determine the character of time. On the contrary, like other phenomena they occur *in*

And I shall offer You verses, in melody and song.
Standing before Your great splendor, my soul longs for You.
Keep Your promise, to Your single-minded treasure –
A Sabbath of serenity.

This day, for Israel, is light and joy, a Sabbath of serenity.

Desire my prayers like the first offering of Nahshon,
And the day of my serenity with happiness and joy,
Beloved like the apple of one's eye, with all successes –
A Sabbath of serenity.

This day, for Israel, is light and joy, a Sabbath of serenity.

We still wait for You to save us, LORD, most glorious of the glorified,
Send, please, to the Hebrews, the child of David, our king.
And declare liberty, relief and respite –
A Sabbath of serenity.

This day, for Israel, is light and joy, a Sabbath of serenity.

Please, Most High, held in awe, see our torments.
Redeem us quickly, be gracious to us, answer us.
Make our souls happy, in light and in joy –
A Sabbath of serenity.

This day, for Israel, is light and joy, a Sabbath of serenity.

Renew our Sanctuary, remember the ruined city.
Bestow Your goodness, Savior, on one who is sad,
Yet still she spends the Sabbath in song and praise –
A Sabbath of serenity.

This day, for Israel, is light and joy, a Sabbath of serenity.

Remember us, Holy One, for the sake of the honored day,
Keep us, please, this day and every day.
My bright, formidable Beloved, bring relief –
A Sabbath of serenity.

This day, for Israel, is light and joy, a Sabbath of serenity.

Let Israel hear a voice of joy and of salvation,
As the vision of redemption is fulfilled, our Rock, who makes salvation flourish,
Make the light of my sun come and shine then always –
A Sabbath of serenity.

This day, for Israel, is light and joy, a Sabbath of serenity.

וְשִׁיר אֶעֱרָךְ לָךְ בְּנִגּוּן וּנְעִימָה
מוּל תִּפְאֶרֶת גָּדְלָךְ נַפְשִׁי לָךְ כָּמַהּ
לִסְגֻלָּה תְמִימָה קַיֵּם הַבְטָחָה שַׁבָּת מְנוּחָה.
יוֹם זֶה לְיִשְׂרָאֵל אוֹרָה וְשִׂמְחָה, שַׁבַּת מְנוּחָה.

רְצֵה תְפִלָּתִי כְּמוֹ קָרְבַּן נַחְשׁוֹן
וְיוֹם מְנוּחָתִי בְּשִׂמְחָה וּבְשָׂשׂוֹן
חָבִיב כְּבַת אִישׁוֹן בְּרֹב הַצְלָחָה שַׁבָּת מְנוּחָה.
יוֹם זֶה לְיִשְׂרָאֵל אוֹרָה וְשִׂמְחָה, שַׁבַּת מְנוּחָה.

יֶשְׁעֲךָ קִוִּינוּ יָהּ אַדִּיר אַדִּירִים
בֶּן דָּוִד מַלְכֵּנוּ שְׁלַח נָא לָעִבְרִים
וְיִקְרָא לִדְרוֹרִים רֶוַח וַהֲנָחָה שַׁבָּת מְנוּחָה.
יוֹם זֶה לְיִשְׂרָאֵל אוֹרָה וְשִׂמְחָה, שַׁבַּת מְנוּחָה.

אָנָּא עֶלְיוֹן נוֹרָא הַבִּיטָה עָנֵינוּ
פְּדֵנוּ בִמְהֵרָה חָנֵּנוּ וַעֲנֵנוּ
שַׂמַּח נַפְשֵׁנוּ בְּאוֹר וְשִׂמְחָה שַׁבָּת מְנוּחָה.
יוֹם זֶה לְיִשְׂרָאֵל אוֹרָה וְשִׂמְחָה, שַׁבַּת מְנוּחָה.

**חַדֵּשׁ מִקְדָּשֵׁנוּ זָכְרָה נֶחֱרֶבֶת**
**טוּבְךָ, מוֹשִׁיעֵנוּ תְּנָה לַנֶּעֱצֶבֶת**
**בְּשַׁבָּת יוֹשֶׁבֶת בְּזֶמֶר וּשְׁבָחָה שַׁבַּת מְנוּחָה.**
**יוֹם זֶה לְיִשְׂרָאֵל אוֹרָה וְשִׂמְחָה, שַׁבַּת מְנוּחָה.**

זְכֹר, קָדוֹשׁ, לָנוּ בִּזְכוּת יְקָרַת הַיּוֹם
שְׁמָר נָא אוֹתָנוּ בְּיוֹם זֶה וּבְכָל יוֹם
דּוֹדִי צַח וְאָיוֹם תָּבִיא רְוָחָה שַׁבָּת מְנוּחָה.
יוֹם זֶה לְיִשְׂרָאֵל אוֹרָה וְשִׂמְחָה, שַׁבַּת מְנוּחָה.

קוֹל רִנָּה וִישׁוּעָה לְיִשְׂרָאֵל הַשְׁמִיעָה
בְּבֹא חֶזְיוֹן תְּשׁוּעָה צוּר, מַצְמִיחַ יְשׁוּעָה
אוֹר שִׁמְשִׁי הוֹפִיעָה תָּמִיד הַזְרִיחָה שַׁבָּת מְנוּחָה.
יוֹם זֶה לְיִשְׂרָאֵל אוֹרָה וְשִׂמְחָה, שַׁבַּת מְנוּחָה.

יָהּ רִבּוֹן Master of all worlds, our God, adored,
King of kings, over all the LORD:
Your wondrous deeds to applaud
We sing to You with one accord.

God of all worlds,
our God, adored;
King of kings,
over all, the LORD.

Early and late my praise shall ring,
To You, holy Author of every thing:
Beasts of the field, birds that take wing.
Angels and mortals to You shall sing.

God of all worlds,
our God, adored;
King of kings,
over all, the LORD.

Your great good deeds are vast in scale,
You humble the proud, You lift the frail.
A thousand years would not avail
Of Your works to tell the tale.

God of all worlds,
our God, adored;
King of kings,
over all, the LORD.

יָהּ רִבּוֹן עָלַם וְעָלְמַיָּא
אַנְתְּ הוּא מַלְכָּא מֶלֶךְ מַלְכַיָּא
עוֹבַד גְּבוּרְתָךְ וְתִמְהַיָּא
שְׁפַר קֳדָמָךְ לְהַחֲוָיָא.

יָהּ רִבּוֹן עָלַם וְעָלְמַיָּא
אַנְתְּ הוּא מַלְכָּא מֶלֶךְ מַלְכַיָּא.

שְׁבָחִין אֲסַדֵּר צַפְרָא וְרַמְשָׁא
לָךְ אֱלָהָא קַדִּישָׁא דִּי בְרָא כָּל נַפְשָׁא
עִירִין קַדִּישִׁין וּבְנֵי אֱנָשָׁא
חֵיוַת בְּרָא וְעוֹפֵי שְׁמַיָּא.

יָהּ רִבּוֹן עָלַם וְעָלְמַיָּא
אַנְתְּ הוּא מַלְכָּא מֶלֶךְ מַלְכַיָּא.

רַבְרְבִין עוֹבְדָיךְ וְתַקִּיפִין
מָכֵךְ רָמַיָּא וְזָקֵף כְּפִיפִין
לוּ יְחֵי גְבַר שְׁנִין אַלְפִין
לָא יֵעֹל גְּבוּרְתָךְ בְּחֻשְׁבְּנַיָּא.

יָהּ רִבּוֹן עָלַם וְעָלְמַיָּא
אַנְתְּ הוּא מַלְכָּא מֶלֶךְ מַלְכַיָּא.

Yours is the glory, the greatness too,
From the lion's jaw, Your flock rescue.
Bring Your exiles home to You:
The people You chose, deliver anew.

God of all worlds,
our God, adored;
King of kings,
over all, the LORD.

Come back to Your Temple, Your sacred shrine,
That there in joy our souls may entwine.
In song our voices to combine,
When Jerusalem's beauty again will shine.

God of all worlds,
our God, adored;
King of kings,
over all, the LORD.

---

of the Temple and their music symbolize in our praise of the Creator? While, on the one hand, we must thank God and praise Him according to our intelligence and understanding, we must also always remember that our praises will inevitably fall short. As the Psalmist rhetorically asks: "Who can relate the mighty deeds of the LORD? Who can pronounce all of His praise?" (Ps. 106:2) or, as this very *zemer* notes, "לוּ יְחֵי גְּבַר שְׁנִין אַלְפִין לָא יֵעֹל גְּבוּרְתָּךְ בְּחֻשְׁבְּנַיָּא, even if man would live for a thousand years, he could not recount Your mighty deeds." The music we play in the Temple expresses this idea, that God's praise cannot be achieved by words, but rather, "To You, silence is praise" (Ps. 65:2). Standing in God's presence, we recognize that we lack the vocabulary to capture His majesty. The ocean of feelings, of thanksgiving, awe, and love within one who stands before the Almighty wants to burst forth, but it cannot be constrained by words or forced into the rational order of sentences. Outside the Temple we recognize and are cognizant of the inadequacy of our praise, but in the Temple we express those feelings. The Levites would play the holy songs on their instruments to symbolize their desire to endlessly sing to God without the limitations of language and the inadequacy of words. (*Shiurim LeZekher Abba Mari*, vol. 2, pp. 80–82)

אֱלָהָא דִּי לֵהּ יְקָר וּרְבוּתָא
פְּרֹק יָת עָנָךְ מִפֻּם אַרְיְוָתָא
וְאַפֵּק יָת עַמָּךְ מִגּוֹ גָלוּתָא
עַמָּא דִּי בְחַרְתְּ מִכָּל אֻמַּיָּא.

יָהּ רִבּוֹן עָלַם וְעָלְמַיָּא
אַנְתְּ הוּא מַלְכָּא מֶֽלֶךְ מַלְכַיָּא.

לְמַקְדְּשָׁךְ תּוּב וּלְקֹֽדֶשׁ קֻדְשִׁין
אֲתַר דִּי בֵהּ יֶחֱדוּן רוּחִין וְנַפְשִׁין
וִיזַמְּרוּן לָךְ שִׁירִין וְרַחֲשִׁין
בִּירוּשְׁלֵם קַרְתָּא דְשֻׁפְרַיָּא.

יָהּ רִבּוֹן עָלַם וְעָלְמַיָּא
אַנְתְּ הוּא מַלְכָּא מֶֽלֶךְ מַלְכַיָּא.

---

YAH RIBON

לְמַקְדְּשָׁךְ תּוּב ... וִיזַמְּרוּן לָךְ שִׁירִין וְרַחֲשִׁין *Come back to Your Temple... in song our voices to combine.* The final stanza of this song is a plea that God return to His Temple so that we may rejoice and sing His praises in His holy abode in Jerusalem, the city of beauty. Indeed, there is a unique *mitzva* and religious experience of *shira bamikdash,* the singing of hymns in the Temple, which, in turn, includes two components: First, there is an obligation for the Levites to sing during the offering of the communal sacrifices as a part of the sacrificial service. And second, there is *shira* which is independent of the sacrificial service, as found most prominently in the case of the *simḥat beit hasho'eiva,* the great celebrations which took place in the Temple on Sukkot. One distinctive aspect of the *shira* in the Temple was that it included musical instruments. (The Talmud [*Sukka* 50b] debates whether the vocal component or the instrumental component was primary, but all agree that both aspects existed.) Although a person may be obligated to recite *shira* outside the Temple as well, as when he experiences a personal salvation, in these cases he is only required to recite the *shira* with his voice. There is no obligation to enhance his *shira* with the accompaniment of musical instruments. What did the instruments

צָמְאָה נַפְשִׁי My soul thirsts for God, the living God *Ps. 42*
My heart and flesh will sing joyfully to the living God. *Ps. 84*
The One God created me, and said "As I live,
No one shall see Me and live."
My soul thirsts for God, the living God
My heart and flesh will sing joyfully to the living God.

He created all with wisdom, design and deliberation,
Deeply hidden though it is from the eyes of all that live.
His glory is high above all, every mouth makes known His splendor,
Blessed is He in whose hands is the life-force of all that lives.
My soul thirsts for God, the living God
My heart and flesh will sing joyfully to the living God.

He set apart the quiet one's offspring, to teach them decrees,
Which if one performs them, thereby he shall live.
Who can vindicate himself? We are like specks of dust,
Truly none can vindicate itself before You, nothing that lives.
My soul thirsts for God, the living God
My heart and flesh will sing joyfully to the living God.

In the heart, the inclination is like a viper's poison,
How then can we return, and be like flesh that lives?
Those who have gone astray, if they wished, could turn from their way,
Before they go to their rest in the place destined for all that lives.
My soul thirsts for God, the living God
My heart and flesh will sing joyfully to the living God.

For everything, I shall thank You, every mouth shall declare Your oneness,
You who open Your hand and satisfy all that lives.
Recall the love of ancient times, and revive those who slumber,
Bring near the days when the Messiah shall live.
My soul thirsts for God, the living God
My heart and flesh will sing joyfully to the living God.

See who is the true mistress, when the handmaid says,
"No, your son is dead while my son lives."
I will bow face down and spread my hands toward you,
When I open my mouth to say: "The soul of all that lives."
My soul thirsts for God, the living God
My heart and flesh will sing joyfully to the living God.

צָמְאָה נַפְשִׁי לֵאלֹהִים לְאֵל חָי: לִבִּי וּבְשָׂרִי יְרַנְּנוּ אֶל אֵל־חָי: תהלים מב
אֵל אֶחָד בְּרָאַנִי, וְאָמַר חַי אָנִי כִּי לֹא יִרְאַנִי הָאָדָם וָחָי. תהלים פד
צָמְאָה נַפְשִׁי לֵאלֹהִים לְאֵל חָי, לִבִּי וּבְשָׂרִי יְרַנְּנוּ אֶל אֵל־חָי.

בָּרָא כֹל בְּחָכְמָה, בְּעֵצָה וּבִמְזִמָּה מְאֹד נֶעְלָמָה מֵעֵינֵי כָּל חָי.
רָם עַל כֹּל כְּבוֹדוֹ, כָּל פֶּה יְחַוֶּה הוֹדוֹ בָּרוּךְ אֲשֶׁר בְּיָדוֹ נֶפֶשׁ כָּל חָי.
צָמְאָה נַפְשִׁי לֵאלֹהִים לְאֵל חָי, לִבִּי וּבְשָׂרִי יְרַנְּנוּ אֶל אֵל־חָי.

הִבְדִּיל נִינֵי תָם, חֻקִּים לְהוֹרוֹתָם אֲשֶׁר יַעֲשֶׂה אוֹתָם הָאָדָם וָחָי.
מִי זֶה יִצְטַדָּק, נִמְשַׁל לְאָבָק דָּק אֱמֶת, כִּי לֹא יִצְדַּק לְפָנֶיךָ כָּל חָי.
צָמְאָה נַפְשִׁי לֵאלֹהִים לְאֵל חָי, לִבִּי וּבְשָׂרִי יְרַנְּנוּ אֶל אֵל־חָי.

בְּלֵב יֵצֶר חָשׁוּב כִּדְמוּת חֲמַת עַכְשׁוּב וְאֵיכָכָה יָשׁוּב הַבָּשָׂר הֶחָי.
נְסוֹגִים אִם אָבוּ, וּמִדַּרְכָּם שָׁבוּ טֶרֶם יִשְׁכָּבוּ בֵּית מוֹעֵד לְכָל חָי.
צָמְאָה נַפְשִׁי לֵאלֹהִים לְאֵל חָי, לִבִּי וּבְשָׂרִי יְרַנְּנוּ אֶל אֵל־חָי.

עַל כֹּל אֲהוֹדֶךָ, כָּל פֶּה תְּיַחֲדֶךָ פּוֹתֵחַ אֶת יָדֶךָ וּמַשְׂבִּיעַ לְכָל חָי.
זְכֹר אַהֲבַת קְדוּמִים, וְהַחֲיֵה נִרְדָּמִים וְקָרֵב הַיָּמִים אֲשֶׁר בֶּן יִשַׁי חָי.
צָמְאָה נַפְשִׁי לֵאלֹהִים לְאֵל חָי, לִבִּי וּבְשָׂרִי יְרַנְּנוּ אֶל אֵל־חָי.

רְאֵה לִגְבֶרֶת אֱמֶת, שִׁפְחָה נוֹאֱמֶת לֹא כִי, בְּנֵךְ הַמֵּת וּבְנִי הֶחָי.
אֶקֹּד עַל אַפִּי, וְאֶפְרֹשׂ לְךָ כַּפִּי עֵת אֶפְתַּח פִּי בְּנִשְׁמַת כָּל חָי.
צָמְאָה נַפְשִׁי לֵאלֹהִים לְאֵל חָי, לִבִּי וּבְשָׂרִי יְרַנְּנוּ אֶל אֵל־חָי.

---

TZAM'A NAFSHI

צָמְאָה נַפְשִׁי לֵאלֹהִים *My soul thirsts for God.* Maimonides (*Hilkhot Yesodei HaTorah* 2:2) employs this same verse in Psalms (42:3) when describing the person who has become intoxicated with the unquenchable desire to know his Creator: "When a person contemplates His great and wondrous works and creatures and from them obtains a glimpse of His wisdom, which is

יָהּ אֶכְסֹף Lord, I yearn the grace of Sabbath, perfectly fitting, one with Your treasured ones.
Draw the grace of Your reverence to a people that seeks Your desire.
Make them holy in the holiness of Shabbat, which is one with Your Torah;
Open up for them the grace and desire to open the gates of Your desire.

He Who Was and Is, keep those who keep and watch for Your holy Shabbat:
As a deer longs for springs of water,
so their soul longs to receive the grace of Shabbat,
which is one with Your holy Name.
Shade those who linger before parting from Shabbat,
so that You will not be closed off from them in the six days
that take holiness from Your holy Shabbat.
And purify their hearts in truth and in faithfulness, to serve You.

(And let Your compassion ripple down through all Your aspects)
Let Your compassion ripple down to Your holy people,
To quench those thirsting for Your kindness
from the river that flows from Eden,
To ornament Israel in the splendor of those
who glorify You in Your holy Shabbat,
To leave them, all six days, the heritage of Jacob whom You chose.

Shabbat, grace of souls; the seventh day, delight of spirits and Eden of life,
where they delight in Your love and in Your awe.
Holy Shabbat, my soul is sick with love for You;
Holy Shabbat, the souls of Israel shall shelter in the shade of Your wings,
Shall be nourished in the plenty of Your house.

---

close and submerge in Him. This ecstatic love also drives man to praise and sing, to compose hymns to God. This attraction to God, though, is not only a moral idea embedded in man, but a cosmic force. Maimonides (*Guide for the Perplexed* 1:72) writes that "the universe, in its entirety, is nothing but one individual being," a macro-anthropos, a great living creature. In truth, the entire universe longs, like every individual, to connect to its Creator and sing His praise. (*And From There You Shall Seek*, p. 174)

יָהּ אֶכְסֹף נֹעַם שַׁבָּת הַמַּתְאֶמֶת וּמְיֻחֶדֶת בִּסְגֻלָּתֶךָ
מְשֹׁךְ נֹעַם יִרְאָתְךָ לְעַם מְבַקְשֵׁי רְצוֹנֶךָ
קַדְּשֵׁם בִּקְדֻשַּׁת הַשַּׁבָּת הַמִּתְאַחֶדֶת בְּתוֹרָתֶךָ
פְּתַח לָהֶם נֹעַם וְרָצוֹן לִפְתֹּחַ שַׁעֲרֵי רְצוֹנֶךָ

הָיָה הֹוֶה, שְׁמֹר שׁוֹמְרֵי וּמְצַפִּים שַׁבָּת קָדְשֶׁךָ
כְּאַיָּל תַּעֲרֹג עַל אֲפִיקֵי מָיִם
כֵּן נַפְשָׁם תַּעֲרֹג לְקַבֵּל נֹעַם שַׁבָּת הַמִּתְאַחֶדֶת בְּשֵׁם קָדְשֶׁךָ
הַצֵּל מְאַחֲרֵי לִפְרֹשׁ מִן הַשַּׁבָּת, לְבִלְתִּי תִּהְיֶה סָגוּר מֵהֶם שִׁשָּׁה יָמִים
הַמְקַבְּלִים קְדֻשָּׁה מִשַּׁבַּת קָדְשֶׁךָ
וְטַהֵר לִבָּם בֶּאֱמֶת וּבֶאֱמוּנָה לְעָבְדֶךָ

(וִיהִיוּ רַחֲמֶיךָ מִתְגּוֹלְלִים עַל מִדּוֹתֶיךָ)
וִיהְיוּ רַחֲמֶיךָ מִתְגּוֹלְלִים עַל עַם קָדְשֶׁךָ
לְהַשְׁקוֹת צְמֵאֵי חַסְדֶּךָ מִנָּהָר הַיּוֹצֵא מֵעֵדֶן
לְעַטֵּר אֶת יִשְׂרָאֵל בְּתִפְאֶרֶת, הַמְפָאֲרִים אוֹתְךָ עַל יְדֵי שַׁבַּת קָדְשֶׁךָ
כָּל שִׁשָּׁה יָמִים, לְהַנְחִילָם נַחֲלַת יַעֲקֹב בְּחִירֶךָ

הַשַּׁבָּת נֹעַם הַנְּשָׁמוֹת, וְהַשְּׁבִיעִי עֹנֶג הָרוּחוֹת וְעֵדֶן הַנְּפָשׁוֹת
לְהִתְעַדֵּן בְּאַהֲבָתְךָ וְיִרְאָתֶךָ
שַׁבַּת קֹדֶשׁ, נַפְשִׁי חוֹלַת אַהֲבָתֶךָ
שַׁבַּת קֹדֶשׁ, נַפְשׁוֹת יִשְׂרָאֵל בְּצֵל כְּנָפֶיךָ יֶחֱסָיוּן
יִרְוְיֻן מִדֶּשֶׁן בֵּיתֶךָ.

---

incomparable and infinite, he will immediately love Him, praise Him, glorify Him, and long with an exceeding longing to know His great Name, as David said, 'My soul thirsts for God, the living God.'" Man has an uncontrollable, powerful longing, an invisible craving and desire to unite with God, to come

בַּר יוֹחַאי Bar Yoḥai,
you are annointed, happy man!
With oil of joy,
more than all your friends.

Bar Yoḥai, with holy anointing oil, holiness anointed you.
You have worn the high priest's headpiece,
marked "holy"; your crown
is dressed with your splendor.

Bar Yoḥai, you settled in a good place
on the day of your flight, when you ran away
to the cave of rocks; there you stood,
and there you gained your glory and honor.

Bar Yoḥai, of the [Tabernacle's] standing acacia planks
do the learned of the Lord learn from you.
It is enchanted light, the altar-light your teachers
burn; is it not they who teach your words?

Bar Yoḥai, you came to the apple orchard
and climbed up to gather sweet spices,
the secrets of the Torah among the buds and the flowers –
"Let Us make man" was said for your sake.

Bar Yoḥai, you dressed yourself in might,
and forced the battle of the Law's fire back to the gate.
You drew your sword out from its sheath
and brandished it against your tormentors.

בַּר יוֹחַאי, נִמְשַׁחְתָּ, אַשְׁרֶיךָ
שֶׁמֶן שָׂשׂוֹן מֵחֲבֵרֶיךָ

בַּר יוֹחַאי, שֶׁמֶן מִשְׁחַת קֹדֶשׁ
נִמְשַׁחְתָּ מִמִּדַּת הַקֹּדֶשׁ
נָשָׂאתָ צִיץ נֵזֶר הַקֹּדֶשׁ
חָבוּשׁ עַל רֹאשְׁךָ, פְּאֵרֶךָ

בַּר יוֹחַאי, מוֹשַׁב טוֹב יָשַׁבְתָּ
יוֹם נַסְתָּ, יוֹם אֲשֶׁר בָּרַחְתָּ
בִּמְעָרַת צוּרִים שֶׁעָמַדְתָּ
שָׁם קָנִיתָ הוֹדְךָ וַהֲדָרֶךָ

בַּר יוֹחַאי, עֲצֵי שִׁטִּים עוֹמְדִים
לְמוּדֵי יהוה הֵם לוֹמְדִים
אוֹר מֻפְלָא, אוֹר הַיְקוֹד הֵם יוֹקְדִים
הֲלֹא הֵמָּה יוֹרוּךָ, מוֹרֶיךָ

בַּר יוֹחַאי, בָּאתָ לִשְׂדֵה תַּפּוּחִים
וְעָלִיתָ לִלְקֹט בּוֹ מֶרְקָחִים
סוֹד תּוֹרָה בְּצִיצִים וּפְרָחִים
״נַעֲשֶׂה אָדָם״ נֶאֱמַר בַּעֲבוּרֶךָ

בַּר יוֹחַאי, נֶאֱזַרְתָּ בִּגְבוּרָה
וּבְמִלְחֶמֶת אֵשׁ דַּת הַשְּׁעָרָה
וְחֶרֶב הוֹצֵאתָ מִתַּעְרָהּ
שָׁלַפְתָּ נֶגֶד צוֹרְרֶיךָ

Bar Yoḥai, to a place of marble stones
you came. to the presence of a lion,
and even the globes atop the pillars above the Great Bear
you saw – but who shall ever see you?

Bar Yoḥai, in the Holy of Holies
stretches the green horizon, the beginning of new things;
seven Sabbaths, the secrets of all fifty [gates of wisdom]
you bound; your knots are the *shin*
knots [of God's tefillin].

Bar Yoḥai, you saw the *yod* of ancient Wisdom,
with its innermost honor,
the thirty-two paths [of creation],
beginning of the offering –
you are the cherub anointed
with the brilliance of your light.

Bar Yoḥai, at the wondrous light which is highest of all,
you were afraid to look, for it is too much,
this mystery – it is called Nothingness –
you, like it, shall be seen by no eye.

Bar Yoḥai, happy the one who gave birth to you,
happy the people who learn from you,
happy those who can reach your secrets,
wearing the priest's breast-plate
of your truth-telling stones.

בַּר יוֹחַאי, לִמְקוֹם אַבְנֵי שַׁיִשׁ
הִגַּעְתָּ, וּפְנֵי אַרְיֵה לַיִשׁ
גַּם גֻּלַּת כֹּתֶרֶת עַל עַיִשׁ
תָּשׁוּרִי, וּמִי יְשׁוּרֶךָ

בַּר יוֹחַאי, בְּקֹדֶשׁ הַקֳּדָשִׁים
קַו יָרֹק מְחַדֵּשׁ חֳדָשִׁים
שֶׁבַע שַׁבָּתוֹת, סוֹד חֲמִשִּׁים
קָשַׁרְתָּ קִשְׁרֵי שי״ן קְשָׁרֶיךָ

בַּר יוֹחַאי, יו״ד חָכְמָה קְדוּמָה
הִשְׁקַפְתָּ, לִכְבוּדוֹ פְּנִימָה
ל״ב נְתִיבוֹת, רֵאשִׁית תְּרוּמָה
אַתְּ כְּרוּב מִמְשַׁח זִיו אוֹרֶךָ

בַּר יוֹחַאי, אוֹר מֻפְלָא, רוּם מַעְלָה
יָרֵאתָ מִלְּהַבִּיט, כִּי רַב לָהּ
תַּעֲלוּמָה, וְאֵין קוֹרֵא לָהּ
נַמְתָּ: עַיִן לֹא תְשׁוּרֶךָ

בַּר יוֹחַאי, אַשְׁרֵי יוֹלַדְתֶּךָ
אַשְׁרֵי הָעָם, הֵם לוֹמְדֶיךָ
אַשְׁרֵי הָעוֹמְדִים עַל סוֹדֶךָ
לְבוּשֵׁי חֹשֶׁן תֻּמֶּיךָ וְאוּרֶיךָ.

צוּר מִשֶּׁלּוֹ The Rock from whom we have eaten:
Bless Him, my faithful friends;
we have sufficed, we have left over,
just as the LORD said.

He feeds His world – our Shepherd, our Father,
we have eaten of His bread, His wine we have drunk.
So let us thank His name, let us praise Him with our mouths,
saying, singing: None is holy like the LORD.

The Rock from whom we have eaten: Bless Him, my faithful friends;
we have sufficed, we have left over, just as the LORD said.

With song and sound of thanks, we shall bless our God,
for the gift He gave our fathers: A lovely land.
With food and sustenance He has satisfied our souls.
His kindness overwhelms us: True is the LORD.

The Rock from whom we have eaten: Bless Him, my faithful friends;
we have sufficed, we have left over, just as the LORD said.

Have compassion in Your love for Your people, our Rock,
for Zion, Your home of glory, Temple of our splendor.
The son of David Your servant: may he come and redeem us,
breath of our life, anointed of the LORD.

The Rock from whom we have eaten: Bless Him, my faithful friends;
we have sufficed, we have left over, just as the LORD said.

May the Temple be rebuilt, Zion's city full again;
there we will sing a new song as we go up in joy,
to the Compassionate, the Holy One –
may He be blessed and raised on high –
with a full cup of wine, sign of the blessing of the LORD.

The Rock from whom we have eaten: Bless Him, my faithful friends;
we have sufficed, we have left over, just as the LORD said.

*Birkat HaMazon can be found on page 124.*

צוּר מִשֶּׁלּוֹ אָכַלְנוּ בָּרְכוּ אֱמוּנַי
שָׂבַעְנוּ וְהוֹתַרְנוּ כִּדְבַר יהוה.

הַזָּן אֶת עוֹלָמוֹ רוֹעֵנוּ אָבִינוּ
אָכַלְנוּ אֶת לַחְמוֹ וְיֵינוֹ שָׁתִינוּ
עַל כֵּן נוֹדֶה לִשְׁמוֹ וּנְהַלְלוֹ בְּפִינוּ
אָמַרְנוּ וְעָנִינוּ אֵין קָדוֹשׁ כַּיהוה.

צוּר מִשֶּׁלּוֹ אָכַלְנוּ, בָּרְכוּ אֱמוּנַי, שָׂבַעְנוּ וְהוֹתַרְנוּ כִּדְבַר יהוה.

בְּשִׁיר וְקוֹל תּוֹדָה נְבָרֵךְ אֱלֹהֵינוּ
עַל אֶרֶץ חֶמְדָּה שֶׁהִנְחִיל לַאֲבוֹתֵינוּ
מָזוֹן וְצֵידָה הִשְׂבִּיעַ לְנַפְשֵׁנוּ
חַסְדּוֹ גָּבַר עָלֵינוּ וֶאֱמֶת יהוה.

צוּר מִשֶּׁלּוֹ אָכַלְנוּ, בָּרְכוּ אֱמוּנַי, שָׂבַעְנוּ וְהוֹתַרְנוּ כִּדְבַר יהוה.

רַחֵם בְּחַסְדֶּךָ עַל עַמְּךָ צוּרֵנוּ
עַל צִיּוֹן מִשְׁכַּן כְּבוֹדֶךָ זְבוּל בֵּית תִּפְאַרְתֵּנוּ
בֶּן דָּוִד עַבְדֶּךָ יָבוֹא וְיִגְאָלֵנוּ
רוּחַ אַפֵּינוּ מְשִׁיחַ יהוה.

צוּר מִשֶּׁלּוֹ אָכַלְנוּ, בָּרְכוּ אֱמוּנַי, שָׂבַעְנוּ וְהוֹתַרְנוּ כִּדְבַר יהוה.

יִבָּנֶה הַמִּקְדָּשׁ עִיר צִיּוֹן תְּמַלֵּא
וְשָׁם נָשִׁיר שִׁיר חָדָשׁ וּבִרְנָנָה נַעֲלֶה
הָרַחֲמָן הַנִּקְדָּשׁ יִתְבָּרַךְ וְיִתְעַלֶּה
עַל כּוֹס יַיִן מָלֵא כְּבִרְכַּת יהוה.

צוּר מִשֶּׁלּוֹ אָכַלְנוּ, בָּרְכוּ אֱמוּנַי, שָׂבַעְנוּ וְהוֹתַרְנוּ כִּדְבַר יהוה.

ברכת המזון *can be found on page 125.*

# יום שבת

# SHABBAT DAY

# Kiddush For Shabbat Morning

*Some say:*

אִם־תָּשִׁיב If you keep your feet from breaking the Sabbath, and from pursuing your affairs on My holy day, if you call the Sabbath a delight, and the LORD's holy day honorable, and if you honor it by not going your own way or attending to your own affairs, or speaking idle words, then you will find joy in the LORD, and I will cause you to ride on the heights of the earth and to feast on the inheritance of your father Jacob, for the mouth of the LORD has spoken. *Is. 58*

*Most begin Kiddush here.*
*On Yom Tov, say the Kiddush on page 66 and on Rosh HaShana, on page 68.*

וְשָׁמְרוּ The children of Israel must keep the Sabbath, *Ex. 31*
observing the Sabbath in every generation
as an everlasting covenant.
It is a sign between Me and the children of Israel for ever,
for in six days the LORD made the heavens and the earth,
but on the seventh day He ceased work
and refreshed Himself.

---

However, these two planes of Shabbat, its particular laws and its covenantal testimony, also exist in the positive sense. A person who properly observes Shabbat not only fulfills the specific commandments of Shabbat, but also affirms the testimony of Shabbat, that God is the Creator of the universe and that He has forged an eternal covenant with the Jewish people. Likewise, just as the violation of Shabbat negatively affects the essence of the religious personality of the person, the proper observance of Shabbat elevates him. By bearing witness to the eternal sign of Shabbat he becomes a signatory of this Godly compact, and his level of *kedushat yisrael* is intensified. This is what the Talmud (*Beitza* 16a) means when it speaks of the "*neshama yeteirah*," the "additional soul" of Shabbat. When a person observes the letter and spirit of Shabbat, when he fulfills its laws and bears its testimony, the holiness of the day is impressed upon his spiritual identity and he becomes a different person. (*Shiurim LeZekher Abba Mari*, vol. 2, pp. 139–140; *Nefesh HaRav*, p. 167)

# קידושא רבה לשבת

*Some say:*

אִם־תָּשִׁיב מִשַּׁבָּת רַגְלֶךָ עֲשׂוֹת חֲפָצֶךָ בְּיוֹם קָדְשִׁי, וְקָרָאתָ לַשַּׁבָּת עֹנֶג ישעיה נח
לִקְדוֹשׁ יהוה מְכֻבָּד, וְכִבַּדְתּוֹ מֵעֲשׂוֹת דְּרָכֶיךָ מִמְּצוֹא חֶפְצְךָ וְדַבֵּר דָּבָר:
אָז תִּתְעַנַּג עַל־יהוה, וְהִרְכַּבְתִּיךָ עַל־בָּמֳתֵי אָרֶץ, וְהַאֲכַלְתִּיךָ נַחֲלַת
יַעֲקֹב אָבִיךָ, כִּי פִּי יהוה דִּבֵּר:

*Most begin* קידוש *here.*
*On* יום טוב *say the* קידוש *on page 67 and on* ראש השנה*, on page 69*

וְשָׁמְרוּ בְנֵי־יִשְׂרָאֵל אֶת־הַשַּׁבָּת שמות לא
לַעֲשׂוֹת אֶת־הַשַּׁבָּת לְדֹרֹתָם בְּרִית עוֹלָם:
בֵּינִי וּבֵין בְּנֵי יִשְׂרָאֵל אוֹת הִוא לְעֹלָם
כִּי־שֵׁשֶׁת יָמִים עָשָׂה יהוה אֶת־הַשָּׁמַיִם וְאֶת־הָאָרֶץ
וּבַיּוֹם הַשְּׁבִיעִי שָׁבַת וַיִּנָּפַשׁ:

---

SHABBAT DAY KIDDUSH

בְּרִית עוֹלָם ... אוֹת הִוא לְעֹלָם *An everlasting covenant… a sign… for ever.* Shabbat is much more than a particular *mitzva*; it is a cornerstone of our faith. On the one hand, it is a symbol of our belief that God created the universe *ex nihilo* and that He is the world's master. On the other hand, it represents the unique bond between the Master of the Universe and the people of Israel, "a sign between Me and the children of Israel for ever" (Ex. 31:17). This is why the Talmud (*Ḥullin* 5a) rules that a person who publicly violates Shabbat is treated according to *halakha* as a non-Jew. Publicly violating Shabbat, and thus negating the testimony it bears, is *per se* an act of blasphemy even for a person with absolute faith in God. He has not only transgressed the specific prohibition of Shabbat; he has violated the covenant of Shabbat that binds man to God which affects the very nature of his religious self. My father, Rav Moshe Soloveitchik, quoted his father, Rav Ḥayyim Soloveitchik, who explained that we treat someone who violates Shabbat publicly so severely not because of the brazenness of the sin, but because he is comparable to a *meisit*, a seducer, one who spreads heretical beliefs and practices.

זָכוֹר Remember the Sabbath day to keep it holy. *Ex. 20*
Six days you shall labor and do all your work,
but the seventh day is a Sabbath of the LORD your God;
on it you shall not do any work –
you, your son or daughter, your male or female slave,
or your cattle, or the stranger within your gates.
For in six days the LORD made heaven and earth
and sea and all that is in them,
and rested on the seventh day;
therefore the LORD blessed the Sabbath day
and declared it holy.

*When saying Kiddush for others, add:*
Please pay attention, my masters.

בָּרוּךְ Blessed are You, LORD our God, King of the Universe,
who creates the fruit of the vine.

*On Shabbat Ḥol HaMo'ed Sukkot, if Kiddush is made in the sukka, add:*
Blessed are You, LORD our God, King of the Universe,
who has made us holy through His commandments,
and has commanded us to dwell in the sukka.

---

help, for she cannot set the process of redemption in motion alone. We must take the first step, to open the door and invite the *Shekhina* into our lives. Thus, on Friday evening, we go out to escort the Shabbat queen to us, for she will not come by herself. However, on Shabbat day, God reveals himself as *Malka Kadisha,* the holy king, who awaits no one and needs no assistance. He is the omnipotent Redeemer who can rescue Israel and the *Shekhina* even before the people repent. This is *Zakhor,* which is related to *zakhar,* the male component of God's revelation, which surges forth, is active and creative. This is why, as Naḥmanides explains, during the daytime we recite the *kiddusha rabba,* which consist of nothing more than the blessing of *borei peri hagafen*. While on Shabbat eve we are God's partner and contribute to the Shabbat's sanctity, on Shabbat day, God acts alone, and we have no part in the process of sanctification. All we can do is stand in awe, offer words of praise and tribute, and recognize the Almighty Creator of our universe. (*Divrei HaRav,* pp. 275–276)

שמות כ

זָכוֹר אֶת־יוֹם הַשַּׁבָּת לְקַדְּשׁוֹ:
שֵׁשֶׁת יָמִים תַּעֲבֹד, וְעָשִׂיתָ כָּל־מְלַאכְתֶּךָ:
וְיוֹם הַשְּׁבִיעִי שַׁבָּת לַיהוה אֱלֹהֶיךָ
לֹא־תַעֲשֶׂה כָל־מְלָאכָה אַתָּה וּבִנְךָ וּבִתֶּךָ
עַבְדְּךָ וַאֲמָתְךָ וּבְהֶמְתֶּךָ, וְגֵרְךָ אֲשֶׁר בִּשְׁעָרֶיךָ:
כִּי שֵׁשֶׁת־יָמִים עָשָׂה יהוה אֶת־הַשָּׁמַיִם וְאֶת־הָאָרֶץ
אֶת־הַיָּם וְאֶת־כָּל־אֲשֶׁר־בָּם
וַיָּנַח בַּיּוֹם הַשְּׁבִיעִי
עַל־כֵּן בֵּרַךְ יהוה אֶת־יוֹם הַשַּׁבָּת וַיְקַדְּשֵׁהוּ:

*When saying* קידוש *for others, add:*

סַבְרִי מָרָנָן

בָּרוּךְ אַתָּה יהוה אֱלֹהֵינוּ מֶלֶךְ הָעוֹלָם, בּוֹרֵא פְּרִי הַגָּפֶן.

*On* שבת חול המועד סוכות *if* קידוש *is made in the* סוכה *add:*

בָּרוּךְ אַתָּה יהוה אֱלֹהֵינוּ מֶלֶךְ הָעוֹלָם
אֲשֶׁר קִדְּשָׁנוּ בְּמִצְוֹתָיו וְצִוָּנוּ לֵישֵׁב בַּסֻּכָּה.

---

**זָכוֹר אֶת־יוֹם הַשַּׁבָּת לְקַדְּשׁוֹ** *Remember the Sabbath day to keep it holy.* Naḥmanides (Ex. 20:8) cites the *Sefer HaBahir* which explains that the two Shabbat commands of *Zakhor* and *Shamor* realate to the two halves of the day, *Shamor* being associated with the nighttime of Shabbat, and *Zakhor* with the daytime. Naḥmanides refers to this concept as a "great mystery" (*sod gadol*), and enigmatically explains that it is because of this mystical distinction that we go out to meet the Shabbat queen, the divine bride, on Shabbat eve, and that we recite *kiddusha rabba* during the day. Let us try to explain these cryptic words of Naḥmanides. Shabbat eve is dedicated to the *Shekhina*, the revelation of God's presence within this world. As the philosophy of Ḥabad stresses, the *Shekhina*, so to speak, is bound in chains and mutely suffers in exile along with Israel. *Shamor*, the attribute of Shabbat night, can be translated as "waiting," passively guarding and protecting; this is the *Shekhina* who awaits Israel's

# Kiddush for Yom Tov Morning

*On Shabbat Ḥol HaMo'ed, turn to page 62.*

*On a Yom Tov that falls on Shabbat, start Kiddush here:*

וְשָׁמְרוּ The children of Israel must keep the Sabbath, observing the Sabbath in every generation as an everlasting covenant. It is a sign between Me and the children of Israel for ever, for in six days the LORD made the heavens and the earth, but on the seventh day He ceased work and refreshed Himself. *Ex. 31*

זָכוֹר Remember the Sabbath day to keep it holy. Six days you shall labor and do all your work, but the seventh day is a Sabbath of the LORD your God; on it you shall not do any work – you, your son or daughter, your male or female slave, or your cattle, or the stranger within your gates. For in six days the LORD made heaven and earth and sea and all that is in them, and rested on the seventh day; *Ex. 20*

*On a Yom Tov that falls on Shabbat, some start Kiddush here instead:*

Therefore the LORD blessed the Sabbath day and declared it holy.

*On a Yom Tov that falls on a weekday, start here:*

אֵלֶּה These are the appointed times of the LORD, *Lev. 23*
sacred assemblies, which you shall announce in their due season.
Thus Moses announced the LORD's appointed seasons
to the children of Israel.

*When saying Kiddush for others, add:* Please pay attention, my masters.

בָּרוּךְ Blessed are You, LORD our God, King of the Universe,
who creates the fruit of the vine.

*On Sukkot, if Kiddush is made in the sukka, add:*

בָּרוּךְ Blessed are You, LORD our God, King of the Universe,
who has made us holy through His commandments
and has commanded us to dwell in the sukka.

---

establish the calendar, and sanctify the festivals only because they act on behalf of the entire people. For this reason, Maimonides (*Hilkhot Kiddush HaḤodesh* 5:13; *Sefer HaMitzvot, Aseh* 153) maintains that the holidays of the

# קידושא רבה לשלוש רגלים

*On* שבת חול המועד *turn to page 63.*

*On* יום טוב *that falls on* שבת*, start* קידוש *here:*

וְשָׁמְרוּ בְנֵי־יִשְׂרָאֵל אֶת־הַשַּׁבָּת, לַעֲשׂוֹת אֶת־הַשַּׁבָּת לְדֹרֹתָם בְּרִית שמות לא
עוֹלָם: בֵּינִי וּבֵין בְּנֵי יִשְׂרָאֵל אוֹת הִוא לְעֹלָם, כִּי־שֵׁשֶׁת יָמִים עָשָׂה
יהוה אֶת־הַשָּׁמַיִם וְאֶת־הָאָרֶץ וּבַיּוֹם הַשְּׁבִיעִי שָׁבַת וַיִּנָּפַשׁ:

זָכוֹר אֶת־יוֹם הַשַּׁבָּת לְקַדְּשׁוֹ: שֵׁשֶׁת יָמִים תַּעֲבֹד, וְעָשִׂיתָ כָּל־ שמות כ
מְלַאכְתֶּךָ: וְיוֹם הַשְּׁבִיעִי שַׁבָּת לַיהוה אֱלֹהֶיךָ, לֹא־תַעֲשֶׂה כָל־
מְלָאכָה אַתָּה וּבִנְךָ וּבִתֶּךָ, עַבְדְּךָ וַאֲמָתְךָ וּבְהֶמְתֶּךָ, וְגֵרְךָ אֲשֶׁר
בִּשְׁעָרֶיךָ: כִּי שֵׁשֶׁת־יָמִים עָשָׂה יהוה אֶת־הַשָּׁמַיִם וְאֶת־הָאָרֶץ אֶת־
הַיָּם וְאֶת־כָּל־אֲשֶׁר־בָּם, וַיָּנַח בַּיּוֹם הַשְּׁבִיעִי

*On* יום טוב *that falls on* שבת*, some start* קידוש *here instead:*

עַל־כֵּן בֵּרַךְ יהוה אֶת־יוֹם הַשַּׁבָּת וַיְקַדְּשֵׁהוּ:

*On* יום טוב *that falls on a weekday, start here:*

אֵלֶּה מוֹעֲדֵי יהוה מִקְרָאֵי קֹדֶשׁ אֲשֶׁר־תִּקְרְאוּ אֹתָם בְּמוֹעֲדָם: ויקרא כג
וַיְדַבֵּר מֹשֶׁה אֶת־מֹעֲדֵי יהוה אֶל־בְּנֵי יִשְׂרָאֵל:

*When saying* קידוש *for others, add* סַבְרִי מָרָנָן

בָּרוּךְ אַתָּה יהוה אֱלֹהֵינוּ מֶלֶךְ הָעוֹלָם, בּוֹרֵא פְּרִי הַגָּפֶן.

*On* סוכות *if* קידוש *is made in the* סוכה *add:*

בָּרוּךְ אַתָּה יהוה אֱלֹהֵינוּ מֶלֶךְ הָעוֹלָם
אֲשֶׁר קִדְּשָׁנוּ בְּמִצְוֹתָיו וְצִוָּנוּ לֵישֵׁב בַּסֻּכָּה.

---

YOM TOV DAY KIDDUSH

There are times when the Sanhedrin acts not based on their own inherent authority as the court comprised of the nation's greatest scholars, but with the power they have as the representative body of the entire nation of Israel. In particular, the Sanhedrin has the ability to declare the new moon,

# Kiddush for Rosh HaShana Day

*On a Rosh HaShana that falls on Shabbat, start Kiddush here:*

וְשָׁמְרוּ The children of Israel must keep the Sabbath, observing the Sabbath in every generation as an everlasting covenant. It is a sign between Me and the children of Israel for ever, for in six days the LORD made the heavens and the earth, but on the seventh day He ceased work and refreshed Himself. *Ex. 31*

זָכוֹר Remember the Sabbath day to keep it holy. Six days you shall labor and do all your work, but the seventh day is a Sabbath of the LORD your God; on it you shall not do any work – you, your son or daughter, your male or female slave, or your cattle, or the stranger within your gates. For in six days the LORD made heaven and earth and sea and all that is in them, and rested on the seventh day; *Ex. 20*

*On a Yom Tov that falls on Shabbat, some start Kiddush here instead:*

Therefore the LORD blessed the Sabbath day and declared it holy.

*On a Yom Tov that falls on a weekday, some start here:*

אֵלֶּה These are the appointed times of the LORD, sacred assemblies, which you shall announce in their due season. Thus Moses announced the LORD's appointed seasons to the children of Israel. *Lev. 23*

*On a Yom Tov that falls on a weekday, start here:*

תִּקְעוּ Sound the shofar on the new moon, *Ps. 81*
on our feast day when the moon is hidden.
For it is a statute for Israel, an ordinance of the God of Jacob.

*When saying Kiddush for others:* Please pay attention, my masters.

בָּרוּךְ Blessed are You, LORD our God, King of the Universe,
who creates the fruit of the vine.

---

praying and observing the holidays according to it, that in itself establishes the dates of the new months and the yearly holidays. It is truly all of Israel, all of the members of the Jewish nation, who, through their actions, declare the festivals and make them holy. (*Kovetz Ḥiddushei Torah*, pp. 58–60; *Iggerot HaGrid*, pp. 82–84; *Shiurim LeZekher Abba Mari*, vol. 1, pp. 148–150)

# קידושא רבה לראש השנה

*On* ראש השנה *that falls on* שבת*, start* קידוש *here:*

שמות לא וְשָׁמְרוּ בְנֵי־יִשְׂרָאֵל אֶת־הַשַּׁבָּת, לַעֲשׂוֹת אֶת־הַשַּׁבָּת לְדֹרֹתָם בְּרִית
עוֹלָם: בֵּינִי וּבֵין בְּנֵי יִשְׂרָאֵל אוֹת הִוא לְעֹלָם, כִּי־שֵׁשֶׁת יָמִים עָשָׂה
יהוה אֶת־הַשָּׁמַיִם וְאֶת־הָאָרֶץ וּבַיּוֹם הַשְּׁבִיעִי שָׁבַת וַיִּנָּפַשׁ:

שמות כ זָכוֹר אֶת־יוֹם הַשַּׁבָּת לְקַדְּשׁוֹ: שֵׁשֶׁת יָמִים תַּעֲבֹד, וְעָשִׂיתָ כָּל־
מְלַאכְתֶּךָ: וְיוֹם הַשְּׁבִיעִי שַׁבָּת לַיהוה אֱלֹהֶיךָ, לֹא־תַעֲשֶׂה כָל־
מְלָאכָה אַתָּה וּבִנְךָ וּבִתֶּךָ, עַבְדְּךָ וַאֲמָתְךָ וּבְהֶמְתֶּךָ, וְגֵרְךָ אֲשֶׁר
בִּשְׁעָרֶיךָ: כִּי שֵׁשֶׁת־יָמִים עָשָׂה יהוה אֶת־הַשָּׁמַיִם וְאֶת־הָאָרֶץ אֶת־
הַיָּם וְאֶת־כָּל־אֲשֶׁר־בָּם, וַיָּנַח בַּיּוֹם הַשְּׁבִיעִי

*On* ראש השנה *that falls on* שבת*, some start* קידוש *here instead:*

עַל־כֵּן בֵּרַךְ יהוה אֶת־יוֹם הַשַּׁבָּת וַיְקַדְּשֵׁהוּ:

*On* ראש השנה *that falls on a weekday, some start here:*

ויקרא כג אֵלֶּה מוֹעֲדֵי יהוה מִקְרָאֵי קֹדֶשׁ אֲשֶׁר־תִּקְרְאוּ אֹתָם בְּמוֹעֲדָם: וַיְדַבֵּר
מֹשֶׁה אֶת־מֹעֲדֵי יהוה אֶל־בְּנֵי יִשְׂרָאֵל:

*On* יום טוב *that falls on a weekday, start here:*

תהלים פא תִּקְעוּ בַחֹדֶשׁ שׁוֹפָר, בַּכֵּסֶה לְיוֹם חַגֵּנוּ:
כִּי חֹק לְיִשְׂרָאֵל הוּא, מִשְׁפָּט לֵאלֹהֵי יַעֲקֹב:

*When saying* קידוש *for others* סַבְרִי מָרָנָן

בָּרוּךְ אַתָּה יהוה אֱלֹהֵינוּ מֶלֶךְ הָעוֹלָם, בּוֹרֵא פְּרִי הַגָּפֶן.

---

present-day set calendar are holy not because of the actions of an earlier court, as Naḥmanides (*Sefer HaMitzvot*, *ibid.*) believes, but because of the activities of the Jewish people today. As there is no recognized court that represents the entire nation to sanctify the calendar, the responsibility and power revert to the general population, and in particular, to those living in the Land of Israel. As the community has accepted the current set calendar,

# Zemirot for Shabbat Day

בָּרוּךְ Blessed be the LORD who, day by day, carries our burden with salvation and redemption. We will rejoice in His name all day long, and raise our head high in His salvation. For He is a stronghold for the poor and a refuge for the needy.

The LORD's tribes are Israel's testimony: He was distressed in their distress, in their suffering and slavery. Through a pavement of sapphire He showed them the strength of His love, He revealed Himself, lifting them from the depths of the pit. For with the LORD is loving-kindness; He abounds in redemption. *Ps. 130*

How precious is His loving-kindness; He shelters them under His shade. For their sake He went with them into exile in Babylon. When they went down in ships, He was counted among them. He ensured that they were treated mercifully by those who took them captive. For the LORD will not forsake His people, for the sake of His great name.

In Eilam He placed His throne, to rescue His beloved, to remove from them the stronghold of His rebels. He redeemed His servants from passing under the sword. He raised the pride of His people, for the glory of all His devoted ones. For though He afflicts, He also shows compassion and loving-kindness. *Lam. 3*

When the he-goat [Greece] extended its power, and the vision of the four ascended to the heights, And in their hearts they intended to destroy those He loved, through His priests He laid low those who rose against Him: The LORD's kindness has not ended nor His compassion ceased. *Lam. 3*

---

When we read God's pledge to Abraham respecting His involvement with his descendants, we are impressed by the weird scene full of undefined dread and grisly uneasiness. "And when the sun was going down, a deep sleep fell upon Abram; and lo, a horror of great darkness fell upon him. And He said to Abram, 'Know of a surety that your seed shall be a stranger in a land that is not theirs and shall serve them; and they shall afflict them four hundred years'" (Gen. 15:12–13). The realization of the covenant is possible only if the people are tested in the crucible of affliction. The basic tendency in man to avoid the painful and search for the pleasant belongs to the original scheme of creation and is implanted in man and animal alike. However, revelation has opened up to man a new existential dimension, one of suffering and sacrifice

# זמירות ליום שבת

בָּרוּךְ אֲדֹנָי יוֹם יוֹם, יַעֲמָס לָנוּ יֶשַׁע וּפִדְיוֹם
וּבִשְׁמוֹ נָגִיל כָּל הַיּוֹם, וּבִישׁוּעָתוֹ נָרִים רֹאשׁ עֶלְיוֹן.
כִּי הוּא מָעוֹז לַדָּל וּמַחְסֶה לָאֶבְיוֹן.

שִׁבְטֵי יָהּ לְיִשְׂרָאֵל עֵדוּת, בְּצָרָתָם לוֹ צָר בְּסִבְלוּת וּבְעַבְדוּת
בְּלִבְנַת הַסַּפִּיר הֶרְאָם עֹז יְדִידוּת, וְנִגְלָה לְהַעֲלוֹתָם מֵעֹמֶק בּוֹר וָדוּת.
כִּי־עִם־יהוה הַחֶסֶד, וְהַרְבֵּה עִמּוֹ פְדוּת: תהלים קל

מַה יָּקָר חַסְדּוֹ בְּצִלּוֹ לְגוֹנְנֵמוֹ, בְּגָלוּת בָּבֶלָה שֻׁלַּח לְמַעֲנֵמוֹ
לְהוֹרִיד בָּרִיחִים נִמְנָה בֵינֵימוֹ, וַיִּתְּנֵם לְרַחֲמִים לִפְנֵי שׁוֹבֵימוֹ.
כִּי לֹא יִטֹּשׁ יהוה אֶת עַמּוֹ, בַּעֲבוּר הַגָּדוֹל שְׁמוֹ.

עֵילָם שָׁת כִּסְאוֹ לְהַצִּיל יְדִידָיו, לְהַאֲבִיד מִשָּׁם מָעֻזְנֵי מוֹרְדָיו
מֵעֲבֹר בַּשֶּׁלַח פָּדָה אֶת עֲבָדָיו, קֶרֶן לְעַמּוֹ יָרִים, תְּהִלָּה לְכָל חֲסִידָיו.
כִּי אִם־הוֹגָה, וְרִחַם כְּרֹב חֲסָדָו: איכה ג

וּצְפִיר הָעִזִּים הִגְדִּיל עֲצוּמָיו, וְגַם חָזוּת אַרְבַּע עָלוּ לִמְרוֹמָיו
וּבְלִבָּם דִּמּוּ לְהַשְׁחִית אֶת רְחוּמָיו, עַל יְדֵי כֹהֲנָיו מִגֵּר מִתְקוֹמְמָיו.
חַסְדֵי יהוה כִּי לֹא־תָמְנוּ, כִּי לֹא כָלוּ רַחֲמָיו: איכה ג

---

BARUCH ADONAI YOM YOM

This song is dedicated to a chronological description of God's care for His people through the course of their exiles. The travails of the Jewish people should not be seen as something incidental to our destiny as God's nation. From the very dawn of our history, with the emergence of Abraham, suffering was considered both a challenge which the covenantal community was expected to meet heroically, and the means of realizing the great metahistorical destiny of this community. Abraham, as the knight of faith, was a great sufferer, a martyr, whose greatness was manifest through his superhuman capacity for endurance and acceptance of sorrow. As a matter of fact, the election of his seed as a covenantal community was to be realized through suffering; the birth of the charismatic community was accompanied by affliction and pain.

I was handed over to Edom [Rome] by my quarrelsome friends, who daily sated their appetite with my treasures. His help was with me, supporting my foundations, He will not forsake me all the days of my age. For the LORD does not reject forever. *Lam. 3*

When He comes from Edom with garments stained crimson, there will be slaughter in Botzra, and an execution of traitors, their blood will turn His garments red, in His great strength He will bring the leaders low. With His mighty blast like a day of the east wind. *Is. 27*

When the oppressor from Edom sees how it will be, He will think Botzra to be a refuge like Betzer, giving protection to angels and men, willful and accidental sinners alike. Love the LORD, all His devoted ones: all His faithful ones He will guard. *Ps. 31*

The Rock in His kindness will command His communities to gather, coming together from the four winds, He will settle them upon the high mountains, He will return with us, gathering the dispersed, for it does not say, "He will bring back" but "He will return" and gather.

Blessed is our God who has bestowed good upon us. In His compassion and abundant kindness, He has done great things for us. Like these and those, may He do yet more for us, to magnify His great, mighty and awesome name, by which we are called.

Blessed is our God who created us for His glory, To praise and laud Him and tell of His majesty, His loving-kindness is greater to us than to any other nation. Therefore with all our heart and soul and might, let us proclaim His kingship and His unity.

May He to whom peace belongs, send us blessing and peace. From left and right, may Israel have peace. May the Compassionate One bless His people with peace, and may they merit to see children and children's children, occupied with Torah and the commandments, bringing Israel peace. Wondrous Counselor, mighty God, everlasting Father, Prince of peace. *Is. 9*

---

dialectic of suffering, through the contradiction implied in a shattered existence, in the mystery of a torn and desolate being. To be means not only to enjoy or to rejoice, but also to suffer and carry the load, to experience great desolation and the dark night of affliction. In order to confront God, man must purge himself and pass through a catharsis. (*Out of the Whirlwind*, pp. 118–120, 129)

נִסְגַּרְתִּי לֶאֱדוֹם בְּיַד רֵעַי מְדָנַי, שֶׁבְּכָל יוֹם מְמַלְּאִים כְּרֵסָם מֵעֲדָנַי
עֶזְרָתוֹ עִמִּי לִסְמֹךְ אֶת אֲדָנַי, וְלֹא נְטַשְׁתַּנִי כָּל יְמֵי עִדָּנַי.
כִּי לֹא יִזְנַח לְעוֹלָם אֲדֹנָי: איכה ג

בְּבוֹאוֹ מֵאֱדוֹם חֲמוּץ בְּגָדִים, זֶבַח לוֹ בְּבָצְרָה וְטֶבַח לוֹ בְּבוֹגְדִים
וְיֵז נִצְחָם מַלְבּוּשָׁיו לְהַאְדִּים, בְּכֹחוֹ הַגָּדוֹל יִבְצֹר רוּחַ נְגִידִים.
הָגָה בְּרוּחוֹ הַקָּשָׁה בְּיוֹם קָדִים: ישעיה כז

רְאוֹתוֹ כִּי כֵן אֲדוֹמִי הָעוֹצֵר, יַחְשָׁב לוֹ בָּצְרָה תִּקְלֹט כְּבֶצֶר
וּמַלְאָךְ כְּאָדָם בְּתוֹכָהּ יִנָּצֵר, וּמֵזִיד כַּשּׁוֹגֵג בְּמִקְלָט יֵעָצֵר.
אֶהֱבוּ אֶת־יהוה כָּל־חֲסִידָיו, אֱמוּנִים נֹצֵר: תהלים לא

יְצַוֶּה צוּר חַסְדּוֹ קְהִלּוֹתָיו לְקַבֵּץ, מֵאַרְבַּע רוּחוֹת עָדָיו לְהִקָּבֵץ
וּבְהַר מְרוֹם הָרִים אוֹתָנוּ לְהַרְבֵּץ, וְאִתָּנוּ יָשׁוּב נִדָּחִים קוֹבֵץ.
יָשִׁיב לֹא נֶאֱמַר, כִּי אִם וְשָׁב וְקִבֵּץ.

בָּרוּךְ הוּא אֱלֹהֵינוּ אֲשֶׁר טוֹב גְּמָלָנוּ, כְּרַחֲמָיו וּכְרֹב חֲסָדָיו הִגְדִּיל לָנוּ
אֵלֶּה וְכָאֵלֶּה יוֹסֵף עִמָּנוּ
לְהַגְדִּיל שְׁמוֹ הַגָּדוֹל הַגִּבּוֹר וְהַנּוֹרָא, שֶׁנִּקְרָא עָלֵינוּ.

בָּרוּךְ הוּא אֱלֹהֵינוּ שֶׁבְּרָאָנוּ לִכְבוֹדוֹ, לְהַלְלוֹ וּלְשַׁבְּחוֹ וּלְסַפֵּר הוֹדוֹ
מִכָּל אֹם גָּבַר עָלֵינוּ חַסְדּוֹ
לָכֵן בְּכָל לֵב וּבְכָל נֶפֶשׁ וּבְכָל מְאוֹדוֹ, נַמְלִיכוֹ וּנְיַחֲדוֹ.

שֶׁהַשָּׁלוֹם שֶׁלּוֹ יָשִׂים עָלֵינוּ בְּרָכָה וְשָׁלוֹם, מִשְּׂמֹאל וּמִיָּמִין עַל יִשְׂרָאֵל שָׁלוֹם
הָרַחֲמָן הוּא יְבָרֵךְ אֶת עַמּוֹ בַשָּׁלוֹם
וְיִזְכּוּ לִרְאוֹת בָּנִים וּבְנֵי בָנִים, עוֹסְקִים, בַּתּוֹרָה וּבְמִצְוֹת, עַל יִשְׂרָאֵל שָׁלוֹם.
פֶּלֶא יוֹעֵץ אֵל גִּבּוֹר אֲבִי־עַד שַׂר־שָׁלוֹם: ישעיה ט

---

through the passional experience. Natural man, whose world is replete with orderliness and beauty, serenity and peace, who is satisfied with himself and his destiny, must forfeit, at least for a while, his neatly arranged world in order to discover God. The person who accepts the covenant must rise above his naturalness, above the order of creation. The covenant is born through the

בָּרוּךְ אֵל עֶלְיוֹן Blessed is God Most High who has given us rest,
To relieve our souls from distress and pain.
May He seek the good of Zion, the outcast city.
How long must she grieve, her spirits downcast?

All who keep the Sabbath,
man and woman alike,
find favor like an offering made to God.

He who rides the heavens, King of worlds,
Gently told His people to rest,
With tasty food and delicacies of all kinds,
With elegant dress, as at a family feast.

All who keep the Sabbath,
man and woman alike,
find favor like an offering made to God.

Happy are all who await a double reward
From the One who sees all, though He dwells in dense dark.
He will grant him a heritage in hill and valley,
A heritage and resting place like [Jacob] on whom the sun shone.

All who keep the Sabbath,
man and woman alike,
find favor like an offering made to God.

Whoever keeps the Sabbath fully, not profaning it,
Shows that he is worthy; holy is his lot.
Happy is he who fulfills the day's duty;
It is like a gift presented to God who fashioned him.

All who keep the Sabbath,
man and woman alike,
find favor like an offering made to God.

בָּרוּךְ אֵל עֶלְיוֹן, אֲשֶׁר נָתַן מְנוּחָה
לְנַפְשֵׁנוּ פִּדְיוֹן מִשֵּׁאת וַאֲנָחָה
וְהוּא יִדְרֹשׁ לְצִיּוֹן, עִיר הַנִּדָּחָה
עַד אָנָה תּוּגְיוֹן נֶפֶשׁ נֶאֱנָחָה.

הַשּׁוֹמֵר שַׁבָּת הַבֵּן עִם הַבַּת
לָאֵל יֵרָצוּ כְּמִנְחָה עַל מַחֲבַת.

רוֹכֵב בָּעֲרָבוֹת, מֶלֶךְ עוֹלָמִים
אֶת עַמּוֹ לִשְׁבֹּת אִזֵּן בַּנְּעִימִים
בְּמַאֲכָלוֹת עֲרֵבוֹת בְּמִינֵי מַטְעַמִּים
בְּמַלְבּוּשֵׁי כָבוֹד זֶבַח מִשְׁפָּחָה.

הַשּׁוֹמֵר שַׁבָּת הַבֵּן עִם הַבַּת
לָאֵל יֵרָצוּ כְּמִנְחָה עַל מַחֲבַת.

וְאַשְׁרֵי כָּל חוֹכֶה לְתַשְׁלוּמֵי כֵפֶל
מֵאֵת כֹּל סוֹכֶה, שׁוֹכֵן בָּעֲרָפֶל
נַחֲלָה לוֹ יִזְכֶּה בָּהָר וּבַשָּׁפֶל
נַחֲלָה וּמְנוּחָה כַּשֶּׁמֶשׁ לוֹ זָרְחָה.

הַשּׁוֹמֵר שַׁבָּת הַבֵּן עִם הַבַּת
לָאֵל יֵרָצוּ כְּמִנְחָה עַל מַחֲבַת.

כָּל שׁוֹמֵר שַׁבָּת כַּדָּת מֵחַלְּלוֹ
הֵן הֶכְשֵׁר חִבַּת קֹדֶשׁ גּוֹרָלוֹ
וְאִם יֵצֵא חוֹבַת הַיּוֹם, אַשְׁרֵי לוֹ
אֶל אֵל אָדוֹן מְחוֹלְלוֹ מִנְחָה הִיא שְׁלוּחָה.

הַשּׁוֹמֵר שַׁבָּת הַבֵּן עִם הַבַּת
לָאֵל יֵרָצוּ כְּמִנְחָה עַל מַחֲבַת.

The Rock, my God, called it "Beloved of days."
Happy are the faithful if it is kept intact.
He will set on their head a close-fitting crown.
On them the Rock of Eternity will make His spirit rest.

All who keep the Sabbath,
man and woman alike,
find favor like an offering made to God.

He who remembers the Sabbath day to keep it holy
Will gain high honor like a diadem on his head.
Therefore let each give to his soul
Delight and joy with which to be exalted.

All who keep the Sabbath,
man and woman alike,
find favor like an offering made to God.

Let her be holy to you – Sabbath the queen –
Placing a blessing in your home.
In all your dwellings, do no work,
Nor your sons and daughters, your servant or maid.

All who keep the Sabbath,
man and woman alike,
find favor like an offering made to God.

---

the seventh day," the word וַיְכַל can also be translated as "desired," in which case this phrase would mean, "God had desire for the seventh day." This alternate translation of the word וַיְכַל is based upon the word כָּלְתָה, as found in Psalms (84:3), "נִכְסְפָה וְגַם כָּלְתָה נַפְשִׁי, my soul pines, indeed it yearns." Consistent with the *Tur*'s explanation, R. Ḥayyim Heller cited an ancient Aramaic translation of the Torah which explicitly translates the words וַיְכַל אֱלֹהִים as "וְחַמֵּיד אֱלֹהִים, and God desired" (see *Al HaTargum HaYerushalmi LaTorah*, pp. 12–13). Shabbat is the most beloved, treasured day of the week; both man and God alike yearn for it. (*MiPeninei HaRav*, p. 66)

חֶמְדַּת הַיָּמִים קְרָאוֹ אֵלִי צוּר
וְאַשְׁרֵי לִתְמִימִים אִם יִהְיֶה נָצוּר
כֶּתֶר הִלּוּמִים עַל רֹאשָׁם יָצוּר
צוּר הָעוֹלָמִים, רוּחוֹ בָּם נָחָה.

הַשּׁוֹמֵר שַׁבָּת הַבֵּן עִם הַבַּת
לָאֵל יֵרָצוּ כְּמִנְחָה עַל מַחֲבַת.

זָכוֹר אֶת יוֹם הַשַּׁבָּת לְקַדְּשׁוֹ
קַרְנוֹ כִּי גָבְהָה נֵזֶר עַל רֹאשׁוֹ
עַל כֵּן יִתֵּן הָאָדָם לְנַפְשׁוֹ
עֹנֶג וְגַם שִׂמְחָה בָּהֶם לְמָשְׁחָה.

הַשּׁוֹמֵר שַׁבָּת הַבֵּן עִם הַבַּת
לָאֵל יֵרָצוּ כְּמִנְחָה עַל מַחֲבַת.

קֹדֶשׁ הִיא לָכֶם שַׁבָּת הַמַּלְכָּה
אֶל תּוֹךְ בָּתֵּיכֶם לְהָנִיחַ בְּרָכָה
בְּכָל מוֹשְׁבוֹתֵיכֶם לֹא תַעֲשׂוּ מְלָאכָה
בְּנֵיכֶם וּבְנוֹתֵיכֶם עֶבֶד וְגַם שִׁפְחָה.

הַשּׁוֹמֵר שַׁבָּת הַבֵּן עִם הַבַּת
לָאֵל יֵרָצוּ כְּמִנְחָה עַל מַחֲבַת.

---

BARUCH EL ELYON

**חֶמְדַּת הַיָּמִים קְרָאוֹ אֵלִי צוּר** *The Rock, my God, called it "Beloved of days."* The appellation "**חֶמְדַּת הַיָּמִים**, beloved of days," which is found in this and other *zemirot,* also appears in the Amida of *shaḥarit* of Shabbat, "**חֶמְדַּת יָמִים אוֹתוֹ קָרָאתָ**, You called it the most cherished of days." In his commentary on the Torah, *Ba'al HaTurim* explains that this is derived from the phrase **וַיְכַל אֱלֹהִים בַּיּוֹם הַשְּׁבִיעִי** (Gen. 2:2). Although usually translated as "God completed on

יוֹם זֶה מְכֻבָּד This day is honored above all others,
For on it He who formed worlds found rest.

For six days, do your work
But the seventh day is God's:
On the Sabbath you shall do no work,
For in six days He made all.

> This day is honored above all others,
> for on it He who formed worlds found rest.

Foremost among sacred days
Is this day of rest, this holy Sabbath.
So let each say Kiddush over wine,
And break bread over two complete loaves.

> This day is honored above all others,
> for on it He who formed worlds found rest.

Eat choice food, drink sweet wine,
For God will give to those who cleave to Him
Clothes to wear, due portions of bread,
Meat and fish, and all tasty foods.

> This day is honored above all others,
> for on it He who formed worlds found rest.

On it you shall lack nothing – so eat,
Be satisfied and bless
The Lord your God, whom you love,
For He has blessed you from all peoples.

> This day is honored above all others,
> for on it He who formed worlds found rest.

The heavens declare His glory
And the earth is full of His loving-kindness.
See all these things His hand has made
For He is the Rock, His work is perfect.

> This day is honored above all others,
> for on it He who formed worlds found rest.

יוֹם זֶה מְכֻבָּד מִכׇּל יָמִים, כִּי בוֹ שָׁבַת צוּר עוֹלָמִים.

שֵׁשֶׁת יָמִים תַּעֲשֶׂה מְלַאכְתֶּךָ / וְיוֹם הַשְּׁבִיעִי לֵאלֹהֶיךָ
שַׁבָּת לֹא תַעֲשֶׂה בוֹ מְלָאכָה / כִּי כֹל עָשָׂה שֵׁשֶׁת יָמִים.
יוֹם זֶה מְכֻבָּד מִכׇּל יָמִים, כִּי בוֹ שָׁבַת צוּר עוֹלָמִים.

רִאשׁוֹן הוּא לְמִקְרָאֵי קֹדֶשׁ / יוֹם שַׁבָּתוֹן יוֹם שַׁבַּת קֹדֶשׁ
עַל כֵּן כׇּל אִישׁ בְּיֵינוֹ יְקַדֵּשׁ / עַל שְׁתֵּי לֶחֶם יִבְצְעוּ תְמִימִים.
יוֹם זֶה מְכֻבָּד מִכׇּל יָמִים, כִּי בוֹ שָׁבַת צוּר עוֹלָמִים.

אֱכֹל מַשְׁמַנִּים, שְׁתֵה מַמְתַּקִּים / כִּי אֵל יִתֵּן לְכֹל בּוֹ דְבֵקִים
בֶּגֶד לִלְבֹּשׁ, לֶחֶם חֻקִּים / בָּשָׂר וְדָגִים וְכׇל מַטְעַמִּים.
יוֹם זֶה מְכֻבָּד מִכׇּל יָמִים, כִּי בוֹ שָׁבַת צוּר עוֹלָמִים.

לֹא תֶחְסַר כֹּל בּוֹ, וְאָכַלְתָּ / וְשָׂבָעְתָּ וּבֵרַכְתָּ
אֶת יהוה אֱלֹהֶיךָ אֲשֶׁר אָהַבְתָּ / כִּי בֵרַכְךָ מִכׇּל הָעַמִּים.
יוֹם זֶה מְכֻבָּד מִכׇּל יָמִים, כִּי בוֹ שָׁבַת צוּר עוֹלָמִים.

הַשָּׁמַיִם מְסַפְּרִים כְּבוֹדוֹ / וְגַם הָאָרֶץ מָלְאָה חַסְדּוֹ
רְאוּ כׇּל אֵלֶּה עָשְׂתָה יָדוֹ / כִּי הוּא הַצּוּר פׇּעֳלוֹ תָמִים.
יוֹם זֶה מְכֻבָּד מִכׇּל יָמִים, כִּי בוֹ שָׁבַת צוּר עוֹלָמִים.

---

YOM ZEH MEKHUBAD

הַשָּׁמַיִם מְסַפְּרִים כְּבוֹדוֹ *The heavens declare His glory.* God did not reveal Himself only to the prophets. He continually reveals Himself to all mankind. The most wondrous revelation of His presence is evident in creation, in the processes of nature, in the cosmic drama. This revelation is unending, appearing in sunrise and sunset, the blooming of the flowers and trees, the waves of the sea and the buzzing of insects. God is reflected in every one of nature's rhythms. When superficial man witnesses the wonders of nature, he does not perceive the Master of the universe. It seems to him that nature was self-created and self-refined. He views the mechanical nature of the universe, and considers its processes as random and meaningless. An individual with an elevated personality, however, with discerning eyes and a sensitive heart, is able to feel and perceive the presence of the Creator. Shabbat, in particular, is the

יוֹם שַׁבָּתוֹן The day of rest should not be forgotten,
Its memory is like sweet fragrance,
On it the dove found rest, And in it the exhausted rest.

This day is honored by the people of faith.
Parents and children guard it with care.
It was engraved on two tablets of stone,
By the greatness of His power and His unfailing strength.
On it the dove found rest, And in it the exhausted rest.

And out of the mist, the darkness shone,
And He lifted the dwellers in low places onto cloud,
And I shall see the tower of my tormentors fall,
But I shall be filled with strength.
On it the dove found rest, And in it the exhausted rest.

Tread on the shoes of enemies and tormentors,
And make the ankles of strangers stumble,
And then my people will answer You with songs,
O God who travels on the wings of the wind.
On it the dove found rest, And in it the exhausted rest.

All came together in a covenant: "We will do and we will obey," they said as one.
Then they responded, saying, "The Lord is One" –
Blessed is He who gives the weary strength.
On it the dove found rest, And in it the exhausted rest.

He spoke in His holiness on the Mount of Myrrh [Sinai]:
"Remember and observe the seventh day."
And learn together all His commands: Gird your loins and muster strength.
On it the dove found rest, And in it the exhausted rest.

The people who have wandered like a straying flock –
May He remember the covenant and the oath,
So that no harm should happen to them, As You swore at the end of Noaḥ's flood.
On it the dove found rest, And in it the exhausted rest.

---

in the market, would purchase it and set it aside for the coming Shabbat. Naḥmanides (*ibid.*) likewise writes that "we must remember the Sabbath every day, and not forget it or supplant it with another day of the week." Naḥmanides cites the *Mekhilta* which explains that Judaism didn't assign

יוֹם שַׁבָּתוֹן אֵין לִשְׁכֹּחַ, זִכְרוֹ כְּרֵיחַ הַנִּיחֹחַ
יוֹנָה מָצְאָה בוֹ מָנוֹחַ וְשָׁם יָנוּחוּ יְגִיעֵי כֹחַ.

הַיּוֹם נִכְבָּד לִבְנֵי אֱמוּנִים, זְהִירִים לְשָׁמְרוֹ אָבוֹת וּבָנִים
חָקוּק בִּשְׁנֵי לוּחוֹת אֲבָנִים, מֵרֹב אוֹנִים וְאַמִּיץ כֹּחַ.
יוֹנָה מָצְאָה בוֹ מָנוֹחַ וְשָׁם יָנוּחוּ יְגִיעֵי כֹחַ.

וּמִתּוֹךְ עֲרָפֶל הָאִיר אֹפֶל, וְעַל עָב, הָרִים יִשְׁבֵי שֶׁפֶל
וּמִגְדַּל צָרֵי אֶרְאֶה נוֹפֵל, אַךְ אָנֹכִי מְלֵאתִי כֹחַ.
יוֹנָה מָצְאָה בוֹ מָנוֹחַ וְשָׁם יָנוּחוּ יְגִיעֵי כֹחַ.

דְּרֹךְ בְּנַעַל אוֹיְבִים וְצָרִים, וְגַם הַמְעַד קַרְסֻלֵּי זָרִים
וְאָז יַעֲנוּ לְךָ עַמִּי, בְּשִׁירִים, אֵל, הַמְהַלֵּךְ עַל כַּנְפֵי רוּחַ.
יוֹנָה מָצְאָה בוֹ מָנוֹחַ וְשָׁם יָנוּחוּ יְגִיעֵי כֹחַ.

וּבָאוּ כֻלָּם בִּבְרִית יַחַד, נַעֲשֶׂה וְנִשְׁמַע אָמְרוּ כְּאֶחָד
וּפָתְחוּ וְעָנוּ יהוה אֶחָד, בָּרוּךְ נֹתֵן לַיָּעֵף כֹּחַ.
יוֹנָה מָצְאָה בוֹ מָנוֹחַ וְשָׁם יָנוּחוּ יְגִיעֵי כֹחַ.

דִּבֶּר בְּקָדְשׁוֹ בְּהַר הַמֹּר, יוֹם הַשְּׁבִיעִי זָכוֹר וְשָׁמוֹר
וְכָל פִּקּוּדָיו יַחַד לִגְמֹר, חַזֵּק מָתְנַיִם וְאַמֵּץ כֹּחַ.
יוֹנָה מָצְאָה בוֹ מָנוֹחַ וְשָׁם יָנוּחוּ יְגִיעֵי כֹחַ.

הָעָם אֲשֶׁר נָע, כַּצֹּאן תָּעָה, יִזְכֹּר לְפָקְדוֹ בְּרִית וּשְׁבוּעָה
לְבַל יַעֲבָר בָּם מִקְרֵה רָעָה, כַּאֲשֶׁר נִשְׁבַּעְתָּ עַל מֵי נֹחַ.
יוֹנָה מָצְאָה בוֹ מָנוֹחַ וְשָׁם יָנוּחוּ יְגִיעֵי כֹחַ.

---

celebration of the cosmic order, the world of nature and its laws that reveal the hand of the divine architect. (*Derashot HaRav*, pp. 109–110; *Rabbi Joseph B. Soloveitchik on Pesach*, p. 201)

YOM SHABBATON

יוֹם שַׁבָּתוֹן אֵין לִשְׁכֹּחַ *The day of rest should not be forgotten.* Rashi (Ex. 20:8) writes that the command to "remember the Sabbath to sanctify it" applies not only on Shabbat, but rather during the entire week. He cites the practice of Shammai the Elder who, when he would come across a desirable item

שַׁבָּת הַיּוֹם Today is the Sabbath of the LORD.
Celebrate greatly with my songs,
Multiply my delicacies,
Keep it like the LORD's command.
Today is the Sabbath of the LORD.

Do not travel beyond boundaries,
Do not labor on this day:
Eat, drink, make merry.
This is the day the LORD has made.
Today is the Sabbath of the LORD.

If you keep it God will guard you like the pupil of His eye,
You, your son and daughter too.
If you call the Sabbath a delight
Then you will find delight before the LORD.
Today is the Sabbath of the LORD.

Eat rich foods and delicacies,
Tasty dishes of many kinds,
Soft-shelled nuts and pomegranates:
Eat, be satisfied and bless the LORD.
Today is the Sabbath of the LORD.

Make ready on the table delicious bread,
And make, this day, three meals.
Bless and thank His glorious name.
Take care, observe and do, my sons.
Today is the Sabbath of the LORD.

---

does not want to share man with anyone else. Hence, He told man to retreat from society. "The seventh day is a Sabbath to the LORD your God" (Ex. 20:9). Everything belongs to Him. Cease to be a slave to your work; discontinue being a servant to society; be exclusively Mine. The idea of Sabbath is man's aloneness. And if man is alone, he is also with God. The *kedushat HaShabbat*, the charisma of the Sabbath, expresses itself in the return of man to himself and to God, the source of *kedusha*. Severance of the individual from the working society establishes a permanent communion with God. (*Days of Deliverance*, p. 113)

שַׁבָּת הַיּוֹם לַיהוה, מְאֹד צַהֲלוּ בְּרִנּוּנַי
וְגַם הַרְבּוּ מַעֲדָנַי, אוֹתוֹ לִשְׁמֹר כְּמִצְוַת יהוה.
שַׁבָּת הַיּוֹם לַיהוה.

מֵעֲבֹר דֶּרֶךְ וּגְבוּלִים, מֵעֲשׂוֹת הַיּוֹם פְּעָלִים
לֶאֱכֹל וְלִשְׁתּוֹת בְּהִלּוּלִים, זֶה הַיּוֹם עָשָׂה יהוה.
שַׁבָּת הַיּוֹם לַיהוה.

וְאִם תִּשְׁמְרֶנּוּ, יָהּ יִנְצָרְךָ כְּבָבַת, אַתָּה וּבִנְךָ וְגַם הַבַּת
וְקָרָאתָ עֹנֶג לַשַּׁבָּת, אָז תִּתְעַנַּג עַל יהוה.
שַׁבָּת הַיּוֹם לַיהוה.

אֱכֹל מַשְׁמַנִּים וּמַעֲדַנִּים, וּמַטְעַמִּים הַרְבֵּה מִינִים
אֱגוֹזֵי פֶרֶךְ וְרִמּוֹנִים, וְאָכַלְתָּ וְשָׂבָעְתָּ וּבֵרַכְתָּ אֶת יהוה.
שַׁבָּת הַיּוֹם לַיהוה.

לַעֲרֹךְ בְּשֻׁלְחָן לֶחֶם חֲמוּדוֹת, לַעֲשׂוֹת הַיּוֹם שָׁלֹשׁ סְעוּדוֹת
אֶת הַשֵּׁם הַנִּכְבָּד לְבָרֵךְ וּלְהוֹדוֹת, שִׁקְדוּ וְשִׁמְרוּ וַעֲשׂוּ בָנַי.
שַׁבָּת הַיּוֹם לַיהוה.

---

names to the days of the week, but rather we refer to each day in relation to Shabbat (i.e., *Yom Rishon BeShabbat, Yom Sheini BeShabbat*). We are to always be thinking about Shabbat and counting towards its arrival. This is why the word *zakhor*, "remember," is written not in the grammatical form of a command, which would imply a defined, one-time action, but rather it is in the participle form, which implies a continuous state. We are commanded to be constantly aware of Shabbat, that the entire week be filled with our love and longing for the most holy of days. (*Divrei HaRav*, pp. 281–282, 298)

SHABBAT HAYOM LADONAI

When Moses revealed the mystery of the Sabbath to the people, he told them, "Remain every man in his place; no man should go out of his place on the seventh day" (Ex. 16:29). Man remains alone, and he should experience the Sabbath as a lone being. On the Sabbath, God tolerates no competition; He

שִׁמְרוּ שַׁבְּתוֹתַי Observe My Sabbaths,
so that you are nourished and sated,
From the radiance of My blessings,
when you come to rest.
Borrow on My account, My children,
Delight in My pleasures:
Today is the Sabbath of the Lord.

Borrow on My account, My children,
Delight in My pleasures:
Today is the Sabbath of the Lord.

Proclaim freedom from toil,
then I will grant My blessing,
joining one to the next,
bringing gladness on My day of joy.
Wear clothes of fine linen and wool.
And learn from My elders:
Today is the Sabbath of the Lord.

Borrow on My account, My children,
Delight in My pleasures:
Today is the Sabbath of the Lord.

Quickly bring the portion,
obey Esther's command.
Make a reckoning with the Creator,
He will repay you for the food, and more.
Trust in Me, My faithful ones,
And drink wine from My plentiful supply.
Today is the Sabbath of the Lord.

Borrow on My account, My children,
Delight in My pleasures:
Today is the Sabbath of the Lord.

---

father and keep my Sabbaths; I am the Lord your God" (Lev. 19:3). While the Torah generally refers to Shabbat in the singular ("Guard the Sabbath,"

שִׁמְרוּ שַׁבְּתוֹתַי
לְמַעַן תִּינְקוּ וּשְׂבַעְתֶּם
מִזִּיו בִּרְכוֹתַי
אֶל הַמְּנוּחָה כִּי בָאתֶם
וּלְווּ עָלַי בָּנַי
וְעִדְנוּ מַעֲדָנַי שַׁבָּת הַיּוֹם לַיהוה.
וּלְווּ עָלַי בָּנַי, וְעִדְנוּ מַעֲדָנַי, שַׁבָּת הַיּוֹם לַיהוה.

לְעָמֵל קִרְאוּ דְרוֹר
וְנָתַתִּי אֶת בִּרְכָתִי
אִשָּׁה אֶל אֲחוֹתָהּ לִצְרוֹר
לְגַלּוֹת עַל יוֹם שִׂמְחָתִי
בִּגְדֵי שֵׁשׁ עִם שָׁנִי
וְהִתְבּוֹנְנוּ מִזְּקֵנַי שַׁבָּת הַיּוֹם לַיהוה.
וּלְווּ עָלַי בָּנַי, וְעִדְנוּ מַעֲדָנַי, שַׁבָּת הַיּוֹם לַיהוה.

מַהֲרוּ אֶת הַמָּנֶה
לַעֲשׂוֹת אֶת דְּבַר אֶסְתֵּר
וְחִשְׁבוּ עִם הַקּוֹנֶה
לְשַׁלֵּם אָכוֹל וְהוֹתֵר
בִּטְחוּ בִי אֱמוּנַי
וּשְׁתוּ יֵין מִשְׁמַנַּי שַׁבָּת הַיּוֹם לַיהוה.
וּלְווּ עָלַי בָּנַי, וְעִדְנוּ מַעֲדָנַי, שַׁבָּת הַיּוֹם לַיהוה.

---

SHIMRU SHABTOTAI

שִׁמְרוּ שַׁבְּתוֹתַי *Observe My Sabbaths.* The opening phrase of this song, which refers to Shabbat in the plural, is based upon the verse "**אִישׁ אִמּוֹ וְאָבִיו תִּירָאוּ וְאֶת־שַׁבְּתֹתַי תִּשְׁמֹרוּ אֲנִי יהוה אֱלֹהֵיכֶם**, Every man shall revere his mother and

Today is a day of redemption,
if you observe the Sabbath;
Then you will be My special treasure.
Stay [for the night of exile], then pass on.
Then you will live before Me.
And be filled from My hidden store.
Today is the Sabbath of the LORD.

Borrow on My account, My children,
Delight in My pleasures:
Today is the Sabbath of the LORD.

Make my city strong,
God, the God most high.
Bring back my Temple,
With joy and words of song.
There may my singers chant,
My Levites and my priests.
Then you will delight in the LORD.
Today is the Sabbath of the LORD.

Borrow on My account, My children,
Delight in My pleasures:
Today is the Sabbath of the LORD.

---

restlessness and fear that characterize competitive society; we are freed from the jealousy and rancor that are often a part of our mundane pursuits. The Torah commands that the family rest together, and the ties between parents and children are renewed on Shabbat. This is the earthly Shabbat, the day's blessing. However, Adam's sin, beyond its repercussions in terms of physical punishment, also drove a wedge between God and humanity. On Shabbat, though, God appears to us and we are reconciled with Him. It hearkens to the future world to come, when all evil will depart, the world will be free of suffering, and even death will be vanquished. This is the eschatological Shabbat, the day when "the LORD will be one and His name will be One" (Zech. 14:9). This is the second Shabbat, the supernal Shabbat that God not only blessed, but also made holy. (*Darosh Darash Yosef*, pp. 249–253)

הִנֵּה יוֹם גְּאֻלָּה
יוֹם שַׁבָּת אִם תִּשְׁמֹרוּ
וִהְיִיתֶם לִי סְגֻלָּה
לִינוּ וְאַחַר תַּעֲבֹרוּ
וְאָז תִּחְיוּ לְפָנַי
וּתְמַלְאוּ צְפוּנַי    שַׁבָּת הַיּוֹם לַיהוה.
וּלְווּ עָלַי בָּנַי, וְעִדְנוּ מַעֲדָנַי, שַׁבָּת הַיּוֹם לַיהוה.

חֲזַק קִרְיָתִי
אֵל אֱלֹהִים עֶלְיוֹן
וְהָשֵׁב אֶת נָוָתִי
בְּשִׂמְחָה וּבְהִגָּיוֹן
יְשׁוֹרְרוּ שָׁם רְנָנַי
לְוִיַּי וְכֹהֲנַי
אָז תִּתְעַנַּג עַל יהוה    שַׁבָּת הַיּוֹם לַיהוה.
וּלְווּ עָלַי בָּנַי, וְעִדְנוּ מַעֲדָנַי, שַׁבָּת הַיּוֹם לַיהוה.

---

"Remember the Sabbath"), this verse refers to "my Sabbaths" in the plural, as if there is more than one kind of Sabbath. The Zohar recounts that once Rabbi Shimon and Rabbi Abba were walking, discussing this grammatical anomaly, when a Bedouin man taught them that in fact there are two different Sabbaths: every Shabbat contains a *Shabbat letata,* a lower, earthly Sabbath, and a *Shabbat le'ela,* a higher, supernal Sabbath. The *KeGavna* prayer which Ḥasidim recite on Shabbat eve contains the same idea. The nature of this twofold Sabbath is explicit in the Torah's text. In Genesis (2:3), we find that God both blessed and sanctified Shabbat; the earthly Shabbat is the day that God blessed, while the supernal Shabbat is the day that God hallowed and sanctified. These two aspects are in fact the inverse of the two levels of the curse of Adam, for Shabbat is the temporary lifting of his punishment. Firstly, Shabbat releases us from Adam's curse by alleviating the weariness and boredom of the workaday world that can lead to despair. We do not suffer from the

כִּי אֶשְׁמְרָה If I keep the Sabbath, God will keep me,
It is an eternal sign between God and me.
It is an eternal sign between God and me.

It is forbidden to engage in business or to travel,
Even to speak about the things we need,
or about matters of trade or state.
Instead I will study God's Torah and it will make me wise.
It is an eternal sign between God and me.

On it I always find refreshment for my soul.
See: My Holy One gave the first generation,
A sign, by giving them a double portion on the sixth day.
So may my food be doubled every sixth day!
It is an eternal sign between God and me.

Engraved in God's law is His priests' decree,
To prepare the Show-Bread in His presence.
So, His sages ruled, on it fasting is forbidden,
except on sins' Atonement Day.
It is an eternal sign between God and me.

It is a day of honor, a day of delight,
with bread and fine wine, meat and fish.
On it those who mourn are turned around,
For it is a joyous day and it will bring me joy.
It is an eternal sign between God and me.

Those who desecrate it by working will, in the end, be cut off.
Therefore I cleanse my heart with it as if with soap.
Evening and morning I will pray to God,
Additional and afternoon prayer also, and He will answer me.
It is an eternal sign between God and me.

---

the verse that on those days, on Rosh Ḥodesh and Shabbat, there is a *mitzva* to visit the prophet or the sage in your midst. Similarly, we find that in the days of the Talmud, everyone would gather on Shabbat afternoon to listen to a scholar's communal lecture, and the Rabbis even created a prohibition to study *Ketuvim* on Shabbat to ensure that people would come to the public *derasha* (see *Shabbat* 115a and Rashi *ibid.*). Thus, on Shabbat learning is a double *kiyyum*: it is a fulfillment of *talmud Torah* as on any other day of the week, but it is also a fulfillment of *lekaddesho*, of imbuing the day with holiness by filling it with spiritual delight. (*Divrei HaRav*, pp. 246–247, 278–279)

כִּי אֶשְׁמְרָה שַׁבָּת אֵל יִשְׁמְרֵנִי. אוֹת הִיא לְעוֹלְמֵי עַד בֵּינוֹ וּבֵינִי.
אוֹת הִיא לְעוֹלְמֵי עַד בֵּינוֹ וּבֵינִי.

אָסוּר מְצֹא חֵפֶץ, עֲשׂוֹת דְּרָכִים, גַּם מִלְּדַבֵּר בּוֹ דִּבְרֵי צְרָכִים
דִּבְרֵי סְחוֹרָה אַף דִּבְרֵי מְלָכִים, אֶהְגֶּה בְּתוֹרַת אֵל וּתְחַכְּמֵנִי.
אוֹת הִיא לְעוֹלְמֵי עַד בֵּינוֹ וּבֵינִי.

בּוֹ אֶמְצָא תָמִיד נֹפֶשׁ לְנַפְשִׁי, הִנֵּה לְדוֹר רִאשׁוֹן נָתַן קְדוֹשִׁי
מוֹפֵת, בְּתֵת לֶחֶם מִשְׁנֶה בַּשִּׁשִּׁי, כָּכָה בְּכָל שִׁשִּׁי יַכְפִּיל מְזוֹנִי.
אוֹת הִיא לְעוֹלְמֵי עַד בֵּינוֹ וּבֵינִי.

רָשַׁם בְּדַת הָאֵל חֹק אֶל סְגָנָיו, בּוֹ לַעֲרֹךְ לֶחֶם פָּנִים בְּפָנָיו
עַל כֵּן לְהִתְעַנּוֹת בּוֹ עַל פִּי נְבוֹנָיו, אָסוּר, לְבַד מִיּוֹם כִּפּוּר עֲוֹנִי.
אוֹת הִיא לְעוֹלְמֵי עַד בֵּינוֹ וּבֵינִי.

הוּא יוֹם מְכֻבָּד, הוּא יוֹם תַּעֲנוּגִים, לֶחֶם וְיַיִן טוֹב, בָּשָׂר וְדָגִים
הַמִּתְאַבְּלִים בּוֹ אָחוֹר נְסוֹגִים, כִּי יוֹם שְׂמָחוֹת הוּא וּתְשַׂמְּחֵנִי.
אוֹת הִיא לְעוֹלְמֵי עַד בֵּינוֹ וּבֵינִי.

מֵחֵל מְלָאכָה בּוֹ סוֹפוֹ לְהַכְרִית, עַל כֵּן אֲכַבֵּס בּוֹ לִבִּי כְּבוֹרִית
וְאֶתְפַּלְּלָה אֶל אֵל עַרְבִית וְשַׁחְרִית, מוּסָף וְגַם מִנְחָה הוּא יַעֲנֵנִי.
אוֹת הִיא לְעוֹלְמֵי עַד בֵּינוֹ וּבֵינִי.

---

KI ESHMERA

אֶהְגֶּה בְּתוֹרַת אֵל *Instead I will study God's Torah.* Sanctity often symbolizes itself in man by withdrawal; for example, *kedushat Shabbat* obligates a person to refrain from productive work and relinquish his ownership of the world. However, we also must sanctify Shabbat through positive actions, not merely through passive abstentions. One such way we hallow the day, Naḥmanides (Ex. 20:7) writes, is "to turn away from preoccupying thoughts about the emptiness of the times, and give our souls pleasure in the ways of God, visiting the sages and the prophets to hear the word of God." (See also Naḥmanides' comments on Lev. 23:2.) When the Shunamite woman tells her husband that she is going to visit the prophet Elisha, he asks her, "Why are you going to him? Today is neither Rosh Ḥodesh nor Shabbat" (II Kings 4:23). Naḥmanides quotes the Talmud (*Rosh HaShana* 16b) which infers from

דְּרוֹר יִקְרָא God proclaims freedom to boy and girl,
And guards you like the pupil of His eye.
Your name is pleasant, never will it cease.
Rest and be at ease on the Sabbath day.

Seek my Temple and my hall,
And show me a sign of salvation.
Plant a shoot in my vineyard.
Hear the cry of my people.

Tread the winepress in Botzra,
And in Babylon which overpowered.
Crush my foes in anger and wrath,
Hear my voice on the day I cry.

God, let there be on the desert mountain,
Myrtle, acacia, cypress and box tree.
To one who warns and one who is warned,
Let peace flow like river waters.

Crush those who rise against me, zealous God,
Melting their heart with grief.
Then we will open and fill our mouths,
And tongues with songs of joy to You.

Know what is wisdom for your soul,
And it will be a crown for your head.
Keep your Holy One's command,
Observe your holy Sabbath day.

*Birkat HaMazon can be found on page 124.*

דְּרוֹר יִקְרָא לְבֵן עִם בַּת
וְיִנְצָרְכֶם כְּמוֹ בָבַת
נְעִים שִׁמְכֶם וְלֹא יֻשְׁבַּת
שְׁבוּ נֽוּחוּ בְּיוֹם שַׁבָּת

דְּרֹשׁ נָוִי וְאוּלַמִּי
וְאוֹת יֶשַׁע עֲשֵׂה עִמִּי
נְטַע שׂוֹרֵק בְּתוֹךְ כַּרְמִי
שְׁעֵה שַׁוְעַת בְּנֵי עַמִּי.

דְּרֹךְ פּוּרָה בְּתוֹךְ בָּצְרָה
וְגַם בָּבֶל אֲשֶׁר גָּבְרָה
נְתֹץ צָרַי בְּאַף עֶבְרָה
שְׁמַע קוֹלִי בְּיוֹם אֶקְרָא.

אֱלֹהִים תֵּן בְּמִדְבָּר הָר
הֲדַס שִׁטָּה בְּרוֹשׁ תִּדְהָר
וְלַמַּזְהִיר וְלַנִּזְהָר
שְׁלוֹמִים תֵּן כְּמֵי נָהָר.

הֲדֹךְ קָמַי, אֵל קַנָּא
בְּמוֹג לֵבָב וּבִמְגִנָּה
וְנַרְחִיב פֶּה וּנְמַלְאֶנָּה
לְשׁוֹנֵנוּ לְךָ רִנָּה.

דְּעֵה חָכְמָה לְנַפְשֶׁךָ
וְהִיא כֶתֶר לְרֹאשֶׁךָ
נְצֹר מִצְוַת קְדוֹשֶׁךָ
שְׁמֹר שַׁבַּת קָדְשֶׁךָ.

ברכת המזון *can be found on page 125.*

# סעודה שלישית
# SE'UDA SHELISHIT

Not far from where our family lived there was a Modzitzer shtiebel where I would occasionally go for *se'uda shelishit*. The Ḥasidim would be singing *Bnei Heikhala, Hashem Ro'i Lo Eḥsar*, then both songs again. It occurred to me that they weren't singing because they wanted to sing, but were singing because they did not want to allow Shabbat to leave. I remember an encounter I had in this shtiebel when I was still a small child. One of the men who had been singing most enthusiastically, wearing a kapota consisting of more holes than material, but a kapota nonetheless, approached me and asked if I recognized him. I told him that I did not, and he introduced himself as Yankel the Porter. During the week I knew Yankel the Porter as someone very ordinary, wearing shabby clothes, walking around with a rope. I could not imagine that this individual of such regal bearing could be the same person. Yet on Shabbat he wore a kapota and shtreimel. On Shabbat his soul wasn't Yankel the Porter, but Yankel the Prince. Well after nightfall I naïvely asked him, "When do we daven *ma'ariv*?" He replied: "Do you miss weekdays that much that you cannot wait to daven *ma'ariv*?" The Jewish soul yearns for holiness and will do anything to not let it go. (*Before Hashem You Shall Be Purified*, pp. 37–38)

# Zemirot for Se'uda Shelishit

אַתְקִינוּ Prepare the feast of perfect faith, joy of the holy King.
Prepare the Royal feast,
this is the feast [mystically known as] "the Small Face,"
and "the Holy Ancient One" and "the Field of Holy Apples" [mystical terms for aspects of the Divine] come to partake in the feast with it.

Children of the palace
who yearn to see the radiance of "the Small Face,"
be here at this table in which the King is engraved.
Long to join this gathering together with the winged angels.
Rejoice now at this time of favor when there is no displeasure.
Come close to me, see my strength, for there are no harsh judgments:
Those brazen dogs are outside, unable to enter.
So I invite the holy Ancient of Days, His brow of desire
as the moment fades,
And His will is revealed, to annul all forces of impurity.
Hurl them into the abyss, hide them in the clefts of rocks,
For now, at Minḥa-time, is a time of joy for "the Small Face."

מִזְמוֹר לְדָוִד A psalm of David. The LORD is my Shepherd, I shall not want. *Ps. 23*
He makes me lie down in green pastures. He leads me beside the still waters. He refreshes my soul. He guides me in the paths of righteousness for His name's sake. Though I walk through the valley of the shadow of death, I will fear no evil, for You are with me; Your rod and Your staff, they comfort me. You set a table before me in the presence of my enemies; You anoint my head with oil; my cup is filled to overflowing. May goodness and kindness follow me all the days of my life, and may I live in the House of the LORD for evermore.

---

is Sabbath, into the dark and frightening, secular workaday week, we sing the psalm "The LORD is my shepherd, I shall not want. He makes me lie down in green pastures; He leads me beside the still waters," etc., and we believe with our entire hearts in the words of the psalmist. However, this psalm only describes the ultimate destination of *homo religious,* not the path leading to that destination. For the path that eventually will lead to the "green pastures" and to the "still waters" is not the royal road, but a narrow, twisting footway that threads its course along the steep mountain slope, as the terrible abyss

# זמירות לסעודה שלישית

אַתְקִֽינוּ סְעוּדְתָא דִּמְהֵימְנוּתָא שְׁלִֽימְתָא, חֶדְוְתָא דְּמַלְכָּא קַדִּישָׁא.
אַתְקִֽינוּ סְעוּדְתָא דְמַלְכָּא.
דָּא הִיא סְעוּדְתָא דִּזְעֵיר אַנְפִּין
וְעַתִּיקָא קַדִּישָׁא וַחֲקַל תַּפּוּחִין קַדִּישִׁין אָתַֽיִן לְסַעֲדָה בַּהֲדֵהּ.

בְּנֵי הֵיכְלָא, דְּכַסִּיפִין לְמֶחֱזֵי זִיו זְעֵיר אַנְפִּין
יְהוֹן הָכָא, בְּהַאי תַּכָּא, דְּבֵהּ מַלְכָּא בְּגִלּוּפִין.
צְבוּ לַחְדָא, בְּהַאי וַעְדָא, בְּגוֹ עִירִין וְכָל גַּדְפִין.
חֲדוּ הַשְׁתָּא, בְּהַאי שַׁעְתָּא, דְּבֵהּ רַעֲוָא וְלֵית זַעְפִין.
קְרִֽיבוּ לִי, חֲזוּ חֵילִי, דְּלֵית דִּינִין דְּתַקִּיפִין.
לְבַר נָטְלִין, וְלָא עָלִין, הָנֵי כַּלְבִין דַּחֲצִיפִין.
וְהָא אַזְמִין עַתִּיק יוֹמִין, לְמִצְחֵהּ עַד יְהוֹן חָלְפִין.
רְעוּ דִי לֵהּ, דְּגַלֵּי לֵהּ, לְבַטָּלָה בְּכָל קְלִיפִין.
יְשַׁוֵּי לוֹן, בִּנְקָבְהוֹן, וִיטַמְּרוּן בְּגוֹ כֵּפִין.
אֲרֵי הַשְׁתָּא, בְּמִנְחָתָא, בְּחֶדְוָתָא דִּזְעֵיר אַנְפִּין.

מִזְמוֹר לְדָוִד, יהוה רֹעִי לֹא אֶחְסָר: בִּנְאוֹת דֶּשֶׁא יַרְבִּיצֵֽנִי, עַל־מֵי תהלים כג
מְנֻחוֹת יְנַהֲלֵֽנִי: נַפְשִׁי יְשׁוֹבֵב, יַנְחֵֽנִי בְמַעְגְּלֵי־צֶֽדֶק לְמַֽעַן שְׁמוֹ:
גַּם כִּי־אֵלֵךְ בְּגֵיא צַלְמָֽוֶת לֹא־אִירָא רָע, כִּי־אַתָּה עִמָּדִי, שִׁבְטְךָ
וּמִשְׁעַנְתֶּֽךָ הֵֽמָּה יְנַחֲמֻֽנִי: תַּעֲרֹךְ לְפָנַי שֻׁלְחָן נֶֽגֶד צֹרְרָי, דִּשַּֽׁנְתָּ
בַשֶּֽׁמֶן רֹאשִׁי, כּוֹסִי רְוָיָה: אַךְ טוֹב וָחֶֽסֶד יִרְדְּפֽוּנִי כָּל־יְמֵי חַיָּי, וְשַׁבְתִּי
בְּבֵית־יהוה לְאֹֽרֶךְ יָמִים:

---

MIZMOR LE'DAVID

יהוה רֹעִי לֹא אֶחְסָר *The Lord is my Shepherd, I shall not want.* Religion is not, at the outset, a refuge of grace and mercy for the despondent and desperate, an enchanted stream for crushed spirits, but a raging, clamorous torrent of man's consciousness with all its crises, pangs, and torments. Yes, it is true that during the third Sabbath meal at dusk, as the day of rest declines and man's soul yearns for its Creator and is afraid to depart from that realm of holiness whose name

יְדִיד Beloved of the soul, Father of compassion,
draw Your servant close to Your will.
Like a deer will Your servant run
and fall prostrate before Your beauty.
To him Your love is sweeter
than honey from the comb, than any taste.

הָדוּר Glorious, beautiful, radiance of the world,
my soul is sick with love for You.
Please, God, heal her now
by showing her Your tender radiance.
Then she will recover her strength and be healed,
Be Your servant for eternity.

וָתִיק Ancient of Days, let Your mercy be aroused;
please have pity on Your beloved child.
How long have I yearned
to see the glory of Your strength.
Please, my God, my heart's desire –
hasten; do not hide Yourself.

הִגָּלֵה Reveal Yourself, beloved, and spread over me
the tabernacle of Your peace.
Let the earth shine with Your glory,
let us be overjoyed and rejoice in You.
Hurry, beloved, for the appointed time has come,
and be gracious to me as in the times of old.

*Birkat HaMazon can be found on page 124.*

---

captures this feeling when he writes, "Like a hind yearning for water brooks, my soul yearns for You, O God." Burning thirst drives the deer to the brook, and the instinctive yearning for existence drives the human being to God. It is the same natural, vital instinct to continue one's biological existence that is implanted in man as a living creature. However, while natural man seeks preservation, spiritual man reveals the secret of preservation, where it can be found and what it is. He redeems the instinct from its subordination to indifferent nature and elevates it to a sublime spiritual height, for he finds the fulfillment of his instinctual yearning in a realm beyond the material by becoming closer to God. Man runs toward the transitory life, *ḥayyei sha'ah*, and he finds eternal life, *ḥayyei olam*. (*And From There You Shall Seek*, pp. 47–48)

יְדִיד נֶפֶשׁ, אָב הָרַחֲמָן, מְשֹׁךְ עַבְדָּךְ אֶל רְצוֹנָךְ
יָרוּץ עַבְדָּךְ כְּמוֹ אַיָּל, יִשְׁתַּחֲוֶה מוּל הֲדָרָךְ
כִּי יֶעֱרַב לוֹ יְדִידוּתָךְ, מִנֹּפֶת צוּף וְכָל טָעַם.

הָדוּר, נָאֶה, זִיו הָעוֹלָם, נַפְשִׁי חוֹלַת אַהֲבָתָךְ
אָנָּא, אֵל נָא, רְפָא נָא לָהּ, בְּהַרְאוֹת לָהּ נֹעַם זִיוָךְ
אָז תִּתְחַזֵּק וְתִתְרַפֵּא, וְהָיְתָה לָךְ שִׁפְחַת עוֹלָם.

וָתִיק, יֶהֱמוּ רַחֲמֶיךָ, וְחוּס נָא עַל בֵּן אוֹהֲבָךְ
כִּי זֶה כַּמֶּה נִכְסֹף נִכְסַף לִרְאוֹת בְּתִפְאֶרֶת עֻזָּךְ
אָנָּא, אֵלִי, מַחְמַד לִבִּי, חוּשָׁה נָּא, וְאַל תִּתְעַלָּם.

הִגָּלֶה נָא וּפְרֹשׂ, חָבִיב, עָלַי אֶת סֻכַּת שְׁלוֹמָךְ
תָּאִיר אֶרֶץ מִכְּבוֹדָךְ, נָגִילָה וְנִשְׂמְחָה בָּךְ.
מַהֵר, אָהוּב, כִּי בָא מוֹעֵד, וְחָנֵּנִי כִּימֵי עוֹלָם.

ברכת המזון *can be found on page 125.*

---

yawns at the traveler's feet. Many see "the LORD passing by; and a great and strong wind rending mountains and shattering rocks … and after the wind an earthquake … and after the earthquake a fire" but only a few prove worthy of hearing "the still small voice" (1 Kings 19:11–12). "Out of the straits have I called unto Thee, O LORD" (Ps. 130:1). Out of the straits of inner oppositions and incongruities, spiritual doubts and uncertainties, out of the depths of a psyche rent with antinomies and contradictions, out of the bottomless pit of a soul that struggles with its own torments I have called, I have called unto Thee, O LORD. (*Halakhic Man*, p. 142)

YEDID NEFESH

יָרוּץ עַבְדָּךְ כְּמוֹ אַיָּל *Like deer will Your servant run.* Man's aspiration for God is essentially the yearning of the lonely individual, bereft of peace of mind or joy, for happiness and repose. The individual, sunk in the depths of secular life, with little purpose or meaning, full of denial and panic, runs to God as to a safe refuge, where he will be liberated from his mute suffering. Man wishes to triumph over death, to turn selfless fate into a spiritual destiny, and to achieve both a joyful temporal existence and eternal life. The Psalmist (42:2)

# הבדלה

# HAVDALA

# Seder Havdala

*On Motza'ei Yom Tov that is not a Motza'ei Shabbat, the first paragraph and the blessings for the spices and flame are omitted. At the end of Yom Kippur, only the blessing for the spices is omitted.*

*Taking a cup of wine in the right hand, say:*

הִנֵּה Behold, God is my salvation. I will trust and not be afraid. *Is. 12*
The LORD, the LORD, is my strength and my song.
He has become my salvation.
With joy you will draw water from the springs of salvation.
Salvation is the LORD's; on Your people is Your blessing, Selah. *Ps. 3*
The LORD of hosts is with us, *Ps. 46*
the God of Jacob is our stronghold, Selah.
LORD of hosts: happy is the one who trusts in You. *Ps. 84*
LORD, save! May the King answer us on the day we call. *Ps. 20*
For the Jews there was light and gladness, joy and honor – *Esther 8*
so may it be for us.
I will lift the cup of salvation and call on the name of the LORD. *Ps. 116*

---

in Shabbat and its restrictions against doing *melakha,* while *kiddush al hakos* introduces the *se'udot* of Shabbat (see the essay "The Mitzva of Kiddush: To Sanctify, to Praise, to Redeem," p. 27). Similarly, the Havdala in *ma'ariv* ends *Shabbat* and makes work permissible, while *havdala al hakos* concludes the *se'udot* of *Shabbat* and marks the beginning of the meals of the week. Thus eating before *havdala al hakos* not only delays the fulfillment of the *mitzva,* but undermines its essential purpose: to serve as the conclusion of the Shabbat meals and the commencement of the weekday meals. Therefore, there is an opinion in the Talmud that if a person improperly eats before reciting *havdala al hakos,* there is no longer any purpose in reciting it at all. Moreover, *havdala al hakos* not only marks the end of the meals of Shabbat, but concludes all of *kevod* and *oneg Shabbat.* Thus, even though Yom Kippur has no *mitzva* of *se'udat Yom Tov,* we still recite *havdala al hakos* at its conclusion to mark the end of the *mitzva* of *kevod Yom Tov* that we fulfill through wearing Yom Tov attire. This also explains the ruling of *Magen Avraham* (262:2) that one should not change out of his Shabbat clothing until after *havdala al hakos.* Even though there is no more prohibition to perform work

# סדר הבדלה

*On* מוצאי יום טוב *that is not a* מוצאי שבת*, the first paragraph and the blessings for the spices and flame are omitted. At the end of* יום כפור*, only the blessing for the spices is omitted.*

*Taking a cup of wine in the right hand, say:*

ישעיה יב הִנֵּה אֵל יְשׁוּעָתִי אֶבְטַח, וְלֹא אֶפְחָד<br>
כִּי־עָזִּי וְזִמְרָת יָהּ יהוה, וַיְהִי־לִי לִישׁוּעָה:<br>
וּשְׁאַבְתֶּם־מַיִם בְּשָׂשׂוֹן, מִמַּעַיְנֵי הַיְשׁוּעָה:<br>
תהלים ג לַיהוה הַיְשׁוּעָה, עַל־עַמְּךָ בִרְכָתֶךָ סֶּלָה:<br>
תהלים מו יהוה צְבָאוֹת עִמָּנוּ, מִשְׂגָּב לָנוּ אֱלֹהֵי יַעֲקֹב סֶלָה:<br>
תהלים פד יהוה צְבָאוֹת, אַשְׁרֵי אָדָם בֹּטֵחַ בָּךְ:<br>
תהלים כ יהוה הוֹשִׁיעָה, הַמֶּלֶךְ יַעֲנֵנוּ בְיוֹם־קָרְאֵנוּ:<br>
אסתר ח לַיְּהוּדִים הָיְתָה אוֹרָה וְשִׂמְחָה וְשָׂשֹׂן וִיקָר: כֵּן תִּהְיֶה לָּנוּ.<br>
תהלים קטז כּוֹס־יְשׁוּעוֹת אֶשָּׂא, וּבְשֵׁם יהוה אֶקְרָא:

HAVDALA

After the conclusion of Shabbat a person may not eat before he recites Havdala over a cup of wine (*havdala al hakos*) even if he has already recited Havdala during *ma'ariv*, removing the prohibition to perform forbidden work. While we find in many contexts a similar prohibition to eat before performing a *mitzva* in order to not delay its performance, the prohibition to eat before *havdala al hakos* is unique, as it is connected to the essence of the *mitzva* itself. For example, the Talmud (*Pesaḥim* 106b) quotes an opinion that if a person inappropriately eats before reciting *havdala al hakos*, he has not only violated the prohibition of eating, but he can also no longer recite Havdala at all. This stands in contrast to other *mitzvot* in which we do not find that eating before their fulfillment would invalidate them. Thus, it is forbidden to eat before praying *shaharit* (*Berakhot* 10b), but if one has eaten, he can (and must) still recite the morning prayers. This discrepancy between Havdala and other *mitzvot* arises from the fact that there are two aspects to Havdala, parallel to the two aspects of Kiddush. Kiddush in the Amida of Shabbat evening ushers

*When making Havdala for others, add:*
Please pay attention, my masters.

Blessed are You, LORD our God, King of the Universe,
who creates the fruit of the vine.

*Hold the spice box and say:*

Blessed are You, LORD our God, King of the Universe,
who creates the various spices.

*Smell the spices and put the spice box down.*
*Lift the hands toward the flame of the Havdala candle and say:*

Blessed are You, LORD our God, King of the Universe,
who creates the lights of fire.

*Holding the cup of wine again in the right hand, say:*

בָּרוּךְ Blessed are You, LORD our God, King of the Universe,
who distinguishes between sacred and secular,
between light and darkness,
between Israel and the nations,
between the seventh day and the six days of work.
Blessed are You, LORD,
who distinguishes between sacred and secular.

---

between Israel and the nations. Should the distinction between Israel and the nations resemble the distinction between light and darkness or should it resemble the distinction between the holy and the profane? Should it be obvious and apparent for all to see or should it be subtle and hidden? In other words, should one act as a Jew only in the recesses of his home, closing the windows and drawing the shades behind him before donning a yarmulke to pray or study the Torah? Or should a Jew's external appearance and actions identify him as such wherever he goes, in both his private and public life? In the Passover Haggada, our Sages deduce from the phrase, "And they were there a great nation," that while Israel lived amongst the Egyptians, "Israel was distinct there." This concept is inferred from the verse because the Hebrew word for nation, "*goy*," is related to the Hebrew word for body, "*geviya*." The connection implies that just as every person is unique and every face different, so too the Jewish people stood apart from the other nations around them.

*When making* הבדלה *for others, add:*

סַבְרִי מָרָנָן

**בָּרוּךְ אַתָּה יהוה אֱלֹהֵינוּ מֶלֶךְ הָעוֹלָם, בּוֹרֵא פְּרִי הַגָּפֶן.**

*Hold the spice box and say:*

**בָּרוּךְ אַתָּה יהוה אֱלֹהֵינוּ מֶלֶךְ הָעוֹלָם, בּוֹרֵא מִינֵי בְשָׂמִים.**

*Smell the spices and put the spice box down.*
*Lift the hands toward the flame of the* הבדלה *candle and say:*

**בָּרוּךְ אַתָּה יהוה אֱלֹהֵינוּ מֶלֶךְ הָעוֹלָם, בּוֹרֵא מְאוֹרֵי הָאֵשׁ.**

*Holding the cup of wine again in the right hand, say:*

**בָּרוּךְ אַתָּה יהוה אֱלֹהֵינוּ מֶלֶךְ הָעוֹלָם**
**הַמַּבְדִּיל בֵּין קֹדֶשׁ לְחֹל**
**בֵּין אוֹר לְחֹשֶׁךְ**
**בֵּין יִשְׂרָאֵל לָעַמִּים**
**בֵּין יוֹם הַשְּׁבִיעִי לְשֵׁשֶׁת יְמֵי הַמַּעֲשֶׂה.**
**בָּרוּךְ אַתָּה יהוה, הַמַּבְדִּיל בֵּין קֹדֶשׁ לְחֹל.**

---

after the Havdala in *tefilla*, it is the *havdala al hakos* which marks the end all aspects of *kevod* and *oneg Shabbat.* (*Shiurim LeZekher Abba Mari*, vol. 2, pp. 131–134)

הַמַּבְדִּיל בֵּין קֹדֶשׁ לְחֹל, בֵּין אוֹר לְחֹשֶׁךְ, בֵּין יִשְׂרָאֵל לָעַמִּים *Who distinguishes between sacred and secular, between light and darkness, between Israel and the nations.* The distinction between light and darkness is an obvious one, clear for all to perceive; indeed, even plants and animals respond to these stimuli. The distinction between holy and profane, however, is a much more subtle one, hidden from the perception of the physical senses. A person needs a special intuition, a spiritual and moral sensitivity, to see with his heart and mind's eye the difference between the sacred and the secular. After the blessing mentions the clearest of *havdalot*, between light and darkness, and the most hidden, between the holy and the profane, the prayer then presents a third *havdala*:

# Zemirot for Havdala

הַמַּבְדִּיל He who distinguishes between sacred and secular,
may He forgive our sins.
May He multiply our offspring and wealth like the sand,
and like the stars at night.

The day has passed like a palm tree's shadow;
I call on God to fulfill what the watchman said: *Is. 21*
"Morning comes, though now it is night."

Your righteousness is as high as Mount Tabor.
May You pass high over my sins.
[Let them be] like yesterday when it has passed, *Ps. 90*
like a watch in the night.

The time of offerings has passed.
Would that I might rest.
I am weary with my sighing, every night I drench [with tears]. *Ps. 6*

Hear my voice; let it not be cast aside.
Open for me the lofty gate.
My head is filled with the dew of dawn, *Song. 5*
my hair with raindrops of the night.

Heed my prayer, revered and awesome God.
When I cry, grant me deliverance at twilight, *Prov. 7*
as the day fades, or in the darkness of the night.

I call to You, LORD: Save me.
Make known to me the path of life.
Rescue me from misery before day turns to night.

Cleanse the defilement of my deeds, lest those who torment me say,
"Where is the God who made me, *Job 35*
who gives cause for songs in the night?"

We are in Your hands like clay: please forgive our sins, light and grave.
Day to day they pour forth speech, *Ps. 19*
and night to night [they communicate knowledge].

---

his *mitzva* observance and Jewish identity be recognizable to all. (*Derashot HaRav*, pp. 180–184)

# זמירות להבדלה

הַמַּבְדִּיל בֵּין קֹדֶשׁ לְחֹל, חַטֹּאתֵֽינוּ הוּא יִמְחֹל
זַרְעֵֽנוּ וְכַסְפֵּֽנוּ יַרְבֶּה כַחוֹל וְכַכּוֹכָבִים בַּלָּֽיְלָה.

יוֹם פָּנָה כְּצֵל תֹּֽמֶר, אֶקְרָא לָאֵל עָלַי גֹּמֵר
אָמַר שֹׁמֵר, אָתָא בֹֽקֶר וְגַם־לָֽיְלָה: ישעיה כא

צִדְקָתְךָ כְּהַר תָּבוֹר, עַל חֲטָאַי עָבוֹר תַּעֲבֹר
כְּיוֹם אֶתְמוֹל כִּי יַעֲבֹר, וְאַשְׁמוּרָה בַלָּֽיְלָה: תהלים צ

חָלְפָה עוֹנַת מִנְחָתִי, מִי יִתֵּן מְנוּחָתִי
יָגַֽעְתִּי בְאַנְחָתִי, אַשְׂחֶה בְכָל־לַֽיְלָה: תהלים ו

קוֹלִי בַּל יֻנְטַל, פְּתַח לִי שַֽׁעַר הַמְנֻטָּל
שֶׁרֹּאשִׁי נִמְלָא טָל, קְוֻצּוֹתַי רְסִֽיסֵי לָֽיְלָה: שיר השירים ה

הֵעָתֵר נוֹרָא וְאָיֹם, אֲשַׁוֵּֽעַ, תְּנָה פִדְיוֹם
בְּנֶֽשֶׁף־בְּעֶֽרֶב יוֹם, בְּאִישׁוֹן לָֽיְלָה: משלי ז

קְרָאתִֽיךָ יָהּ, הוֹשִׁיעֵֽנִי, אֹֽרַח חַיִּים תּוֹדִיעֵֽנִי
מִדַּלָּה תְבַצְּעֵֽנִי, מִיּוֹם עַד לָֽיְלָה.

טַהֵר טִנּוּף מַעֲשַׂי, פֶּן יֹאמְרוּ מַכְעִיסַי
אַיֵּה אֱלֽוֹהַּ עֹשָׂי, נֹתֵן זְמִרוֹת בַּלָּֽיְלָה: איוב לה

נַֽחְנוּ בְיָדְךָ כַּֽחֹֽמֶר, סְלַח נָא עַל קַל וָחֹֽמֶר
יוֹם לְיוֹם יַבִּֽיעַ אֹֽמֶר, וְלַֽיְלָה לְּלָֽיְלָה: תהלים יט

---

However, our Sages were not merely communicating with this exegetical comment a historical fact; they were relating a religious imperative as well: the distinctiveness of a Jew must be evident for all to see. The *havdala* between Israel and other nations is not meant to be a hidden one, but rather one that is as apparent and obvious as the distinction between light and darkness. Judaism does not merely require a Jew to perform the *mitzvot*; it requires that

אֱלֹהִים יִסְעָדֵנוּ God sustain us
with blessing, in all we have,
and grant us goodness
in all we put our hands to,
God sustain us.

On Sunday as we set to work,
may He order blessing to us,
and so too on Monday,
may He sweeten the secret
hidden in wait for us.
God sustain us.

Multiply my hosts, Savior,
on Tuesday and on Wednesday.
On Thursday, without suffering,
may He send us our redeemer.
God sustain us.

Prepare fresh meat
on Friday for the sacred meal.
Holiness, praise, honor,
on all that we desire.
God sustain us.

We shall offer our souls
delights on our holy day,
and our couch is luscious with life,
and the night, lit up for us.
God sustain us.

אֱלֹהִים יִסְעָדֵֽנוּ
בְּרָכָה בִּמְאוֹדֵֽנוּ
וְזֶֽבֶד טוֹב יִזְבְּדֵֽנוּ
בְּכָל מִשְׁלַח יָדֵֽינוּ.
אֱלֹהִים יִסְעָדֵֽנוּ.

בְּיוֹם רִאשׁוֹן לִמְלָאכָה
יְצַו אִתָּֽנוּ בְּרָכָה
וְיוֹם הַשֵּׁנִי כָּֽכָה
יַמְתִּיק אֶת סוֹדֵֽנוּ.
אֱלֹהִים יִסְעָדֵֽנוּ.

רַבֵּה צְבָאַי, יִשְׁעִי
בַּשְּׁלִישִׁי וּבָרְבִיעִי
בַּחֲמִישִׁי אַךְ לֹא בְעִי
יִשְׁלַח אֶת פּוֹדֵֽנוּ.
אֱלֹהִים יִסְעָדֵֽנוּ.

הָכֵן טְבֹחַ טֶֽבַח
בְּיוֹם הַשִּׁשִּׁי זֶֽבַח
קֹֽדֶשׁ הִלּוּל וָשֶֽׁבַח
עַל כָּל מַחְמַדֵּֽנוּ.
אֱלֹהִים יִסְעָדֵֽנוּ.

מַעֲדַנִּים לְנַפְשֵֽׁנוּ
נָתַן בְּיוֹם קָדְשֵֽׁנוּ
וְרַעֲנַנָּה עַרְשֵֽׁנוּ
וְלַֽיְלָה אוֹר בַּעֲדֵֽנוּ.
אֱלֹהִים יִסְעָדֵֽנוּ.

אִישׁ חָסִיד הָיָה Once upon a time there was a devoted man. So poor was he that he had no food or sustenance; and in his shame he stayed at home to study, for he had no clothes to wear either. What is more, he was responsible for the upkeep of his wife, an honorable woman, and five sons.

One day his wife said, "I cannot be distracted any longer. We have no bread to eat, no clothes, nothing at all to call our own. You have searched the Torah and found what you looked for – but what are we to eat now?

"Listen. Go out to the marketplace, fearless as a knight in arms. Gracious, compassionate God above might perhaps take pity on us with some act of kindness. He is a shelter for those who place trust in Him; He grants the wishes of those who fear Him."

"You advise me soundly and wisely," he said, "but I cannot agree to what you say. I cannot go out in shame and humiliation with nothing to cover me at all, with nothing in my hand to trade with, not even a penny."

But the woman hurried round to her neighbors and borrowed a fine set of handsome clothes. And her husband put them on and cast all his trust onto the God he loved so much. The children, in their prayers, said, "Please, do not make this poor man come home shamed."

Full of hope, he came to the marketplace. And who should be there to greet him but Elijah the prophet? The seer said to him, "Today you shall indeed become rich. Now command me, with all the honor you have: I am your slave.

"Call out to anyone who may have a mind to buy a slave unmatched in all the world." The man was disturbed: how could he overturn all the laws? How can a servant sell his own master? But Elijah placed his wisdom within the man, and he then held onto Elijah as if he were indeed the prophet's master.

A merchant eagerly bought the slave – for eight hundred thousand gold pieces. He demanded of Elijah what kind of work he did; asked whether he was skilled at building. "Build me a palace – a mansion," he said. "When it is finished – you are a free man."

אִישׁ חָסִיד הָיָה, בְּלִי מָזוֹן וּמִחְיָה.
בְּבֵיתוֹ עָסַק מִלְּבוּשׁ, וְאֵין בֶּגֶד לִלְבֹּשׁ.
גּוֹנֵן בַּחֲשׁוּבָה אִשָּׁה, וְגַם בְּבָנִים חֲמִשָּׁה.

דִּבְּרָה לוֹ הָאִשָּׁה, יוֹתֵר אֵין לְהִתְיָאֲשָׁה.
הֲמִבְּלִי לֶחֶם לֶאֱכֹל, בְּעֵרֹם וּבְחֹסֶר כֹּל.
וְתוֹרָה מָצָאתָ כִּי יָגַעְתָּ, מַה נֹּאכַל מֵעַתָּה.

זָהִיר כְּבַר נָשׁוּק, הֲלֹא תֵצֵא לַשּׁוּק.
חַנּוּן וְרַחוּם בִּמְרוֹמָיו, אוּלַי יִגְמְלֵנוּ בְּרַחֲמָיו.
טוֹב לְקַוֹּ מַחֲסֶה, רְצוֹן יְרֵאָיו יַעֲשֶׂה.

יָעַצְתְּ בְּדַעַת וּבְחָכְמָה, עֲצָתֵךְ בְּלִי לְהַסְכִּימָה.
כְּצֵאתִי לְבֹשֶׁת וְלִכְלִמָּה, מִבְּלִי כְסוּת וְשַׂלְמָה.
לְאֵין בְּיָדִי לִפְרֻטָה, אֲפִלּוּ שָׁוֶה פְּרוּטָה.

מִהֲרָה וְשָׁאֲלָה מִשְּׁכֵנִים, מַלְבּוּשִׁים נָאִים מְתֻקָּנִים.
נִלְבַּשׁ וְהִשְׁלִיךְ יְהָבוֹ, עַל יהוה אֲשֶׁר אֲהֵבוֹ.
סָחוּ יְלָדָיו בִּפְלוּלָם, אַל יָשֹׁב דַּךְ נִכְלָם.

עָבַר בַּשּׁוּק בְּשִׁבְרָתוֹ, וְהִנֵּה אֵלִיָּהוּ הַנָּבִיא לִקְרָאתוֹ.
פָּץ לוֹ הַמְבַשֵּׂר, בֶּאֱמֶת הַיּוֹם תִּתְעַשֵּׁר.
צַוֵּנִי בְּכָל כְּבוֹדֶךָ, כִּי הִנְנִי עַבְדֶּךָ.

קְרָא לְמִי בְּדַעְתּוֹ, קְנוֹת עֶבֶד אֵין כְּמוֹתוֹ.
רָחַשׁ אֵיךְ יְשַׁנֶּה דִּינוֹ, עֶבֶד לִמְכֹּר אֶת אֲדוֹנוֹ.
שָׁת לוֹ חָכְמָתוֹ בְּקִרְבּוֹ, וְהֶחֱזִיק בּוֹ כְּמוֹ רַבּוֹ.

תַּגָּר קְנָאוֹ בַּאֲהָבִים, בִּשְׁמוֹנֶה מֵאוֹת אֶלֶף זְהוּבִים.
תְּבָעוֹ מַה מְּלַאכְתֶּךָ, אִם בְּבִנְיַן חָכְמָתֶךָ.
תַּכְלִית טְרַקְלִין וּפַלְטְרִין, הֲרֵי אַתָּה בֶּן חוֹרִין.

On the first day at work, Elijah toiled with all the other laborers. But at midnight he prayed, "Answer me, answer me, Performer of Wonders. I took this upon myself and had myself sold into slavery, not for my own honor's sake, but for Yours.

"Now, God who created Your whole world, finish off this building. As I entreat You, show Your mercy, for my intentions are good." Angels of Mercy from high above, then came down and began to build.

The children of Majesty were many and soon all the work was done. The merchant was overjoyed when he saw that the task was finished, the most beautiful of handsome towers, exactly as the architects had planned.

"Now," said Elijah, "Remember what you told me yesterday. Set me free, clearly and certainly, as you said you would when you spoke of liberty." The merchant was true to his word, and the man of truth, Elijah – vanished away.

יוֹם רִאשׁוֹן בְּמִפְעָלִים, פָּעַל עִם פּוֹעֲלִים.
שִׁוַּע בַּחֲצִי הַלַּיְלָה, עֲנֵנִי נוֹרָא עֲלִילָה.
יָזַמְתִּי וְנִמְכַּרְתִּי לְהַעֲבִידִי, לִכְבוֹדְךָ וְלֹא לִכְבוֹדִי.

בּוֹרֵא עוֹלָם בְּקִנְיָן, הַשְׁלֵם זֶה הַבִּנְיָן.
רַחֲמֶיךָ יִכְמְרוּ בַּחֲנִינָתִי, כִּי לְטוֹבָה כַּוָּנָתִי.
מַלְאֲכֵי רַחֲמִים מִמְּעוֹנָתוֹ, אָז הֵחֵלּוּ לִבְנוֹתוֹ.

רַבּוּ בְּנֵי הַמְּלוּכָה, וַתִּשְׁלַם כָּל הַמְּלָאכָה.
דָּץ הַסּוֹחֵר בִּרְאוֹתוֹ, כִּי נִגְמְרָה מְלַאכְתּוֹ.
כְּלוּלַת מִגְדָּלִים נָאִים, לְפִי עִנְיַן הַבַּנָּאִים.

יִזָּכֵר לְךָ עַתָּה, אֶתְמוֹל אֲשֶׁר דִּבַּרְתָּ.
חָפְשֵׁנִי בְּוַדַּאי וּבְבֵרוּר, כְּנַמְתָּ לְעִנְיַן שִׁחְרוּר.
זֶה קִיְּמוֹ בֶּאֱמֶת, וּפָרַח לוֹ אִישׁ הָאֱמֶת.

| | |
|---|---|
| אָמַר יהוה לְיַעֲקֹב The LORD said to Jacob, | "Do not be afraid, my servant Jacob." |
| The LORD chose Jacob, | "Do not be afraid, my servant Jacob." |
| The LORD redeemed Jacob, | "Do not be afraid, my servant Jacob." |
| A star is to come forth from Jacob, | "Do not be afraid, my servant Jacob." *Num. 24* |
| In coming times he shall take root, Jacob, | "Do not be afraid, my servant Jacob." *Is. 27* |
| A ruler shall rise up from Jacob, | "Do not be afraid, my servant Jacob." *Num. 24* |
| Remember but this of Jacob, | "Do not be afraid, my servant Jacob." |
| The bliss of the salvation of Jacob, | "Do not be afraid, my servant Jacob." |
| Goodly are your tents, O Jacob, | "Do not be afraid, my servant Jacob." |
| They shall teach Your laws to Jacob, | "Do not be afraid, my servant Jacob." *Deut. 33* |
| There is no sorcery in Jacob, | "Do not be afraid, my servant Jacob." *Num. 23* |
| He has seen no sin in Jacob, | "Do not be afraid, my servant Jacob." |
| Who can count the dust of Jacob? | "Do not be afraid, my servant Jacob." |
| The LORD swore an oath to Jacob, | "Do not be afraid, my servant Jacob." |
| Please, forgive the sins of Jacob, | "Do not be afraid, my servant Jacob." |
| Restore the fortunes, now, of Jacob, | "Do not be afraid, my servant Jacob." |
| The LORD has recalled Jacob, | "Do not be afraid, my servant Jacob." |
| He ordered the salvations of Jacob, | "Do not be afraid, my servant Jacob." |
| This voice, it is the voice of Jacob, | "Do not be afraid, my servant Jacob." |
| Sing out in the joy of Jacob, | "Do not be afraid, my servant Jacob." |
| LORD, restore the might of Jacob, | "Do not be afraid, my servant Jacob." |
| You shall grant truth to Jacob. | "Do not be afraid, my servant Jacob." *Micha 7* |

אָמַר יהוה לְיַעֲקֹב, אַל תִּירָא עַבְדִּי יַעֲקֹב.
בָּחַר יהוה בְּיַעֲקֹב, אַל תִּירָא עַבְדִּי יַעֲקֹב.
גָּאַל יהוה אֶת יַעֲקֹב, אַל תִּירָא עַבְדִּי יַעֲקֹב.
דָּרַךְ כּוֹכָב מִיַּעֲקֹב, אַל תִּירָא עַבְדִּי יַעֲקֹב. במדבר כד
הַבָּאִים יַשְׁרֵשׁ יַעֲקֹב, אַל תִּירָא עַבְדִּי יַעֲקֹב. ישעיה כז
וְיֵרְדְּ מִיַּעֲקֹב, אַל תִּירָא עַבְדִּי יַעֲקֹב. במדבר כד
זְכֹר זֹאת לְיַעֲקֹב, אַל תִּירָא עַבְדִּי יַעֲקֹב.
חֶדְוַת יְשׁוּעוֹת יַעֲקֹב, אַל תִּירָא עַבְדִּי יַעֲקֹב.
טֹבוּ אֹהָלֶיךָ יַעֲקֹב, אַל תִּירָא עַבְדִּי יַעֲקֹב.
יוֹרוּ מִשְׁפָּטֶיךָ לְיַעֲקֹב, אַל תִּירָא עַבְדִּי יַעֲקֹב. דברים לג
כִּי לֹא נַחַשׁ בְּיַעֲקֹב, אַל תִּירָא עַבְדִּי יַעֲקֹב. במדבר כג
לֹא הִבִּיט אָוֶן בְּיַעֲקֹב, אַל תִּירָא עַבְדִּי יַעֲקֹב.
מִי מָנָה עֲפַר יַעֲקֹב, אַל תִּירָא עַבְדִּי יַעֲקֹב.
נִשְׁבַּע יהוה לְיַעֲקֹב, אַל תִּירָא עַבְדִּי יַעֲקֹב.
סְלַח נָא לַעֲוֹן יַעֲקֹב, אַל תִּירָא עַבְדִּי יַעֲקֹב.
עַתָּה הָשֵׁב שְׁבוּת יַעֲקֹב, אַל תִּירָא עַבְדִּי יַעֲקֹב.
פָּדָה יהוה אֶת יַעֲקֹב, אַל תִּירָא עַבְדִּי יַעֲקֹב.
צַוֵּה יְשׁוּעוֹת יַעֲקֹב, אַל תִּירָא עַבְדִּי יַעֲקֹב.
קוֹל קוֹל יַעֲקֹב, אַל תִּירָא עַבְדִּי יַעֲקֹב.
רָנּוּ שִׂמְחָה לְיַעֲקֹב, אַל תִּירָא עַבְדִּי יַעֲקֹב.
שָׁב יהוה אֶת גְּאוֹן יַעֲקֹב, אַל תִּירָא עַבְדִּי יַעֲקֹב.
תִּתֵּן אֱמֶת לְיַעֲקֹב, אַל תִּירָא עַבְדִּי יַעֲקֹב. מיכה ז

אֵלִיָּהוּ הַנָּבִיא Elijah the Prophet,
Elijah the Tishbite, Elijah the Gileadite –
he will come to us quickly with the Messiah, son of David.

The man who acted with zeal in God's name;
The man for whom Yekutiel [Moses] declared endless peace;
The man who stepped forward and atoned Israel's sin.

The man whose eyes saw twelve generations.
The man who was recognized as the "hairy one";
The man whose loins were girded with leather.

The man who raged against idol worshipers;
The man who swore that there would be no season's rain;
The man who stalled rain and dew for three whole years.

The man who went out to find his soul a hiding place,
The man sustained by ravens, the man who would not be killed;
The man for whose sake jug and flour-basket were blessed.

The man whose instruction was heard with yearning,
The man who was answered with fire from high heavens.
The man after whom they would say, "The LORD is God!" *1 Kings 18*

The man who will be sent from the highest heaven.
The man appointed over all good tidings.
The man trusted as mediator, to reconcile fathers with sons.

The man who cried gloriously, "I have been zealous for the LORD!" *1 Kings 19*
The man who rode horses of fire in the storm.
The man who never tasted death or burial.

Man of Tishbe, save us from the lion's mouth.
Bring us tidings of good things to come.
Make us happy, all, fathers with sons,
At the ends of our Sabbaths.

That man who is called "the Man of Tishbe,"
Let us prevail in the Torah with his aid.
Let us hear good tidings soon, from his mouth.
Bring us out of darkness into light.

Happy the one who saw his face in a dream.
Happy the one who has greeted or answered him, "Peace."
The LORD will bless His people with peace. *Ps. 29*

As is written, "I shall send Elijah the Prophet to you *Mal. 3*
before the coming of the great and terrifying day of the LORD.
And he shall reconcile fathers to sons and sons to fathers."

## אֵלִיָּהוּ הַנָּבִיא

אֵלִיָּהוּ הַתִּשְׁבִּי, אֵלִיָּהוּ הַגִּלְעָדִי
בִּמְהֵרָה יָבוֹא אֵלֵינוּ עִם מָשִׁיחַ בֶּן דָּוִד.

אִישׁ אֲשֶׁר קִנֵּא לְשֵׁם הָאֵל
אִישׁ בֻּשַּׂר שָׁלוֹם עַל יַד יְקוּתִיאֵל
אִישׁ גַּשׁ וַיְכַפֵּר עַל בְּנֵי יִשְׂרָאֵל.
אֵלִיָּהוּ הַנָּבִיא

אִישׁ דּוֹרוֹת שְׁנֵים עָשָׂר רָאוּ עֵינָיו
אִישׁ הַנִּקְרָא בַּעַל שֵׂעָר בְּסִמָּנָיו
אִישׁ וְאֵזוֹר עוֹר אָזוּר בְּמָתְנָיו.
אֵלִיָּהוּ הַנָּבִיא

אִישׁ זָעַף עַל עוֹבְדֵי חַמָּנִים
אִישׁ חָשׁ וְנִשְׁבַּע מִהְיוֹת גִּשְׁמֵי מְעוֹנִים
אִישׁ טַל וּמָטָר עָצַר שָׁלֹשׁ שָׁנִים.
אֵלִיָּהוּ הַנָּבִיא

אִישׁ יָצָא לִמְצֹא לְנַפְשׁוֹ נַחַת
אִישׁ כִּלְכְּלוּהוּ הָעוֹרְבִים וְלֹא מֵת לַשַּׁחַת
אִישׁ לְמַעֲנוֹ נִתְבָּרְכוּ כַּד וְצַפַּחַת.
אֵלִיָּהוּ הַנָּבִיא

אִישׁ מוּסָרָיו הִקְשִׁיבוּ כְמֵהִים
אִישׁ נַעֲנָה בָאֵשׁ מִשְּׁמֵי גְבוֹהִים
אִישׁ סָחוּ אַחֲרָיו יהוה הוּא הָאֱלֹהִים.
אֵלִיָּהוּ הַנָּבִיא

אִישׁ עָתִיד לְהִשְׁתַּלֵּחַ מִשְּׁמֵי עֲרָבוֹת
אִישׁ פָּקִיד עַל כָּל בְּשׂוֹרוֹת טוֹבוֹת
אִישׁ צִיר נֶאֱמָן לְהָשִׁיב לֵב בָּנִים עַל אָבוֹת. מלכים א׳ יח
אֵלִיָּהוּ הַנָּבִיא

אִישׁ קָרָא קַנֹּא קִנֵּאתִי לַיהוה
בְּתִפְאָרָה
אִישׁ רָכַב עַל סוּסֵי אֵשׁ בִּסְעָרָה
אִישׁ שֶׁלֹּא טָעַם טַעַם מִיתָה וּקְבוּרָה.
אֵלִיָּהוּ הַנָּבִיא

אִישׁ תִּשְׁבִּי תַּצִּילֵנוּ מִפִּי אֲרָיוֹת מלכים א׳ יט
תְּבַשְּׂרֵנוּ בְּשׂוֹרוֹת טוֹבוֹת
תְּשַׂמְּחֵנוּ בָּנִים עַל אָבוֹת
בְּמוֹצָאֵי שַׁבָּתוֹת.
אֵלִיָּהוּ הַנָּבִיא

אִישׁ תִּשְׁבִּי עַל שְׁמוֹ נִקְרָא
תַּצְלִיחֵנוּ עַל יָדוֹ בַּתּוֹרָה
תַּשְׁמִיעֵנוּ מִפִּיו בְּשׂוֹרָה טוֹבָה בִּמְהֵרָה
תּוֹצִיאֵנוּ מֵאֲפֵלָה לְאוֹרָה.
אֵלִיָּהוּ הַנָּבִיא

אַשְׁרֵי מִי שֶׁרָאָה פָנָיו בַּחֲלוֹם
אַשְׁרֵי מִי שֶׁנָּתַן לוֹ שָׁלוֹם
וְהֶחֱזִיר לוֹ שָׁלוֹם
יהוה יְבָרֵךְ אֶת עַמּוֹ בַשָּׁלוֹם. תהלים כט
אֵלִיָּהוּ הַנָּבִיא

כַּכָּתוּב: הִנֵּה אָנֹכִי שֹׁלֵחַ לָכֶם אֵת אֵלִיָּה הַנָּבִיא מלאכי ג
לִפְנֵי בּוֹא יוֹם יהוה הַגָּדוֹל וְהַנּוֹרָא:
וְהֵשִׁיב לֵב־אָבוֹת עַל־בָּנִים, וְלֵב בָּנִים עַל־אֲבוֹתָם:

לָעַד Always it lived on in our hearts,
this loyal faith
That we shall return to our Holy Land,
the city where David camped.

> Always it lived on in our hearts, this loyal faith
> That we shall return to our Holy Land,
> the city where David camped.

There we shall serve our God
in happiness, in joy and in delight;
There we shall go up at feasts of pilgrimage,
three times a year.

> Always it lived on in our hearts, this loyal faith
> That we shall return to our Holy Land,
> the city where David camped.

There we shall stand up to meet our destiny,
that which the father of many received.
There we shall live out our lives,
the lives of the nation that cannot be counted.

> Always it lived on in our hearts, this loyal faith
> That we shall return to our Holy Land,
> the city where David camped.

The Torah of life is our desire,
given at the mouth of the Most High.
That is our inheritance always –
a gift of the desert.

> Always it lived on in our hearts, this loyal faith
> That we shall return to our Holy Land,
> the city where David camped.

לָעַד חַיָּה בִּלְבָבֵנוּ
הָאֱמוּנָה הַנֶּאֱמָנָה
לָשׁוּב לְאֶרֶץ קָדְשֵׁנוּ
עִיר בָּהּ דָּוִד חָנָה.

לָעַד חַיָּה בִּלְבָבֵנוּ, הָאֱמוּנָה הַנֶּאֱמָנָה
לָשׁוּב לְאֶרֶץ קָדְשֵׁנוּ, עִיר בָּהּ דָּוִד חָנָה.

שָׁמָּה נַעֲבֹד אֱלֹהֵינוּ
בְּחֶדְוָה בְּגִילָה וּבִרְנָנָה
שָׁמָּה נַעֲלֶה לִרְגָלֵינוּ
שָׁלֹשׁ פְּעָמִים בַּשָּׁנָה.

לָעַד חַיָּה בִּלְבָבֵנוּ, הָאֱמוּנָה הַנֶּאֱמָנָה
לָשׁוּב לְאֶרֶץ קָדְשֵׁנוּ, עִיר בָּהּ דָּוִד חָנָה.

שָׁמָּה נַעֲמֹד לְגוֹרָלֵנוּ
אַב הֲמוֹן קָנָה
שָׁמָּה נִחְיֶה חַיֵּינוּ
חַיֵּי עֲדַת מִי מָנָה.

לָעַד חַיָּה בִּלְבָבֵנוּ, הָאֱמוּנָה הַנֶּאֱמָנָה
לָשׁוּב לְאֶרֶץ קָדְשֵׁנוּ, עִיר בָּהּ דָּוִד חָנָה.

תּוֹרַת חַיִּים חֶמְדָּתֵנוּ
מִפִּי עֶלְיוֹן נִתָּנָה
נֶצַח הִיא נַחֲלָתֵנוּ
מִמִּדְבָּר מַתָּנָה.

לָעַד חַיָּה בִּלְבָבֵנוּ, הָאֱמוּנָה הַנֶּאֱמָנָה
לָשׁוּב לְאֶרֶץ קָדְשֵׁנוּ, עִיר בָּהּ דָּוִד חָנָה.

# סעודה וברכותיה

# THE MEAL AND ITS BLESSINGS

What does it mean to bless God? What can flesh and blood, temporal man, referred to in our liturgy as a fading flower and a broken shard offer the everlasting King of Kings? The answer is that while the Divine Presence indeed resides with us on earth – "For I am the Lord who dwells with them in their impurity" (Lev. 16:17) – God is not clearly revealed to us. In fact, He is hidden from view: "Behold I come to you in a cloud" (Ex. 19:9). God has chosen not to reveal His hand in human events, but to remain the One who "dwells concealed… in the shadow" (Ps. 91:1). It is true that God is so close that man can almost touch Him, yet not everyone can penetrate the cloud that surrounds and conceals Him. This obscuring cloud takes on any number of guises. For the physicist, the cloud is a mathematical formula. For the physiologist, it is an instinct, for the psychologist, a drive, and for the general, the power of his army. The cloud is any manifestation of nature or man that promotes the illusion that the world operates autonomously, concealing the reality that God is responsible for all that occurs on earth. Sometimes God decides to disperse the obscuring clouds, and occasionally in history He has revealed Himself and proclaimed "I am the Lord your God." More often, however, God remains obscure, a God whose "abode is in transcendence."

The underlying meaning of all our blessings is the spreading of holiness by revealing God's presence in this world. When one recites a *berakha*, he in essence is saying, "Master of the Universe, You are hidden behind a cloud; no one sees You. Yet, as I drink this glass of water, I reveal Your presence. The very fact that I can eat, that my body absorbs food, that I can digest, indeed the entire biological process behind food consumption and the creation of food itself, is testimony to Your presence. Through this recognition I am removing the obscuring cloud: I am revealing You." For this reason, blessings are addressed to God in the second person: "Blessed are You," rather than "Blessed is He," to affirm God's very presence before us; as if to say, "Where are You, God? You are right here with me! How do I know? Because Your presence is evident in this water that I am about to drink!" The purpose of a *berakha* is to transform the Hidden into Presence, and through use of the second person singular we reveal the Divine Presence that is directly in front of us. (*Derashot HaRav*, pp. 8–11)

# Birkat HaMazon / Grace After Meals

*On days when Taḥanun is said, say the below.*

עַל־נַהֲרוֹת By the rivers of Babylon we sat and wept Ps. 137
as we remembered Zion.
There on the willow trees we hung up our harps,
for there our captors asked us for songs, our tormentors, for amusement,
said: "Sing us one of the songs of Zion!"
How can we sing the LORD's song on foreign soil?
If I forget you, Jerusalem, may my right hand forget its skill.
May my tongue cling to the roof of my mouth if I do not remember you,
if I do not set Jerusalem above my highest joy.
Remember, LORD, what the Edomites did on the day Jerusalem fell.
They said, "Tear it down, tear it down to its very foundations!"
Daughter of Babylon, doomed to destruction,
happy is he who repays you for what you have done to us,
who seizes your infants and dashes them against the rocks.

*On days when Taḥanun is omitted, say the below:*

שִׁיר הַמַּעֲלוֹת A song of ascents. Ps. 126
When the LORD brought back the exiles of Zion
we were like people who dream.

---

as the king of Babylon, and in another period he appears as a different king in another place and with a different language. There is an identity of events, and, of course, an identity of destiny spread over thousands of years. In fact, our enemy is still alive. He has still not reconciled himself to the fundamental reality of the existence of the Jewish people and the desire of our people to return to our land. (*The Lord is Righteous*, pp. 221–222)

SHIR HAMA'ALOT

בְּשׁוּב יהוה אֶת־שִׁיבַת צִיּוֹן *When the LORD brought back the exiles of Zion.* The Almighty has promised us that eventually He will end the exile and return us to Zion. Indeed the language of this Psalm echoes the wording of God's guarantee in Deuteronomy (30:3), "וְשָׁב יהוה אֱלֹהֶיךָ אֶת־שְׁבוּתְךָ וְרִחֲמֶךָ, And the LORD your God will return you from your captivity and have mercy upon you." However, how can we be certain that the redemption will in fact take

# ברכת המזון

*On days when תחנון is said, say the below.*

תהלים קלז
עַל־נַהֲרוֹת בָּבֶל, שָׁם יָשַׁבְנוּ גַּם־בָּכִינוּ, בְּזָכְרֵנוּ אֶת־צִיּוֹן:
עַל־עֲרָבִים בְּתוֹכָהּ תָּלִינוּ כִּנֹּרוֹתֵינוּ:
כִּי שָׁם שְׁאֵלוּנוּ שׁוֹבֵינוּ דִּבְרֵי־שִׁיר וְתוֹלָלֵינוּ שִׂמְחָה
שִׁירוּ לָנוּ מִשִּׁיר צִיּוֹן:
אֵיךְ נָשִׁיר אֶת־שִׁיר־יהוה עַל אַדְמַת נֵכָר:
אִם־אֶשְׁכָּחֵךְ יְרוּשָׁלָםִ, תִּשְׁכַּח יְמִינִי:
תִּדְבַּק לְשׁוֹנִי לְחִכִּי אִם־לֹא אֶזְכְּרֵכִי
אִם־לֹא אַעֲלֶה אֶת־יְרוּשָׁלַםִ עַל רֹאשׁ שִׂמְחָתִי:
זְכֹר יהוה לִבְנֵי אֱדוֹם אֵת יוֹם יְרוּשָׁלָםִ
הָאֹמְרִים עָרוּ עָרוּ עַד הַיְסוֹד בָּהּ:
בַּת־בָּבֶל הַשְּׁדוּדָה, אַשְׁרֵי שֶׁיְשַׁלֶּם־לָךְ אֶת־גְּמוּלֵךְ שֶׁגָּמַלְתְּ לָנוּ:
אַשְׁרֵי שֶׁיֹּאחֵז, וְנִפֵּץ אֶת־עֹלָלַיִךְ אֶל־הַסָּלַע:

*On days when תחנון is omitted, say the below:*

תהלים קכו
שִׁיר הַמַּעֲלוֹת, בְּשׁוּב יהוה אֶת־שִׁיבַת צִיּוֹן
הָיִינוּ כְּחֹלְמִים:

---

AL NAHAROT BAVEL

זְכֹר יהוה לִבְנֵי אֱדוֹם *Remember, Lord, what the Edomites did.* This Psalm begins by describing the weeping of the Jews after the destruction of the First Temple at the hands of the Babylonians, but then shifts to the Edomites, referring to Rome and the destruction of the Second Temple. Similarly, in Lamentations, Jeremiah, who prophesied in the aftermath of the first destruction, already vows that God will avenge the "daughter of Edom" (Lam. 4:21–22) for destroying the Second Temple. This association teaches that the two destructions are closely related, and are really one. Ultimately, there is no difference between the exiles of Babylonia, Rome, Germany and Spain. They are all essentially one *galut*, one experience of exile. The enemy is the same, all that changes is its name. In one time the enemy is disguised

Then were our mouths filled with laughter,
and our tongues with songs of joy.
Then was it said among the nations,
"The LORD has done great things for them."
The LORD did do great things for us and we rejoiced.
Bring back our exiles, LORD, like streams in a dry land.
May those who sowed in tears, reap in joy.
May one who goes out weeping, carrying a bag of seed,
come back with songs of joy, carrying his sheaves.

*Some say:*

תְּהִלַּת My mouth shall speak the praise of God, *Ps. 145*
and all creatures shall bless His holy name for ever and all time.
We will bless God now and for ever. *Ps. 115*
Halleluya! Thank the LORD for He is good; *Ps. 136*
His loving-kindness is for ever.
Who can tell of the LORD's mighty acts and make all His praise be heard? *Ps. 106*

---

in the messianic future when all the nations will declare that "The LORD has done great things for them," only then, in the end of days, will we be permitted to indulge in complete celebration. On the one hand, this teaching is a *halakha* which requires us to restrain our celebrations even at times of joy. Undisciplined frivolity is forbidden. At the same time, Rabbi Yoḥanan's teaching is an insight into the nature of human life. True happiness flows from the attainment of our hopes and the fruition of our dreams. However, the Rabbis teach that "no person dies with even half of his desires fulfilled." Moreover, even when we do achieve a goal or find a dream of ours within reach, we never fully attain what we imagined for ourselves. In this world, the dream will always be more beautiful than the reality, and, thus, it is simply impossible for the reflective person to completely fill his mouth with laughter. However, when the Messiah returns us to Zion, the Psalm promises that "we will be like dreamers." In other words, it will be just as we envisioned it in our dreams, with every hope and prayer fulfilled entirely. We will recover the original vision of the Land of Israel with all of its bounty and holiness. At that time our entire being will be filled with joy and our mouths will be completely filled with laughter, for reality and dream will have become one. (*Nefesh HaRav*, p. 93)

אָז יִמָּלֵא שְׂחוֹק פִּינוּ וּלְשׁוֹנֵנוּ רִנָּה
אָז יֹאמְרוּ בַגּוֹיִם הִגְדִּיל יהוה לַעֲשׂוֹת עִם־אֵלֶּה:
הִגְדִּיל יהוה לַעֲשׂוֹת עִמָּנוּ, הָיִינוּ שְׂמֵחִים:
שׁוּבָה יהוה אֶת־שְׁבִיתֵנוּ, כַּאֲפִיקִים בַּנֶּגֶב:
הַזֹּרְעִים בְּדִמְעָה בְּרִנָּה יִקְצֹרוּ:
הָלוֹךְ יֵלֵךְ וּבָכֹה נֹשֵׂא מֶשֶׁךְ־הַזָּרַע
בֹּא־יָבֹא בְרִנָּה נֹשֵׂא אֲלֻמֹּתָיו:

*Some say:*

תְּהִלַּת יהוה יְדַבֶּר פִּי, וִיבָרֵךְ כָּל־בָּשָׂר שֵׁם קָדְשׁוֹ לְעוֹלָם וָעֶד: תהלים קמה
וַאֲנַחְנוּ נְבָרֵךְ יָהּ מֵעַתָּה וְעַד־עוֹלָם, הַלְלוּיָהּ: תהלים קטו
הוֹדוּ לַיהוה כִּי־טוֹב, כִּי לְעוֹלָם חַסְדּוֹ: תהלים קלו
מִי יְמַלֵּל גְּבוּרוֹת יהוה, יַשְׁמִיעַ כָּל־תְּהִלָּתוֹ: תהלים קו

---

place? To understand God's promise of redemption, we must first understand the nature of exile. The Talmud Yerushalmi (*Sukka* 4:3; see *Korban HaEida* ad loc.) re-reads the opening verse of the Decalogue not as "I am the Lord, your God, who took you out of the Land of Egypt," but rather as "I am the Lord, your God, who went out with you from the Land of Egypt." God, so to speak, was also in bondage in Egypt, in exile and captivity with His children. Similarly, the verse in Deuteronomy can be translated as "And the Lord your God will return with you from captivity." When the Jewish nation went into exile, the divine presence attached itself to the people and went into exile with them. He too exposes Himself to the exile and suffers as a hostage in an alien land. This is the greatest guarantee that the day of redemption will arrive. The divine presence cannot remain a prisoner, suffering forever. God accompanies us into the exile to assure that we will return. God must liberate Himself, and He has promised that when He returns to Zion, He will take His captive children with him. (*The Lord is Righteous*, pp. 177–179)

**אָז יִמָּלֵא שְׂחוֹק פִּינוּ** *Then were our mouths filled with laughter.* Understanding this verse as a reference to the Messianic Age, Rabbi Yoḥanan taught (*Berakhot* 31a) that "it is forbidden to fill our mouths with laughter in this world." Only

# Zimmun / Invitation

*For the zimmun said at a wedding or during the week of Sheva Berakhot,* *see page 164. At a Brit, see page 182.*

*When three or more men say Birkat HaMazon together, the following zimmun is said. When three or more women say Birkat HaMazon, substitute "Friends" for "Gentlemen." The leader should ask permission from those with precedence to lead the Birkat HaMazon.*

*Leader* Gentlemen, let us say grace.

*Others* May the name of the LORD be blessed from now and for ever. *Ps. 113*

*Leader* May the name of the LORD be blessed from now and for ever.
With your permission, (my father and teacher / my mother and teacher / the Kohanim present / our teacher the Rabbi / the master of this house / the mistress of this house)
my masters and teachers,
let us bless (*in a minyan:* our God,) the One
from whose food we have eaten.

*Others* Blessed be (*in a minyan:* our God,) the One
from whose food we have eaten, and by whose goodness we live.

**People present who have not taken part in the meal say:*
*Blessed be (*in a minyan:* our God,) the One
whose name is continually blessed for ever and all time.

*Leader* Blessed be (*in a minyan:* our God,) the One
from whose food we have eaten, and by whose goodness we live.
Blessed be He, and blessed be His name.

---

craftsman has no rights in the finished object and must only be paid wages for his labor and work. Maimonides (*Hilkhot Sekhirut* 10:4) and the majority of medieval authorities rule that the craftsman has no ownership rights in the object, while Rosh (*Bava Kama* 9:14) argues that he does. However, this dispute has no relevance to God's ownership of the universe. The craftsman doesn't acquire rights in the newly formed object because the raw material already belonged to a different individual; however, when the raw material was ownerless there is no competing claim to the craftsman's acquisition of the object. Therefore, we find that the Talmud Yerushalmi (*Ma'aserot* 1:5) rules that "One who sows a field that is *hefker* [ownerless] is obligated to tithe [the produce]." In a field with an owner, the owner of the field owns the produce. But in an ownerless field, the person who planted the seed and created the produce acquires it along with all obligations associated with such ownership. Regarding

# סדר הזימון

*For the* זימון *said at a wedding or during the week of* שבע ברכות*, see page 165.*
*At a* ברית*, see page 183.*

*When three or more men say* ברכת המזון *together, the following* זימון *is said.*
*When three or more women say* ברכת המזון*, substitute* חֲבֵרוֹתַי *for* רַבּוֹתַי*.*
*The leader should ask permission from those with precedence to lead the* ברכת המזון*.*

*Leader* רַבּוֹתַי, נְבָרֵךְ.

*Others* יְהִי שֵׁם יהוה מְבֹרָךְ מֵעַתָּה וְעַד־עוֹלָם: תהלים קיג

*Leader* יְהִי שֵׁם יהוה מְבֹרָךְ מֵעַתָּה וְעַד־עוֹלָם:
בִּרְשׁוּת (אָבִי מוֹרִי / אִמִּי מוֹרָתִי / כֹּהֲנִים / מוֹרֵנוּ הָרַב / בַּעַל הַבַּיִת הַזֶּה / בַּעֲלַת הַבַּיִת הַזֶּה)
מָרָנָן וְרַבָּנָן וְרַבּוֹתַי
נְבָרֵךְ (במנין: אֱלֹהֵינוּ) שֶׁאָכַלְנוּ מִשֶּׁלּוֹ.

*Others* בָּרוּךְ (במנין: אֱלֹהֵינוּ) שֶׁאָכַלְנוּ מִשֶּׁלּוֹ וּבְטוּבוֹ חָיִינוּ.

**People present who have not taken part in the meal say:*
*בָּרוּךְ (במנין: אֱלֹהֵינוּ) וּמְבֹרָךְ שְׁמוֹ תָּמִיד לְעוֹלָם וָעֶד.

*Leader* בָּרוּךְ (במנין: אֱלֹהֵינוּ) שֶׁאָכַלְנוּ מִשֶּׁלּוֹ וּבְטוּבוֹ חָיִינוּ.
בָּרוּךְ הוּא וּבָרוּךְ שְׁמוֹ.

---

ZIMMUN

שֶׁאָכַלְנוּ מִשֶּׁלּוֹ *From whose food we have eaten.* The verse in Psalms declares (24:1–2), "The earth and its fullness belong to the Lord, for He has founded it upon the seas, and established it upon the rivers." This means to say that God is the true owner and master of the world because He created it, formed and fashioned it. Everything that exists, from the tiniest of insects to the starry expanses of outer space, was created by the hand of God, and thus belongs to Him. This is not merely a philosophical concept; the derivation of ownership from creation is a halakhic principle as well. We find a dispute in the Talmud (*Bava Kama* 98b) regarding how to conceptualize the rights of a craftsman who was given raw material by a second party. One opinion maintains that "a craftsman acquires the object by improving it," meaning, he acquires the value added to the raw material through his work. Another opinion maintains that the

BLESSING OF NOURISHMENT

בָּרוּךְ Blessed are You, LORD our God, King of the Universe,
who in His goodness feeds the whole world
with grace, kindness and compassion.
He gives food to all living things,
for His kindness is for ever.

---

ברכת הזן – BLESSING OF NOURISHMENT

Human economic behavior fluctuates between two poles: economic activism (which the Bible sanctions) and trust in God. The latter is an important motif which should guide the *homo economicus* in his actions. Judaism has never forbidden man to strive for economic security or shelter from the vicissitudes of a not-always-friendly world. God, in His infinite mercy, allows man to work for his sustenance and to devise means of increasing the yield of his labors. He also permits him to strive for material comfort and riches. Yet man must never entertain the illusion that the bread he eats is his. This would result in the profanation of the bread and in man's self-absolutization and self-deification. Man must know that he is not a creator in either the metaphysical or the economic sense. His world of material wealth was given to him gratuitously by the Creator of the universe.

Theologians speak with indignation of Marxist arrogance and Communist pride. If abhorrent impudence based on philosophical and metaphysical ignorance has ever come to expression in the annals of human history, it is in the Marxist pronouncements and manifestoes. Our philosophy of the *homo economicus* is opposed to so erroneous and obnoxious a glorification of the universal economic determinant.

The first sacrificial act by which food becomes the bread of the LORD is the acknowledgment that God is the Master who feeds His world and to Whom we are indebted for His loving-kindness. This idea comes to full expression in both the blessing prior to the meal and particularly in the Grace recited after the meal: "Who in His goodness feeds the whole world with grace, kindness and compassion. He gives food to all living things, for His kindness is forever." (*Festival of Freedom*, pp. 7–11)

הַזָּן אֶת הָעוֹלָם כֻּלּוֹ בְּטוּבוֹ *Who in His goodness feeds the whole world.* In the first blessing of *Birkat HaMazon* we do not recognize God as the One who provides for us, our family, or our community. We do not single out the Jewish people, the Land of Israel, or even mankind in general. Rather, we

ברכת הזן

בָּרוּךְ אַתָּה יהוה אֱלֹהֵינוּ מֶלֶךְ הָעוֹלָם
הַזָּן אֶת הָעוֹלָם כֻּלּוֹ בְּטוּבוֹ
בְּחֵן בְּחֶסֶד וּבְרַחֲמִים
הוּא נוֹתֵן לֶחֶם לְכָל בָּשָׂר כִּי לְעוֹלָם חַסְדּוֹ.

---

the creation of the universe, all the more so, there exists no competing claim to God's ownership. The Almighty both created the raw material *ex nihilo* and formed it into the world which we inhabit. In this case, all would agree that "the craftsman acquires the object by improving it." (*Yemei Zikaron*, pp. 40–41)

בָּרוּךְ שֶׁאָכַלְנוּ מִשֶּׁלּוֹ וּבְטוּבוֹ חָיִינוּ *Blessed be the One from whose food we have eaten, and by whose goodness we live (previous page).* Although there is no obligation to recite the *zimmun* unless three people eat together, the Talmud (*Berakhot* 45a) records a dispute as to whether or not two people who share a meal may recite the *zimmun* if they wish. The Babylonian Talmud does not present the reasoning of each opinion; however, the Jerusalem Talmud (*Berakhot* 7:1) relates this disagreement to the question of whether or not two judges, instead of the standard court of three, can adjudicate a case. Those who maintain that two judges can act as a court also hold that two individuals may make a *zimmun,* while those who believe that a court is not valid with less than three judges also maintain that a *zimmun* requires a minimum of three participants. However, the connection between these two debates, the number of judges needed for a court and the number of participants necessary for a *zimmun,* is quite perplexing. What do the laws of court proceedings have in common with the laws of *zimmun*? This analogy suggests that *zimmun* is not merely a call and response between a leader and chorus, but rather is somewhat akin to a judicial verdict. *Zimmun* represents the resolution of a group that it is proper to bless God. Thus the Jerusalem Talmud assumes that the number of judges necessary to create a balanced consideration (*shikkul hada'at*) and issue a binding ruling also suffices to create the declaration of the *zimmun.* When a group recites the *Birkat HaMazon* together, the leader's call, "Blessed be the One from whose food we have eaten," in essence means, "Let us now be in accord that it was God who provided our food." The others in turn respond: "We agree with this ruling. Blessed is the One from whose food we have eaten." (*Shiur on Birkat HaMazon*, 1961)

Because of His continual great goodness,
we have never lacked food,
nor may we ever lack it, for the sake of His great name.
For He is God who feeds and sustains all,
does good to all,
and prepares food for all creatures He has created.
Blessed are You, LORD, who feeds all.

BLESSING FOR THE LAND

**נוֹדֶה** We thank You, LORD our God,
for having granted as a heritage to our ancestors
a desirable, good and spacious land;
for bringing us out, LORD our God, from the land of Egypt,
freeing us from the house of slavery;

---

child to school. In *Birkat HaMazon* we recognize God not just for the food that we eat, but for all of the ways in which He sustains us. (*Shiur on Birkat HaMazon,* 1969)

**ברכת הארץ** – BLESSING FOR THE LAND

**עַל שֶׁהִנְחַלְתָּ לַאֲבוֹתֵינוּ** *For having granted as a heritage to our ancestors.* It is interesting to note that this is the only place in the regular liturgy where a Jew thanks God for giving us *Eretz Yisrael.* We recite *Birkat HaTorah* every morning for the gift of God's Law, but there is no blessing for His Land. In the Amida, the core text of our prayers, we do not mention it. It is only here in *Birkat HaMazon* that we express our gratitude to God for bequeathing to our ancestors the Land of Israel. (*Shiur on Birkat HaMazon,* 1969)

**אֶרֶץ חֶמְדָּה** *A desirable land.* The Torah (Gen. 3:6) uses the word *neḥmad* (from the same root as *ḥemda*) to describe the allure of the Tree of Knowledge in the Garden of Eden. The word *neḥmad* does not simply mean beautiful or desirable as most render it; Onkelos translates it into Aramaic as *rogeg* which means fascinating, attracting, pulling. There is one type of beauty that is esthetically pleasing, but it does not necessarily attract a person. However, there is another kind of beauty that pulls a person to it like a magnet. The

וּבְטוּבוֹ הַגָּדוֹל, תָּמִיד לֹא חָסַר לָנוּ
וְאַל יֶחְסַר לָנוּ מָזוֹן לְעוֹלָם וָעֶד
בַּעֲבוּר שְׁמוֹ הַגָּדוֹל.
כִּי הוּא אֵל זָן וּמְפַרְנֵס לַכֹּל
וּמֵטִיב לַכֹּל
וּמֵכִין מָזוֹן לְכָל בְּרִיּוֹתָיו אֲשֶׁר בָּרָא.
בָּרוּךְ אַתָּה יהוה, הַזָּן אֶת הַכֹּל.

ברכת הארץ

נוֹדֶה לְךָ, יהוה אֱלֹהֵינוּ
עַל שֶׁהִנְחַלְתָּ לַאֲבוֹתֵינוּ אֶרֶץ חֶמְדָּה טוֹבָה וּרְחָבָה
וְעַל שֶׁהוֹצֵאתָנוּ יהוה אֱלֹהֵינוּ מֵאֶרֶץ מִצְרַיִם
וּפְדִיתָנוּ מִבֵּית עֲבָדִים

---

bless God who "gives food to all living things," human and animal alike. We proclaim that He is the One who "feeds and sustains all … and prepares food for all creatures He has created." For this reason, the blessing contains no elements of thanksgiving or gratitude. Genuine gratitude must be personal; it requires the person to offer thanks on his own behalf. However, the first idea of *Birkat HaMazon* is a universal one in which we recognize that God provides food for every living creature. He is the Master and Sustainer of the entire biological realm. He feeds man, fowl, the beasts of the field, every reptile and every insect without distinction. (*Shiur on Birkat HaMazon,* 1969)

**כִּי הוּא אֵל זָן וּמְפַרְנֵס לַכֹּל** *For He is God who feeds and sustains all.* We refer to God as both *zan* and *mefarnes–zan* means that He provides the actual food that we eat, while *mefarnes* refers to the larger recognition that He sustains us in every way. Not only does God give us our food, but He is also the source of the strength and vitality that our bodies need to take in the food, and to digest and assimilate it. In the colloquial Yiddish, *parnassah* is not food alone but it includes clothing, a roof over your head, even sending a

for Your covenant which You sealed in our flesh;
for Your Torah which You taught us;
for Your laws which You made known to us;
for the life, grace and kindness You have bestowed on us;
and for the food by which You continually feed and sustain us,
every day, every season, every hour.

---

*On Ḥanukka:*

עַל הַנִּסִּים [We thank You also] for the miracles, the redemption, the mighty deeds, the salvations, and the victories in battle which You performed for our ancestors in those days, at this time.

בִּימֵי מַתִּתְיָהוּ In the days of Mattityahu, son of Yoḥanan, the High Priest, the Hasmonean, and his sons, the wicked Greek kingdom rose up against Your people Israel to make them forget Your Torah and to force them to transgress the statutes of Your will. It was then that You in Your great compassion stood by them in the time of their distress. You championed their cause, judged their claim, and avenged their wrong.

---

remember that he is a Jew. Here in the second blessing we offer personal thanksgiving not to God the Creator, but to *our* God who redeemed *our* forefathers from Egypt and brought them to the Land of Israel. Moreover, we thank God not only for granting us His chosen land, but for selecting us as His chosen people, "for Your covenant which You sealed in our flesh; for Your Torah which You taught us." It is not a secular ideology of a people's homeland. The Land of Israel is significant only because it is associated with the uniqueness of the Jewish people, intertwined with the covenant and the Torah. We hear in this blessing an echo of the phrase from the Yom Tov prayers, "אַתָּה בְחַרְתָּנוּ מִכָּל הָעַמִּים, You have chosen us from among all peoples." This is why we refer to God as *Elokeinu, our* God, because He has set us apart as a unique, singular community and charged us with a special mission. However, this should not be confused with an attitude of racial superiority. We do not enjoy any extra rights or privileges. On the contrary, we have more obligations and duties than anyone else. We have a greater task, and thus we are required to sacrifice more than others. Indeed, we have paid a high price for this assignment. (*Shiur on Birkat HaMazon*, 1969)

וְעַל בְּרִיתְךָ שֶׁחָתַמְתָּ בִּבְשָׂרֵנוּ
וְעַל תּוֹרָתְךָ שֶׁלִּמַּדְתָּנוּ
וְעַל חֻקֶּיךָ שֶׁהוֹדַעְתָּנוּ
וְעַל חַיִּים חֵן וָחֶסֶד שֶׁחוֹנַנְתָּנוּ
וְעַל אֲכִילַת מָזוֹן שָׁאַתָּה זָן וּמְפַרְנֵס אוֹתָנוּ תָּמִיד
בְּכָל יוֹם וּבְכָל עֵת וּבְכָל שָׁעָה.

---

בחנוכה:

עַל הַנִּסִּים וְעַל הַפֻּרְקָן וְעַל הַגְּבוּרוֹת וְעַל הַתְּשׁוּעוֹת וְעַל הַמִּלְחָמוֹת שֶׁעָשִׂיתָ לַאֲבוֹתֵינוּ בַּיָּמִים הָהֵם בַּזְּמַן הַזֶּה.

בִּימֵי מַתִּתְיָהוּ בֶּן יוֹחָנָן כֹּהֵן גָּדוֹל חַשְׁמוֹנַאי וּבָנָיו, כְּשֶׁעָמְדָה מַלְכוּת יָוָן הָרְשָׁעָה עַל עַמְּךָ יִשְׂרָאֵל לְהַשְׁכִּיחָם תּוֹרָתֶךָ וּלְהַעֲבִירָם מֵחֻקֵּי רְצוֹנֶךָ, וְאַתָּה בְּרַחֲמֶיךָ הָרַבִּים עָמַדְתָּ לָהֶם בְּעֵת צָרָתָם, רַבְתָּ אֶת רִיבָם, דַּנְתָּ

---

person somehow becomes intoxicated in the face of such beauty and cannot resist it. When Eve saw the tree she fell under its spell and, like a sleepwalker, almost involuntarily reached out for its fruit. She couldn't control herself. This is *ḥemda*. When we refer to *Eretz Yisrael* as the *eretz ḥemda* we mean that the land attracts the Jewish people. It enchants us and will never let us go. Indeed, at no point in our long, painful diaspora did we ever give up on *Eretz Yisrael*. No matter how distant we are we cannot escape the pull of *Eretz Yisrael*. This is why we call it the *eretz ḥemda*. (*Shiur on Birkat HaMazon*, 1969)

וְעַל בְּרִיתְךָ שֶׁחָתַמְתָּ בִּבְשָׂרֵנוּ, וְעַל תּוֹרָתְךָ שֶׁלִּמַּדְתָּנוּ, וְעַל חֻקֶּיךָ שֶׁהוֹדַעְתָּנוּ *For Your covenant which You sealed in our flesh; for Your Torah which You taught us; for Your laws which You made known to us.* In the first blessing of *Birkat HaMazon* we see God from a universalistic perspective, proclaiming the majesty of the Creator who sustains all life. However, the universal element that we share with all mankind, while important, is not enough. If there is no private aspect, then all universal philosophy is meaningless; a Jew must also always

You delivered the strong into the hands of the weak, the many into the hands of the few, the impure into the hands of the pure, the wicked into the hands of the righteous, and the arrogant into the hands of those who were engaged in the study of Your Torah. You made for Yourself great and holy renown in Your world, and for Your people Israel You performed a great salvation and redemption as of this very day. Your children then entered the holiest part of Your House, cleansed Your Temple, purified Your Sanctuary, kindled lights in Your holy courts, and designated these eight days of Ḥanukka for giving thanks and praise to Your great name.

*Continue with "For all this" on the next page.*

---

them the strength to fight and helped them defeat the enemy and emerge triumphant from the engagement, yet there is human participation in the *Al HaNissim* of Ḥanukka. The role of the Hasmoneans has been emphasized, while there is not a single word about the role which Esther and Mordecai played.

We learn from this that when the fight is spiritual, God invites the Jew to participate. Even though man is under the guidance of the Almighty, when spiritual survival is at stake, man must take the initiative, and therefore his role is recorded. However, when it is only a question of physical struggle, God acts differently. When there is a physical menace or the threat of physical destruction, God uses the human hand as a mere instrument of His will. He recruits man. He uses human energy, human resources, to implement the plan which He has devised. But Judaism has said that in this case, the man who is the messenger of God should not be credited with the salvation. Spiritual achievements are attributed to man; military achievements are attributed to God. No matter how much the human being accomplishes as far as political and material achievements are concerned he cannot attribute them to himself. He must not claim credit, because the worst sin is to say: "My power and the might of my hand has gotten me this wealth" (Deut. 8:17). Therefore, on Purim, when we celebrate a physical victory, the liturgy makes no mention of Mordecai and Esther's deeds because, if the achievements are in the realm of military conquest and of a material nature, victory should be attributed to the Almighty. On Ḥanukka, though, the story was different. Antiochus was interested in destroying the Jews spiritually, and when the menace is of a spiritual nature, the initiative belongs to man. For this reason, we remember the Hasmoneans' efforts when we commemorate their victory on Ḥanukka. (*Days of Deliverance*, pp. 121–124)

אֶת דִּינָם, נָקַמְתָּ אֶת נִקְמָתָם, מָסַרְתָּ גִבּוֹרִים בְּיַד חַלָּשִׁים, וְרַבִּים בְּיַד מְעַטִּים, וּטְמֵאִים בְּיַד טְהוֹרִים, וּרְשָׁעִים בְּיַד צַדִּיקִים, וְזֵדִים בְּיַד עוֹסְקֵי תוֹרָתֶךָ, וּלְךָ עָשִׂיתָ שֵׁם גָּדוֹל וְקָדוֹשׁ בְּעוֹלָמֶךָ, וּלְעַמְּךָ יִשְׂרָאֵל עָשִׂיתָ תְּשׁוּעָה גְדוֹלָה וּפֻרְקָן כְּהַיּוֹם הַזֶּה. וְאַחַר כֵּן בָּאוּ בָנֶיךָ לִדְבִיר בֵּיתֶךָ, וּפִנּוּ אֶת הֵיכָלֶךָ, וְטִהֲרוּ אֶת מִקְדָּשֶׁךָ, וְהִדְלִיקוּ נֵרוֹת בְּחַצְרוֹת קָדְשֶׁךָ, וְקָבְעוּ שְׁמוֹנַת יְמֵי חֲנֻכָּה אֵלּוּ, לְהוֹדוֹת וּלְהַלֵּל לְשִׁמְךָ הַגָּדוֹל.

*Continue with* וְעַל הַכֹּל *on the next page.*

---

על הנסים – FOR THE MIRACLES

מָסַרְתָּ גִבּוֹרִים *You delivered the strong.* In *Al HaNissim* we thank God for the military victory, for delivering the mighty, wicked Greeks into the hands of the small band of righteous Hasmoneans; however, we do not even mention the miracle of the oil burning for eight days when it should have run out after only one. *Al HaNissim* forms part of the *hoda'ah,* thanksgiving, section of the Amida and of *Birkat HaMazon.* In these sections we thank God for the material blessings of our lives and for His protection of our physical existence throughout our history. We do not, though, include thanksgiving for purely spiritual miracles. Thus, in *Al HaNissim* we thank God for vanquishing the Greek enemy and protecting our physical existence, but we do not include praise for the miracle of the light, which was a miracle for the glory of the Temple. (*Harerei Kedem,* vol. 1, p. 351)

וְאַחַר כֵּן בָּאוּ בָנֶיךָ לִדְבִיר בֵּיתֶךָ *Your children then entered the holiest part of Your House.* If you compare the *Al HaNissim* that we recite on Purim with the *Al HaNissim* that we recite on Ḥanukka, you will find an important distinction. In the *Al HaNissim* of Purim, there is nothing mentioned of Mordecai and Esther's role in the unfolding of the dramatic events about which the Megilla tells us. We know from the Megilla that Mordecai took the initiative and Esther was ready to sacrifice herself. But in the *Al HaNissim,* the names of Mordecai and Esther are mentioned only as an indication of the period during which the events transpired. Though the Megilla depicts the human role and human action, these are completely ignored in the *Al HaNissim* of Purim. However, the *Al HaNissim* of Ḥanukka does not shy away from mentioning human action: "Your children then entered the holiest part of Your House, cleansed Your Temple, purified Your Sanctuary, kindled lights in Your holy courts…" Of course, God made it possible; He gave

*On Purim:*

עַל הַנִּסִּים [We thank You also] for the miracles, the redemption, the mighty deeds, the salvations, and the victories in battle which You performed for our ancestors in those days, at this time.

בִּימֵי מָרְדְּכַי In the days of Mordekhai and Esther, in Shushan the capital, the wicked Haman rose up against them and sought to destroy, slay and exterminate all the Jews, young and old, children and women, on one day, the thirteenth day of the twelfth month, which is the month of Adar, and to plunder their possessions. Then You in Your great compassion thwarted his counsel, frustrated his plans, and caused his scheme to recoil on his own head, so that they hanged him and his sons on the gallows. *Esther 3*

*Continue with "For all this."*

---

וְעַל הַכֹּל For all this, LORD our God, we thank and bless You.
May Your name be blessed continually
by the mouth of all that lives, for ever and all time –
for so it is written: "You will eat and be satisfied, then you shall bless the LORD your God for the good land He has given you." *Deut. 8*
Blessed are You, LORD, for the land and for the food.

---

וְעַל הַכֹּל *For all this.* Every demonstration of God's loving-kindness that we experience obligates a response of gratitude and appreciation. However, the thanksgiving that we offer should not be limited to the specific act of divine kindness that triggered our outpouring. Instead, each expression of God's kindness should remind us of all of the ways that He lovingly watches over us, and our feelings of gratitude should overflow to include every way in which He provides for us. When a person survives a dangerous situation he recites *Birkat HaGomel* and declares "Blessed are You … who bestows good on the unworthy, who has bestowed on me much good." While the focus of the praise remains on the act of divine kindness that the person is celebrating, he also includes an acknowledgement for other acts of divine compassion. This is why, after we thank God for the food we just enjoyed, for the Exodus and for the land that He gave to our forefathers, we add "and for everything," for our health, our families, our happiness. We likewise proclaim our gratitude for everything that we enjoy in this world. (*Harerei Kedem*, vol. 1, p. 352)

וְאָכַלְתָּ וְשָׂבָעְתָּ *You will eat and be satisfied.* The Talmud (*Berakhot* 34b) writes that although we bow in the thanksgiving (*hoda'ah*) section of the Amida, to

בפורים:

עַל הַנִּסִּים וְעַל הַפֻּרְקָן וְעַל הַגְּבוּרוֹת וְעַל הַתְּשׁוּעוֹת וְעַל הַמִּלְחָמוֹת
שֶׁעָשִׂיתָ לַאֲבוֹתֵינוּ בַּיָּמִים הָהֵם בַּזְּמַן הַזֶּה.

בִּימֵי מָרְדְּכַי וְאֶסְתֵּר בְּשׁוּשַׁן הַבִּירָה, כְּשֶׁעָמַד עֲלֵיהֶם הָמָן הָרָשָׁע,
אסתר ג בִּקֵּשׁ לְהַשְׁמִיד לַהֲרֹג וּלְאַבֵּד אֶת־כָּל־הַיְּהוּדִים מִנַּעַר וְעַד־זָקֵן טַף
וְנָשִׁים בְּיוֹם אֶחָד, בִּשְׁלוֹשָׁה עָשָׂר לְחֹדֶשׁ שְׁנֵים־עָשָׂר, הוּא־חֹדֶשׁ אֲדָר,
וּשְׁלָלָם לָבוֹז: וְאַתָּה בְּרַחֲמֶיךָ הָרַבִּים הֵפַרְתָּ אֶת עֲצָתוֹ, וְקִלְקַלְתָּ אֶת
מַחֲשַׁבְתּוֹ, וַהֲשֵׁבוֹתָ לּוֹ גְּמוּלוֹ בְּרֹאשׁוֹ, וְתָלוּ אוֹתוֹ וְאֶת בָּנָיו עַל הָעֵץ.

*Continue with* וְעַל הַכֹּל.

---

וְעַל הַכֹּל, יהוה אֱלֹהֵינוּ, אֲנַחְנוּ מוֹדִים לָךְ וּמְבָרְכִים אוֹתָךְ
יִתְבָּרַךְ שִׁמְךָ בְּפִי כָּל חַי תָּמִיד לְעוֹלָם וָעֶד
דברים ח כַּכָּתוּב: וְאָכַלְתָּ וְשָׂבָעְתָּ, וּבֵרַכְתָּ אֶת־יהוה אֱלֹהֶיךָ
עַל־הָאָרֶץ הַטֹּבָה אֲשֶׁר נָתַן־לָךְ:
בָּרוּךְ אַתָּה יהוה, עַל הָאָרֶץ וְעַל הַמָּזוֹן.

---

בִּקֵּשׁ לְהַשְׁמִיד לַהֲרֹג וּלְאַבֵּד אֶת־כָּל־הַיְּהוּדִים *Sought to destroy, slay and exterminate all the Jews.* Eighteen thousand and five hundred Jews, according to our tradition, were invited to the reception given by Ahasuerus for the population of Shushan (*Esther Rabba* 7:13). Apparently, 18,500 Jews were prominent enough and integrated into the general society to such an extent that Ahasuerus deemed it necessary to invite them to attend the festivities. Nevertheless, when Haman's edict "to destroy, kill and annihilate every Jew, both young and old, children and women" (Esther 3:13) was published, the 18,500 prominent Jews were not excluded; there was no exemption. The hostility toward the Jew by Amalek, by man-Satan, is not directed exclusively against the religious Jew, who is conspicuous in his exoticism, who is different and unique. The hatred embraces religious as well as agnostic Jews, the nationalist as well as the assimilationist Jew, the Jewish home adorned with a *mezuza* and the home stripped of everything Jewish. The hatred of Amalek is commodious enough to encompass and embrace every Jew and every Jewish home. At this point, the Jews realized and understood the idea of common destiny. Haman united them. All Jews are alike, all Jews are equal, and all share in the same predicament. The Megilla is the book that proclaimed the oneness of the Jewish people and their common fate and destiny. (*Days of Deliverance*, pp. 17–19)

BLESSING FOR JERUSALEM

רַחֵם נָא Have compassion, please, Lord our God,
on Israel Your people,
on Jerusalem Your city,
on Zion the dwelling place of Your glory,
on the royal house of David Your anointed,
and on the great and holy House that bears Your name.
Our God, our Father,
tend us, feed us, sustain us and support us,
relieve us and send us relief, Lord our God,
swiftly from all our troubles.
Please, Lord our God, do not make us dependent
on the gifts or loans of other people,
but only on Your full, open, holy and generous hand
so that we may suffer neither shame nor humiliation
for ever and all time.

---

the attitude of prayer, but is incongruous with *Birkat HaMazon*. Similarly, we find that one who is drunk may not pray (*Berakhot* 31a), but the Talmud Yerushalmi (*Terumot* 1:4) states that one who is drunk may still recite *Birkat HaMazon*. This reflects the same distinction. One who is drunk reflects an attitude of satiety and abundance, having enjoyed the earth's produce. This disposition conflicts with the prayer experience of feeling totally dependent upon God, but it is compatible with *Birkat HaMazon* which is meant to follow the experience of enjoying the material blessings of God and feeling totally content and satisfied by them. (*Reshimot Shiurim, Berakhot*, pp. 396–397)

ברכת ירושלים – BLESSING FOR JERUSALEM

רַחֵם *Have compassion.* When man is economically secure and there is no poverty in the land, it is easy to eat and offer gratitude to God. When a person dwells in a "good land, a land of… olive oil and honey, a land where you will eat without scarceness" (Deut. 8:7–9), as God promised the Jewish people, it is natural to fulfill the command "You will eat and be satisfied, then you shall bless the Lord, your God." There is no Biblical obligation to recite *Birkat HaMazon* unless the person eats and is truly satisfied, as the verse states.

ברכת ירושלים

רַחֵם נָא, יהוה אֱלֹהֵינוּ
עַל יִשְׂרָאֵל עַמֶּךָ
וְעַל יְרוּשָׁלַיִם עִירֶךָ
וְעַל צִיּוֹן מִשְׁכַּן כְּבוֹדֶךָ
וְעַל מַלְכוּת בֵּית דָּוִד מְשִׁיחֶךָ
וְעַל הַבַּיִת הַגָּדוֹל וְהַקָּדוֹשׁ שֶׁנִּקְרָא שִׁמְךָ עָלָיו.
אֱלֹהֵינוּ, אָבִינוּ
רְעֵנוּ, זוּנֵנוּ, פַּרְנְסֵנוּ וְכַלְכְּלֵנוּ
וְהַרְוִיחֵנוּ, וְהַרְוַח לָנוּ יהוה אֱלֹהֵינוּ מְהֵרָה מִכָּל צָרוֹתֵינוּ.
וְנָא אַל תַּצְרִיכֵנוּ, יהוה אֱלֹהֵינוּ
לֹא לִידֵי מַתְּנַת בָּשָׂר וָדָם
וְלֹא לִידֵי הַלְוָאָתָם
כִּי אִם לְיָדְךָ הַמְּלֵאָה, הַפְּתוּחָה, הַקְּדוֹשָׁה וְהָרְחָבָה
שֶׁלֹּא נֵבוֹשׁ וְלֹא נִכָּלֵם לְעוֹלָם וָעֶד.

---

bow during the recitation of *Birkat HaMazon* is inappropriate. This distinction in practice is rooted in the fundamentally different modes of approaching God that we experience in prayer versus the grace after meals. Prayer is the act of insubstantial man lacking the wherewithal to subsist appearing before the all-powerful Being upon whom his existence depends. When one prays, one is afflicted with troubles and is unable to overcome them without the help of God. The Talmud quotes the verse "A prayer of the afflicted, when he is overwhelmed" (Ps. 102:1) as proof that one may not pray from a highly situated place in a room. In prayer, "there is no elevation before the Omnipresent" (*Berakhot* 10b). *Birkat HaMazon*, on the other hand, encapsulates an entirely different attitude. The Bible commands "You will eat and be satisfied, then you shall bless." *Birkat HaMazon* is recited on a full stomach to thank God for the bounty and material blessings that He has given us. Therefore, bowing, which is symbolic of dependence and the insufficiency of the person, reflects

*On Shabbat, say:*

רְצֵה Favor and strengthen us, LORD our God,
through Your commandments,
especially through the commandment of the seventh day,
this great and holy Sabbath.
For it is, for You, a great and holy day.
On it we cease work and rest in love
in accord with Your will's commandment.
May it be Your will, LORD our God,
to grant us rest without distress, grief, or lament on our day of rest.
May You show us the consolation of Zion Your city,
and the rebuilding of Jerusalem Your holy city,
for You are the Master of salvation and consolation.

---

temptations of the evil inclination. The Jewish people, though, have remained loyal to God and have continued to thank and praise Him even in the most trying times. As proof, God shows the angels that the Jewish people recite *Birkat HaMazon* as if it was a sumptuous meal when they have nothing more than an olive-sized piece of bread to eat. In return for their sacrifice and struggle, the Jewish people do indeed deserve God's favor and mercy. (*Shiur on Birkat HaMazon*, 1969)

רצה והחליצנו – FAVOR AND STRENGTHEN US

שֶׁלֹּא תְהֵא צָרָה *Grant us rest without distress.* The day of Shabbat is meant to be filled with contentment, devoid of any sadness or pain. For this reason the Talmud Yerushalmi (*Shabbat* 15:3) states that it is forbidden to beseech God on Shabbat for personal needs as this would imply that we feel deficient and incomplete, that something is not as it should be. In the same vein, the *Mekhilta* (20:9) writes that when Shabbat begins, a person should feel that he has completed all of his work; his state of mind should be as if no project remains unfinished, no issue unresolved. Shabbat should resemble the world to come where everything exists in its perfected state. Nevertheless, the Talmud Yerushalmi notes that the prayers of the regular liturgy, even if they include petitions, may be recited. Similarly, we allow prayers on behalf of the community as a whole (see Rama, *Oraḥ Ḥayyim* 284). However, there is one type of prayer that is forbidden on Shabbat even as part of the regular *tefillot* or on behalf of the community. Maimonides (*Hilkhot Shabbat* 30:12) writes, "It is forbidden to fast, to cry out, to beseech, and to ask for mercy

*On* שבת*, say:*

רְצֵה וְהַחֲלִיצֵנוּ, יהוה אֱלֹהֵינוּ, בְּמִצְוֹתֶיךָ
וּבְמִצְוַת יוֹם הַשְּׁבִיעִי הַשַּׁבָּת הַגָּדוֹל וְהַקָּדוֹשׁ הַזֶּה
כִּי יוֹם זֶה גָּדוֹל וְקָדוֹשׁ הוּא לְפָנֶיךָ
לִשְׁבָּת בּוֹ, וְלָנְוּחַ בּוֹ בְּאַהֲבָה כְּמִצְוַת רְצוֹנֶךָ
וּבִרְצוֹנְךָ הָנִיחַ לָנוּ, יהוה אֱלֹהֵינוּ
שֶׁלֹּא תְהֵא צָרָה וְיָגוֹן וַאֲנָחָה בְּיוֹם מְנוּחָתֵנוּ
וְהַרְאֵנוּ, יהוה אֱלֹהֵינוּ, בְּנֶחָמַת צִיּוֹן עִירֶךָ
וּבְבִנְיַן יְרוּשָׁלַיִם עִיר קָדְשֶׁךָ
כִּי אַתָּה הוּא בַּעַל הַיְשׁוּעוֹת וּבַעַל הַנֶּחָמוֹת.

---

However, the great strength of the Jew is that he can bless God even when he has eaten practically nothing and has not satisfied his hunger. Across the centuries, the Jewish people have always thanked God for their portion, even if it was no more than an egg or an olive. Similarly, when the Temple stood, the third blessing of *Birkat HaMazon* was an expression of thanksgiving for Jerusalem, the royal house of David, and the holy Temple as it stood. However, after the destruction of the Temple and exile of the people, the blessing was converted into a prayer for the restoration of these lost institutions. Yet despite the long exile, despite the mourning and pain, the Jew has never ceased to thank God. This is the almost supernatural ability of the Jewish people. In this regard, the Talmud (*Berakhot* 20b) relates the following:

> The ministering angels said before the Holy One Blessed Be He: Sovereign of the Universe, it is written in Your Torah, "Who favors no person [*asher lo yisa panim*] and takes no bribe," yet You indeed favor Israel, as it is written, "The Lord will lift His countenance upon you [*yisa Hashem panav eilekha*]." He answered them: How shall I not favor Israel? I have written in the Torah "You shall eat, be satiated, and bless the Lord your God," and yet they are careful [to say the grace] if the quantity is but the size of an olive or an egg.

The angels know and understand only absolute justice. They carry out their assignments perfectly, fulfilling the will of God to the last iota. Although in this regard the angels are indeed superior to man, man possesses a capability that the angels do not. In this world, the human is surrounded by an indifferent or hostile environment, and is exposed to the inner conflict and

*On Rosh Ḥodesh and Festivals, say:*

אֱלֹהֵינוּ Our God and God of our ancestors,
may there rise, come, reach, appear, be favored, heard, regarded
and remembered before You, our recollection and remembrance,
as well as the remembrance of our ancestors,
and of the Messiah son of David Your servant,
and of Jerusalem Your holy city,
and of all Your people the house of Israel –
for deliverance and well-being, grace,
loving-kindness and compassion,
life and peace, on this day of:

*On Rosh Ḥodesh:* Rosh Ḥodesh.
*On Rosh HaShana:* the Day of Memorial.
*On Pesaḥ:* the Festival of Matzot.
*On Shavuot:* the Festival of Shavuot.
*On Sukkot:* the Festival of Sukkot.
*On Shemini Atzeret & Simḥat Torah:* the Festival of Shemini Atzeret.

On it remember us, LORD our God, for good;
recollect us for blessing,
and deliver us for life.
In accord with Your promise of salvation and compassion,
spare us and be gracious to us;
have compassion on us and deliver us,
for our eyes are turned to You because You are God,
gracious and compassionate (*on Rosh HaShana:* King).

---

יעלה ויבא – MAY THERE RISE, COME…

רֹאשׁ הַחֹדֶשׁ הַזֶּה *This day of Rosh Ḥodesh.* There are two kinds of sanctities that mark the days of the Jewish calendar. The first type of sanctity totally transforms the character of the day. Its holiness, apparent to all, overflows into every moment, every area of life, and removes any sense of the ordinary or mundane. This is the nature of *kedushat Shabbat* and *kedushat Yom Tov.* On these holy days the Jew ceases from all forbidden labor, throws off the yoke of the week, and enters a new realm. Dressed in his best clothing, he sits before a magnificently set table and recites the Kiddush before sumptuous

*On* ראש חודש *and* חגים, *say:*

אֱלֹהֵֽינוּ וֵאלֹהֵי אֲבוֹתֵֽינוּ
יַעֲלֶה וְיָבוֹא וְיַגִּֽיעַ, וְיֵרָאֶה וְיֵרָצֶה וְיִשָּׁמַע
וְיִפָּקֵד וְיִזָּכֵר זִכְרוֹנֵֽנוּ וּפִקְדוֹנֵֽנוּ, וְזִכְרוֹן אֲבוֹתֵֽינוּ
וְזִכְרוֹן מָשִֽׁיחַ בֶּן דָּוִד עַבְדֶּֽךָ
וְזִכְרוֹן יְרוּשָׁלַֽיִם עִיר קָדְשֶֽׁךָ
וְזִכְרוֹן כָּל עַמְּךָ בֵּית יִשְׂרָאֵל
לְפָנֶֽיךָ, לִפְלֵיטָה לְטוֹבָה, לְחֵן וּלְחֶֽסֶד וּלְרַחֲמִים
לְחַיִּים וּלְשָׁלוֹם בְּיוֹם

בראש חודש: רֹאשׁ הַחֹֽדֶשׁ הַזֶּה.
בראש השנה: הַזִּכָּרוֹן הַזֶּה.
בפסח: חַג הַמַּצּוֹת הַזֶּה.
בשבועות: חַג הַשָּׁבוּעוֹת הַזֶּה.
בסוכות: חַג הַסֻּכּוֹת הַזֶּה.
בשמיני עצרת ושמחת תורה: הַשְּׁמִינִי חַג הָעֲצֶֽרֶת הַזֶּה.

זָכְרֵֽנוּ יהוה אֱלֹהֵֽינוּ בּוֹ לְטוֹבָה
וּפָקְדֵֽנוּ בוֹ לִבְרָכָה
וְהוֹשִׁיעֵֽנוּ בוֹ לְחַיִּים.
וּבִדְבַר יְשׁוּעָה וְרַחֲמִים, חוּס וְחָנֵּֽנוּ וְרַחֵם עָלֵֽינוּ, וְהוֹשִׁיעֵֽנוּ
כִּי אֵלֶֽיךָ עֵינֵֽינוּ, כִּי אֵל (בראש השנה: מֶֽלֶךְ) חַנּוּן וְרַחוּם אָֽתָּה.

---

on Shabbat even for a calamity for which the community would declare a fast and public prayer." While regular petitions can sometimes be tolerated, prayers of crisis and despair, the prayers of an *eit tzara*, are totally incongruous on Shabbat. Maimonides equates such prayers with fasting on Shabbat which contradicts the obligation of *oneg Shabbat*, the requirement to make Shabbat a day of beauty and pleasure. Even in times of pain, a person must suppress his cry so as to not give voice to his pain, for Shabbat is to be a day of peace and replenishment, not a day of "distress, grief, or lament." (*Harerei Kedem*, vol. 3, pp. 237–238)

**וּבְנֵה** And may Jerusalem the holy city be rebuilt soon, in our time.
Blessed are You, Lord, who in His compassion
will rebuild Jerusalem. Amen.

BLESSING OF GOD'S GOODNESS

**בָּרוּךְ** Blessed are You, Lord our God, King of the Universe –
God our Father, our King, our Sovereign,
our Creator, our Redeemer, our Maker,
our Holy One, the Holy One of Jacob.
He is our Shepherd, Israel's Shepherd,
the good King who does good to all.

---

the Jordan in which he pleads to be able to see "that good mountain and the *Levanon*" (Deut. 3:25). The Rabbis (*Sifrei* ad loc., *Berakhot* 48b) explain that the "good mountain" is the Temple Mount, and "*Levanon*" is a poetic reference to the Temple itself. Accordingly, Moses yearned not to see Jerusalem, the political concept, the symbol of Israel's sovereignty, but rather he prayed to see Jerusalem, the home of God's Temple. "Good," therefore, doesn't mean prosperous, powerful, or successful; it means holy. Modern man and his great nation-states have everything, but they don't have holiness, and even the best of all lands and the greatest of nations is not good without a center of holiness. Without holiness there is confusion, perplexity, and rebellion in society. The Land of Israel, though, is the "good land" because it is the land whose sanctity culminates in Jerusalem and the Temple. (*Shiur on Birkat HaMazon*, 1969)

**ברכת הטוב והמטיב** – BLESSING OF GOD'S GOODNESS

**הַמֶּלֶךְ הַטּוֹב וְהַמֵּיטִיב לַכֹּל** *The good King who does good to all.* The Talmud (*Berakhot* 48b) records that the fourth and final blessing of *Birkat HaMazon* was instituted by the court in Yavneh when the martyrs of Betar were buried. In the year 135 CE, the Romans conquered the city, massacred every adult and child inside, and would not allow the Jewish community to bury the victims. After seven years, the emperor allowed the bodies to receive a proper burial, and miraculously the bodies had not decomposed over that time. In response to the miracle, the Rabbis composed this blessing. The Talmud explains that

וּבְנֵה יְרוּשָׁלַיִם עִיר הַקֹּדֶשׁ בִּמְהֵרָה בְיָמֵינוּ.
בָּרוּךְ אַתָּה יהוה, בּוֹנֶה בְרַחֲמָיו יְרוּשָׁלָיִם, אָמֵן.

ברכת הטוב והמטיב

בָּרוּךְ אַתָּה יהוה אֱלֹהֵינוּ מֶלֶךְ הָעוֹלָם
הָאֵל אָבִינוּ, מַלְכֵּנוּ, אַדִּירֵנוּ
בּוֹרְאֵנוּ, גּוֹאֲלֵנוּ, יוֹצְרֵנוּ, קְדוֹשֵׁנוּ, קְדוֹשׁ יַעֲקֹב
רוֹעֵנוּ, רוֹעֵה יִשְׂרָאֵל, הַמֶּלֶךְ הַטּוֹב וְהַמֵּטִיב לַכֹּל

---

meals. Wherever he looks, in the synagogue and in his home, the Jew sees and experiences the holiness of the day. Everyone can feel that Shabbat and Yom Tov are holy, different, and completely incomparable to the rest of the week. However, there is a different type of holiness, a hidden, unseen sanctity that can elevate a day, even if most people don't notice it. Specifically, on Rosh Ḥodesh, in the days of the Temple they would offer a *korban mussaf*, and, today as well, we recite a partial Hallel and *tefillat mussaf*. However, beyond that, Rosh Ḥodesh resembles every other day of the year. There is no recitation of Kiddush or performance of special *mitzvot*; there is no obligation of *simḥa* or *oneg*. After the morning prayers, the Jew leaves the synagogue and goes to his office to work, encumbered with all of his worries and struggles. The sanctity of Rosh Ḥodesh doesn't dispel the mundane, but rather somehow lives within it. As opposed of the holiness of Shabbat and Yom Tov, the *kedusha* of Rosh Ḥodesh represents the subtle, almost secret holiness that can quietly reside within our everyday lives. (*Divrei Hagut VeHa'arakha*, pp. 163–166)

וּבְנֵה יְרוּשָׁלַיִם עִיר הַקֹּדֶשׁ *And may Jerusalem the holy city be rebuilt.* The Talmud (*Berakhot* 48b) explains that the command to thank God for "the good land which He gave you" includes two distinct ideas: The word "land" refers to the entire Land of Israel, and the adjective "good" alludes specifically to Jerusalem. Consequently, the second blessing of *Birkat HaMazon* elaborates upon the theme of the Land of Israel, while the third blessing focuses on Jerusalem. The Talmud sees this allusion to Jerusalem in the verse based upon the parallel phrase found in Moses' petition to God to allow him to cross

Every day He has done, is doing, and will do good to us.
He has acted, is acting, and will always act kindly
toward us for ever,
granting us grace, kindness and compassion, relief and rescue,
prosperity, blessing, redemption and comfort,
sustenance and support, compassion,
life, peace and all good things,
and of all good things may He never let us lack.

ADDITIONAL REQUESTS

הָרַחֲמָן May the Compassionate One
reign over us for ever and all time.

May the Compassionate One
be blessed in heaven and on earth.

May the Compassionate One
be praised from generation to generation,
be glorified by us to all eternity,
and honored among us for ever and all time.

---

was a greater tragedy than the fall of Jerusalem, and in the ensuing years after the tragedy, many Jews lost their faith and committed apostasy, including the infamous Elisha ben Avuyah. However, despite the persecutions of those dark years, most Jews remained faithful. When seven years later the victims of Betar were released for burial and everyone witnessed the miracle that their bodies remained intact, the Jews understood this as a sign that God hadn't abandoned them. It revived their spirits and gave them the strength to withstand the Roman oppression. Just as the bodies had miraculously remained intact, the Jewish people would survive. They knew that they would persevere and outlive their Roman tormentors. (*Notes of Rabbi Hershel Schachter*)

הרחמן – MAY THE COMPASSIONATE ONE

הָרַחֲמָן הוּא יִשְׁתַּבַּח לְדוֹר דּוֹרִים *May the Compassionate One be praised from generation to generation.* The kabbalists explain that the word יִשְׁתַּבַּח implies that God's true praise can only emanate from God Himself. The word is a

שֶׁבְּכָל יוֹם וָיוֹם
הוּא הֵיטִיב, הוּא מֵיטִיב, הוּא יֵיטִיב לָנוּ
הוּא גְמָלָנוּ, הוּא גוֹמְלֵנוּ, הוּא יִגְמְלֵנוּ לָעַד
לְחֵן וּלְחֶסֶד וּלְרַחֲמִים, וּלְרֶוַח, הַצָּלָה וְהַצְלָחָה
בְּרָכָה וִישׁוּעָה, נֶחָמָה, פַּרְנָסָה וְכַלְכָּלָה
וְרַחֲמִים וְחַיִּים וְשָׁלוֹם וְכָל טוֹב, וּמִכָּל טוּב לְעוֹלָם אַל יְחַסְּרֵנוּ.

בקשות נוספות

הָרַחֲמָן הוּא יִמְלֹךְ עָלֵינוּ לְעוֹלָם וָעֶד.
הָרַחֲמָן הוּא יִתְבָּרַךְ בַּשָּׁמַיִם וּבָאָרֶץ.
הָרַחֲמָן הוּא יִשְׁתַּבַּח לְדוֹר דּוֹרִים
וְיִתְפָּאַר בָּנוּ לָעַד וּלְנֵצַח נְצָחִים
וְיִתְהַדַּר בָּנוּ לָעַד וּלְעוֹלְמֵי עוֹלָמִים.

---

the phrase "the good King" refers to the miracle of the bodies' lack of decay, and the additional phrase "who does good to all" is in gratitude for the honorable burial these martyrs ultimately received.

To fully appreciate the significance of this miracle, though, one must understand the context of the time and the tragedy that the defeat of Betar constituted. In the immediate decades after the fall of Jerusalem, it is very possible that individuals continued to offer the Paschal sacrifices at the site of the Temple (see *Pesaḥim* 3b and *Shu"t Maharatz Chajes* 76:3). Many hoped that they would soon regain their autonomy and rededicate the Temple. With Bar Kochba's revolt, it seemed indeed that a Jewish state might be reestablished. The destruction of Betar and its fortress, however, put an end to the rebellion and crushed any possibility of a return to Jewish autonomy. To demonstrate their control, the Romans mercilessly killed everyone "until their blood ran into the great sea" (*Gittin* 57a).The fall of Betar also marked the beginning of the period of the religious persecutions by Rome including the murder of the ten martyred rabbis. In some ways the destruction of Betar and its aftermath

May the Compassionate One
grant us an honorable livelihood.

May the Compassionate One
break the yoke from our neck
and lead us upright to our land.

May the Compassionate One
send us many blessings to this house
and this table at which we have eaten.

May the Compassionate One
send us Elijah the prophet – may he be remembered for good –
to bring us good tidings of salvation and consolation.

May the Compassionate One
bless the State of Israel.

May the Compassionate One
bless the members of Israel's Defense Forces,
who stand guard over our land.

*A guest says:*

יְהִי רָצוֹן May it be Your will that the master of this house shall not suffer shame in this world, nor humiliation in the World to Come. May all he owns prosper greatly, and may his and our possessions be successful and close to hand. Let not the Accuser hold sway over his deeds or ours, and may no thought of sin, iniquity or transgression enter him or us from now and for evermore.

---

which constrains this inner desire of man: "Who can express the power of God or relate all of His praise?" (Ps. 106:2). In other words, it is impossible for a mortal, finite man, to properly praise the eternal King of kings. The idea that man could offer praise of his Creator is nothing less than absurd. Therefore, King David also teaches us, "For You, silence is praise" (Ps. 65:2). The ultimate glorification of God is to be silent, to realize that we do not have the capability to express or even to comprehend God's infinite benevolence. Moreover, silence also represents our recognition that God is beyond our praise; while we may feel the need to praise God, we must always remember that He is in no need of it. (*Shiurim LeZekher Abba Mari*, vol. 2, pp. 25–28)

הָרַחֲמָן הוּא יְפַרְנְסֵנוּ בְּכָבוֹד.
הָרַחֲמָן הוּא יִשְׁבֹּר עֻלֵּנוּ מֵעַל צַוָּארֵנוּ
וְהוּא יוֹלִיכֵנוּ קוֹמְמִיּוּת לְאַרְצֵנוּ.
הָרַחֲמָן הוּא יִשְׁלַח לָנוּ בְּרָכָה מְרֻבָּה בַּבַּיִת הַזֶּה
וְעַל שֻׁלְחָן זֶה שֶׁאָכַלְנוּ עָלָיו.
הָרַחֲמָן הוּא יִשְׁלַח לָנוּ אֶת אֵלִיָּהוּ הַנָּבִיא זָכוּר לַטּוֹב
וִיבַשֶּׂר לָנוּ בְּשׂוֹרוֹת טוֹבוֹת יְשׁוּעוֹת וְנֶחָמוֹת.
הָרַחֲמָן הוּא יְבָרֵךְ אֶת מְדִינַת יִשְׂרָאֵל.
הָרַחֲמָן הוּא יְבָרֵךְ אֶת חַיָּלֵי צְבָא הַהֲגָנָה לְיִשְׂרָאֵל
הָעוֹמְדִים עַל מִשְׁמַר אַרְצֵנוּ.

*A guest says:*

יְהִי רָצוֹן שֶׁלֹּא יֵבוֹשׁ בַּעַל הַבַּיִת בָּעוֹלָם הַזֶּה, וְלֹא יִכָּלֵם לָעוֹלָם הַבָּא, וְיִצְלַח מְאֹד בְּכָל נְכָסָיו, וְיִהְיוּ נְכָסָיו וּנְכָסֵינוּ מֻצְלָחִים וּקְרוֹבִים לָעִיר, וְאַל יִשְׁלֹט שָׂטָן לֹא בְּמַעֲשֵׂה יָדָיו וְלֹא בְּמַעֲשֵׂה יָדֵינוּ. וְאַל יִזְדַּקֵּק לֹא לְפָנָיו וְלֹא לְפָנֵינוּ שׁוּם דְּבַר הִרְהוּר חֵטְא, עֲבֵירָה וְעָוֹן, מֵעַתָּה וְעַד עוֹלָם.

reflexive verb meaning, "may the Compassionate One be praised" – by Himself. There are two seemingly contradictory principles in Judaism which are both absolutely true, and both ideas are expressed by King David in Psalms. On the one hand, man is obligated to praise God, to sing hymns about His awesome power and boundless kindness. "Offer praise, servants of God, praise the name of God. Let His name be blessed from this time forth and forever" (Ps. 135:1). This is not merely an obligation, but part of the basic nature of man. The religious personality yearns to praise his Creator, yearns to express the overwhelming awe he feels when he reflects upon God's handiwork and to articulate the sense of thanksgiving which overcomes him when he ponders the blessings of his life. At the same time, we find a second principle

הָרַחֲמָן May the Compassionate One bless –

*When eating at one's own table, say (include the words in parentheses that apply):*
me, (my wife/husband, / my father, my teacher / my mother, my teacher/ my children,) and all that is mine,

*A guest at someone else's table says (include the words in parentheses that apply):*
the master of this house, him (and his wife, the mistress of this house / and his children,) and all that is his,

*Children at their parents' table say (include the words in parentheses that apply):*
my father, my teacher, (master of this house,) and my mother, my teacher, (mistress of this house,) them, their household, their children, and all that is theirs.

*For all other guests, add:*
and all the diners here,

אוֹתָנוּ – together with us and all that is ours.
Just as our forefathers
Abraham, Isaac and Jacob were blessed in all, from all, with all,
so may He bless all of us together with a complete blessing,
and let us say: Amen.

בַּמָּרוֹם On high, may grace be invoked for them and for us,
as a safeguard of peace.
May we receive a blessing from the Lord
and a just reward from the God of our salvation,
and may we find grace and good favor in the eyes of God and man.

*At a circumcision feast add here "May the Compassionate One bless the father" on page 184.*

*On Shabbat:* May the Compassionate One let us inherit the time,
that will be entirely Shabbat and rest for life everlasting.

*On Rosh Ḥodesh:* May the Compassionate One renew this month for us,
for good and blessing.

*On Rosh HaShana:* May the Compassionate One renew for us this year,
for good and blessing.

*On Yom Tov:* May the Compassionate One let us inherit the day,
that is all good.

*On Sukkot:* May the Compassionate One restore for us,
the fallen Tabernacle of David.

## הָרַחֲמָן הוּא יְבָרֵךְ

*When eating at one's own table, say (include the words in parentheses that apply):*

אוֹתִי (וְאֶת אִשְׁתִּי / וְאֶת בַּעֲלִי / וְאֶת אָבִי מוֹרִי /
וְאֶת אִמִּי מוֹרָתִי / וְאֶת זַרְעִי) וְאֶת כָּל אֲשֶׁר לִי.

*A guest at someone else's table says (include the words in parentheses that apply):*

אֶת בַּעַל הַבַּיִת הַזֶּה, אוֹתוֹ (וְאֶת אִשְׁתּוֹ בַּעֲלַת הַבַּיִת הַזֶּה /
וְאֶת זַרְעוֹ) וְאֶת כָּל אֲשֶׁר לוֹ.

*Children at their parents' table say (include the words in parentheses that apply):*

אֶת אָבִי מוֹרִי (בַּעַל הַבַּיִת הַזֶּה), וְאֶת אִמִּי מוֹרָתִי (בַּעֲלַת הַבַּיִת
הַזֶּה), אוֹתָם וְאֶת בֵּיתָם וְאֶת זַרְעָם וְאֶת כָּל אֲשֶׁר לָהֶם

*For all other guests, add:*

וְאֶת כָּל הַמְּסֻבִּין כָּאן

אוֹתָנוּ וְאֶת כָּל אֲשֶׁר לָנוּ, כְּמוֹ שֶׁנִּתְבָּרְכוּ אֲבוֹתֵינוּ
אַבְרָהָם יִצְחָק וְיַעֲקֹב, בַּכֹּל, מִכֹּל, כֹּל
כֵּן יְבָרֵךְ אוֹתָנוּ כֻּלָּנוּ יַחַד בִּבְרָכָה שְׁלֵמָה, וְנֹאמַר אָמֵן.

בַּמָּרוֹם יְלַמְּדוּ עֲלֵיהֶם וְעָלֵינוּ זְכוּת שֶׁתְּהֵא לְמִשְׁמֶרֶת שָׁלוֹם
וְנִשָּׂא בְרָכָה מֵאֵת יהוה וּצְדָקָה מֵאֱלֹהֵי יִשְׁעֵנוּ
וְנִמְצָא חֵן וְשֵׂכֶל טוֹב בְּעֵינֵי אֱלֹהִים וְאָדָם.

*At a meal after a* ברית *add here* הָרַחֲמָן הוּא יְבָרֵךְ אֲבִי הַיֶּלֶד *on page 185.*

בשבת: הָרַחֲמָן הוּא יַנְחִילֵנוּ יוֹם שֶׁכֻּלּוֹ שַׁבָּת וּמְנוּחָה לְחַיֵּי הָעוֹלָמִים.

בראש חודש: הָרַחֲמָן הוּא יְחַדֵּשׁ עָלֵינוּ אֶת הַחֹדֶשׁ הַזֶּה לְטוֹבָה וְלִבְרָכָה.

בראש השנה: הָרַחֲמָן הוּא יְחַדֵּשׁ עָלֵינוּ אֶת הַשָּׁנָה הַזֹּאת לְטוֹבָה וְלִבְרָכָה.

ביום טוב: הָרַחֲמָן הוּא יַנְחִילֵנוּ יוֹם שֶׁכֻּלּוֹ טוֹב.

בסוכות: הָרַחֲמָן הוּא יָקִים לָנוּ אֶת סֻכַּת דָּוִד הַנּוֹפֶלֶת.

הָרַחֲמָן May the Compassionate One make us worthy
of the Messianic Age and life in the World to Come.
He gives great / *On Shabbat, Festivals, and Rosh Ḥodesh:* He is a tower of / *II Sam. 22*
salvation to His king, showing kindness to His anointed,
to David and his descendants for ever.
He who makes peace in His high places,
may He make peace for us and all Israel, and let us say: Amen.

יְראוּ Fear the LORD, you His holy ones; *Ps. 34*
those who fear Him lack nothing.
Young lions may grow weak and hungry,
but those who seek the LORD lack no good thing.
Thank the LORD for He is good; *Ps. 118*
His loving-kindness is for ever.
You open Your hand, and satisfy every living thing with favor. *Ps. 145*
Blessed is the person who trusts in the LORD, *Jer. 17*
whose trust is in the LORD alone.
Once I was young, and now I am old, *Ps. 37*
yet I have never watched a righteous man forsaken
or his children begging for bread.
The LORD will give His people strength. *Ps. 29*
The LORD will bless His people with peace.

*If Birkat HaMazon was made on a cup of wine, then the blessing over wine is made and the majority of the cup is drunk, after which the Berakha Me'Ein Shalosh,* *page 156**, is said.*

*At a wedding or Sheva Berakhot, turn to page 166.*

---

the verses in Deuteronomy which promise that after the exile, "you will return to the LORD, your God, and you will listen to His voice… and the LORD, your God, will return you from captivity and have mercy upon you." We have a guarantee that the Jewish people as a whole will never be totally destroyed through spiritual assimilation and alienation despite the persecutions or seductions of the exile. Individuals may wander astray and become lost, but the nation as a whole will find her way back. Israel will repent. It emerges that our faith in the arrival of the Messiah is dependent upon our faith in Israel's eventual repentance. Just as a person must believe in the coming of the Messiah, he must also believe in the Jewish people. (*On Repentance*, pp. 122–125)

הָרַחֲמָן הוּא יְזַכֵּנוּ לִימוֹת הַמָּשִׁיחַ וּלְחַיֵּי הָעוֹלָם הַבָּא
שמואל ב׳ כב מַגְדִּל/ *On* ראש חודש *and* ,חגים ,שבת מִגְדּוֹל/ יְשׁוּעוֹת מַלְכּוֹ
וְעֹשֶׂה־חֶסֶד לִמְשִׁיחוֹ, לְדָוִד וּלְזַרְעוֹ עַד־עוֹלָם:
עֹשֶׂה שָׁלוֹם בִּמְרוֹמָיו
הוּא יַעֲשֶׂה שָׁלוֹם עָלֵינוּ וְעַל כָּל יִשְׂרָאֵל, וְאִמְרוּ אָמֵן.

תהלים לד יְראוּ אֶת־יהוה קְדֹשָׁיו, כִּי־אֵין מַחְסוֹר לִירֵאָיו:
כְּפִירִים רָשׁוּ וְרָעֵבוּ, וְדֹרְשֵׁי יהוה לֹא־יַחְסְרוּ כָל־טוֹב:
תהלים קיח הוֹדוּ לַיהוה כִּי־טוֹב, כִּי לְעוֹלָם חַסְדּוֹ:
תהלים קמה פּוֹתֵחַ אֶת־יָדֶךָ, וּמַשְׂבִּיעַ לְכָל־חַי רָצוֹן:
ירמיה יז בָּרוּךְ הַגֶּבֶר אֲשֶׁר יִבְטַח בַּיהוה, וְהָיָה יהוה מִבְטַחוֹ:
תהלים לז נַעַר הָיִיתִי גַּם־זָקַנְתִּי, וְלֹא־רָאִיתִי צַדִּיק נֶעֱזָב וְזַרְעוֹ מְבַקֶּשׁ־לָחֶם:
תהלים כט יהוה עֹז לְעַמּוֹ יִתֵּן, יהוה יְבָרֵךְ אֶת־עַמּוֹ בַשָּׁלוֹם:

*If* ברכת המזון *was made on a cup of wine, then* בּוֹרֵא פְּרִי הַגָּפֶן *is said and the majority of the cup is drunk, after which* ברכה מעין שלוש*, page 157, is said.*

*At a wedding or* שבע ברכות*, turn to page 167.*

---

הָרַחֲמָן הוּא יְזַכֵּנוּ לִימוֹת הַמָּשִׁיחַ *May the Compassionate One make us worthy of the Messianic Age.* The Talmud (*Sanhedrin* 97b) records a dispute whether the final redemption depends upon the repentance of the Jewish people or if the advent of the Messiah is guaranteed without any preconditions. Maimonides (*Hilkhot Teshuva* 7:5) rules that *teshuva* is absolutely necessary: "Israel will not be redeemed without repentance." However, if this is true, it would seem to undermine our faith in the coming of the Messiah which is a cornerstone of Jewish belief. How can Maimonides himself rule that a person must believe that the Messiah will definitely come? How can a person declare, "I believe with complete faith in the coming of the Messiah and although he may tarry I will await his arrival every day"? Perhaps the Jewish people will not repent, perhaps we will not be worthy, and if so there is no assurance that the Messiah will ever arrive. Maimonides was aware of this problem, and he therefore continues: "and the Torah has guaranteed us that in the end of their exile Israel will repent and will be immediately redeemed." This is based upon

# Berakha Me'Ein Shalosh

*Grace after eating from the "seven species" of produce with which Israel is blessed: food made from the five grains (but not bread or matza); wine or grape juice; grapes, figs, pomegranates, olives, or dates.*

בָּרוּךְ Blessed are You, LORD our God, King of the Universe,

| *After grain products:* | *After wine or grape juice:* | *After grapes, figs, olives, pomegranates or dates:* |
|---|---|---|
| for the nourishment and sustenance, | for the vine and the fruit of the vine, | for the tree and the fruit of the tree, |

*After grain products, and wine or grape juice:*
for the nourishment and sustenance
and for the vine and the fruit of the vine,

and for the produce of the field; for the desirable, good and spacious land that You willingly gave as heritage to our ancestors, that they might eat of its fruit and be satisfied with its goodness. Have compassion, please, LORD our God, on Israel Your people, on Jerusalem, Your city, on Zion the home of Your glory, on Your altar and Your Temple. May You rebuild Jerusalem, the holy city swiftly in our time, and may You bring us back there, rejoicing in its rebuilding, eating from its fruit, satisfied by its goodness, and blessing You for it in holiness and purity.

---

performs entirely on His own without the participation of man, like the miraculous Exodus from Egypt, when the Jews remained in their homes and watched the events unfold. *Ezra*, on the other hand, means that man begins and the Almighty finishes. The human must also contribute to the process. In a similar vein, the creation of fruit is a miracle of *yeshua*, one that God accomplishes without man's participation. Bread, though, falls into the category of *ezra*. The Creator helps man by causing the wheat to grow, but man must transform it into bread. *A priori*, we may have thought that we must thank God more for His salvation, for providing fruit without human labor, than for assistance, the process of making bread in which man plays a part. Yet we arrive at the opposite conclusion. We must bless the Almighty for His gift of the seven species, but here a single blessing suffices. With respect to bread, however, where man takes the initiative, we must bless the Almighty even more intensely. The more man participates, the more he must thank his Creator; for he must bless God not only for His aid and assistance, but also for giving him the honor of becoming a partner with God. (*Derashot HaRav*, pp. 169–170; *MiPeninei HaRav*, p. 371)

# ברכה מעין שלוש

*Grace after eating from the "seven species" of produce with which ארץ ישראל is blessed: food made from the five grains (but not bread or מצה); wine or grape juice; grapes, figs, pomegranates, olives, or dates.*

בָּרוּךְ אַתָּה יהוה אֱלֹהֵינוּ מֶלֶךְ הָעוֹלָם, עַל

*After grain products:*
הַמִּחְיָה וְעַל הַכַּלְכָּלָה

*After wine or grape juice:*
הַגֶּפֶן וְעַל פְּרִי הַגֶּפֶן

*After grapes, figs, olives, pomegranates or dates:*
הָעֵץ וְעַל פְּרִי הָעֵץ

*After grain products, and wine or grape juice:*
הַמִּחְיָה וְעַל הַכַּלְכָּלָה וְעַל הַגֶּפֶן וְעַל פְּרִי הַגֶּפֶן

וְעַל תְּנוּבַת הַשָּׂדֶה וְעַל אֶרֶץ חֶמְדָּה טוֹבָה וּרְחָבָה, שֶׁרָצִיתָ וְהִנְחַלְתָּ לַאֲבוֹתֵינוּ לֶאֱכֹל מִפִּרְיָהּ וְלִשְׂבֹּעַ מִטּוּבָהּ. רַחֶם נָא יהוה אֱלֹהֵינוּ עַל יִשְׂרָאֵל עַמֶּךָ וְעַל יְרוּשָׁלַיִם עִירֶךָ וְעַל צִיּוֹן מִשְׁכַּן כְּבוֹדֶךָ וְעַל מִזְבְּחֶךָ וְעַל הֵיכָלֶךָ. וּבְנֵה יְרוּשָׁלַיִם עִיר הַקֹּדֶשׁ בִּמְהֵרָה בְיָמֵינוּ, וְהַעֲלֵנוּ לְתוֹכָהּ וְשַׂמְּחֵנוּ בְּבִנְיָנָהּ וְנֹאכַל מִפִּרְיָהּ וְנִשְׂבַּע מִטּוּבָהּ, וּנְבָרֶכְךָ עָלֶיהָ בִּקְדֻשָּׁה וּבְטָהֳרָה.

---

**ברכה מעין שלש – BERAKHA ME'EIN SHALOSH**

After eating bread, we recite the three full blessings of *Birkat HaMazon* (together with a fourth blessing of Rabbinic origin), while after eating the fruit for which the Land of Israel is praised, we recite "*berakha aḥat me'ein shalosh*," a single blessing abstracted from the original three. This distinction illustrates a startling but fundamental principle. In the formation of a fruit, man's participation is minimal. The fruit tree grows and blossoms by itself each year; the fruit ripens by itself and can even fall off the tree unaided. All that is left for man to do is to pick up the fruit and eat it. God provides this food in its complete and final form, in a way not fundamentally different from how He provided the manna during Israel's years in the wilderness. However, in order to eat bread, not only must one plow and sow annually, and ensure that there is adequate water, but one must harvest and thresh the grain, grind it and knead it and bake it. Man is so integral to the process of making bread that we may call him a partner with God in this enterprise.

In general, we can speak of two types of divine intervention: *yeshua* (salvation) and *ezra* (assistance). *Yeshua* refers to something that the Almighty

| | |
|---|---|
| *On Shabbat:* | Be pleased to refresh us<br>on this Sabbath Day. |
| *On Rosh Ḥodesh:* | Remember us for good<br>on this day of the New Moon. |
| *On Rosh HaShana:* | Remember us for good<br>on this Day of Remembrance. |
| *On Pesaḥ:* | Grant us joy on this Festival of Matzot. |
| *On Shavuot:* | Grant us joy on this Festival of Shavuot. |
| *On Sukkot:* | Grant us joy on this Festival of Sukkot. |
| *On Shemini Atzeret & Simḥat Torah:* | Grant us joy on this Festival of Shemini Atzeret. |

For You, LORD, are good and do good to all and we thank You for the land

| *After grain products:* | *After wine or grape juice:* | *After grapes, figs, olives, pomegranates or dates:* |
|---|---|---|
| and for the nourishment. Blessed are You, LORD, for the land and for the nourishment. | and for the fruit of the vine.* Blessed are You, LORD, for the land and for the fruit of the vine.* | and for the fruit.** Blessed are You, LORD, for the land and for the fruit.** |

*After grain products, and wine or grape juice:*

and for the nourishment and for the fruit of the vine.*
Blessed are You, LORD, for the land and for the nourishment
and the fruit of the vine.*

** If the wine is from Israel, then substitute "her vine" for "the vine."*
*** If the fruit is from Israel, then substitute "her fruit" for "the fruit."*

# Blessing After Food – Borei Nefashot

*After food or drink that does not require Birkat HaMazon or Berakha Me'Ein Shalosh – such as meat, fish, dairy products, vegetables, beverages, or fruit other than grapes, figs, pomegranates, olives or dates – say:*

בָּרוּךְ Blessed are You, LORD our God, King of the Universe,
who creates the many forms of life and their needs.
For all You have created to sustain the life of all that lives,
blessed be He, Giver of life to the worlds.

| | |
|---|---|
| בשבת: | וּרְצֵה וְהַחֲלִיצֵנוּ בְּיוֹם הַשַּׁבָּת הַזֶּה |
| בראש חודש: | וְזָכְרֵנוּ לְטוֹבָה בְּיוֹם רֹאשׁ הַחֹדֶשׁ הַזֶּה |
| בראש השנה: | וְזָכְרֵנוּ לְטוֹבָה בְּיוֹם הַזִּכָּרוֹן הַזֶּה |
| בפסח: | וְשַׂמְּחֵנוּ בְּיוֹם חַג הַמַּצּוֹת הַזֶּה |
| בשבועות: | וְשַׂמְּחֵנוּ בְּיוֹם חַג הַשָּׁבוּעוֹת הַזֶּה |
| בסוכות: | וְשַׂמְּחֵנוּ בְּיוֹם חַג הַסֻּכּוֹת הַזֶּה |
| בשמיני עצרת ושמחת תורה: | וְשַׂמְּחֵנוּ בְּיוֹם הַשְּׁמִינִי חַג הָעֲצֶרֶת הַזֶּה |

כִּי אַתָּה יהוה טוֹב וּמֵטִיב לַכֹּל, וְנוֹדֶה לְּךָ עַל הָאָרֶץ

*After grain products:*

וְעַל הַמִּחְיָה.
בָּרוּךְ אַתָּה יהוה, עַל הָאָרֶץ וְעַל הַמִּחְיָה.

*After wine or grape juice:*

וְעַל פְּרִי הַגָּפֶן.*
בָּרוּךְ אַתָּה יהוה, עַל הָאָרֶץ וְעַל פְּרִי הַגָּפֶן.*

*After grapes, figs, olives, pomegranates or dates:*

וְעַל הַפֵּרוֹת.**
בָּרוּךְ אַתָּה יהוה, עַל הָאָרֶץ וְעַל הַפֵּרוֹת.**

*After grain products, and wine or grape juice:*

וְעַל הַמִּחְיָה וְעַל פְּרִי הַגָּפֶן.*
בָּרוּךְ אַתָּה יהוה, עַל הָאָרֶץ וְעַל הַמִּחְיָה וְעַל פְּרִי הַגָּפֶן.*

**If the wine is from* ארץ ישראל, *then substitute* גַּפְנָהּ *for* הַגָּפֶן.
***If the fruit is from* ארץ ישראל, *then substitute* פֵּרוֹתֶיהָ *for* הַפֵּרוֹת.

# בורא נפשות

*After food or drink that does not require* ברכת המזון *or* מעין שלוש *– such as meat, fish, dairy products, vegetables, beverages, or fruit other than grapes, figs, pomegranates, olives or dates – say:*

בָּרוּךְ אַתָּה יהוה אֱלֹהֵינוּ מֶלֶךְ הָעוֹלָם
בּוֹרֵא נְפָשׁוֹת רַבּוֹת וְחֶסְרוֹנָן
עַל כָּל מַה שֶּׁבָּרָאתָ לְהַחֲיוֹת בָּהֶם נֶפֶשׁ כָּל חָי.
בָּרוּךְ חֵי הָעוֹלָמִים.

# חופה, קידושין ושבע ברכות

# THE WEDDING CEREMONY AND MEAL

# Marriage Service

## BLESSINGS OF BETROTHAL

*The Rabbi performing the ceremony takes a cup of wine and says:*

בָּרוּךְ Blessed are You, LORD our God, King of the Universe, who creates the fruit of the vine.

בָּרוּךְ Blessed are You, LORD our God, King of the Universe, who has made us holy through His commandments, and has commanded us concerning forbidden unions, forbidding us those who are betrothed, permitting us those who are wedded to us through the rite of the canopy and sacred covenant of marriage. Blessed are You, LORD, who sanctifies His people Israel by the rite of the canopy and sacred covenant of marriage.

*The bride and bridegroom both drink from the wine. The bridegroom takes the ring and, holding it ready to be placed on the forefinger of the bride's right hand, says:*

הֲרֵי Behold you are consecrated to me by this ring
in accordance with the law of Moses and of Israel.

*He then places the ring on the forefinger of the bride's right hand. The Ketuba is read and the bridegroom hands it to the bride. A second cup of wine is taken, and over it, the Sheva Berakhot are recited, beginning with the final blessing of "who creates the fruit of the vine," and proceeding with the remaining six blessings. The same person should preferably recite the first two blessings, "who creates the fruit of the vine" and "who has created all for His glory."*

*Following the Sheva Berakhot, the bridegroom and the bride both drink from the wine.*

*The bridegroom breaks a glass in memory of the destruction of the Temple. Some say the following beforehand:*

אִם־אֶשְׁכָּחֵךְ If I forget you, O Jerusalem, may my right hand forget its skill. *Ps. 137*
May my tongue cling to the roof of my mouth if I do not remember you, if I do not set Jerusalem above my highest joy.

---

to the frailty of man or his sinful nature and did not consider marriage as a bridle and a cure for sin. There is no need for the healing power of God to absolve man of the sin which marriage necessarily incurs. On the contrary, marriage was blessed by Judaism with dignity, sacredness and purity. The wedding's *nissuin* blessings, which deal with the dignity of man and his divine charisma, are very indicative of our attitude towards a purged and remedied sexual desire. (*Family Redeemed*, pp. 77–78)

מְקַדֵּשׁ עַמּוֹ יִשְׂרָאֵל עַל יְדֵי חֻפָּה וְקִדּוּשִׁין *Who sanctifies His people Israel by the rite*

# סדר קידושין ונישואין

## ברכות האירוסין

*The* מסדר קידושין *takes a cup of wine and says:*

בָּרוּךְ אַתָּה יהוה אֱלֹהֵינוּ מֶלֶךְ הָעוֹלָם, בּוֹרֵא פְּרִי הַגָּפֶן.

בָּרוּךְ אַתָּה יהוה אֱלֹהֵינוּ מֶלֶךְ הָעוֹלָם, אֲשֶׁר קִדְּשָׁנוּ בְּמִצְוֹתָיו וְצִוָּנוּ עַל הָעֲרָיוֹת, וְאָסַר לָנוּ אֶת הָאֲרוּסוֹת, וְהִתִּיר לָנוּ אֶת הַנְּשׂוּאוֹת לָנוּ עַל יְדֵי חֻפָּה וְקִדּוּשִׁין. בָּרוּךְ אַתָּה יהוה, מְקַדֵּשׁ עַמּוֹ יִשְׂרָאֵל עַל יְדֵי חֻפָּה וְקִדּוּשִׁין.

*The* חתן *and* כלה *both drink from the wine. The* חתן *takes the ring and, holding it ready to be placed on the forefinger of the* כלה*'s right hand, says:*

הֲרֵי אַתְּ מְקֻדֶּשֶׁת לִי בְּטַבַּעַת זוֹ כְּדַת מֹשֶׁה וְיִשְׂרָאֵל.

*He then places the ring on the forefinger of the* כלה*'s right hand. The* כתובה *is read and the* חתן *hands it to the* כלה*. A second cup of wine is taken, and over it, the* שבע ברכות *are recited, beginning with the final blessing of* בּוֹרֵא פְּרִי הַגָּפֶן*, and proceeding with the remaining six blessings. The same person should preferably recite the first two blessings,* בּוֹרֵא פְּרִי הַגָּפֶן *and* שֶׁהַכֹּל בָּרָא לִכְבוֹדוֹ*.*

*Following the* שבע ברכות*, the* חתן *and* כלה *both drink from the wine.*

*The* חתן *breaks a glass in memory of the destruction of the* בית המקדש*. Some say the following beforehand:*

אִם־אֶשְׁכָּחֵךְ יְרוּשָׁלָםִ, תִּשְׁכַּח יְמִינִי: תִּדְבַּק לְשׁוֹנִי לְחִכִּי אִם־לֹא אֶזְכְּרֵכִי, אִם־לֹא אַעֲלֶה אֶת־יְרוּשָׁלַםִ עַל רֹאשׁ שִׂמְחָתִי: תהלים קלז

---

**סדר קידושין ונישואין – MARRIAGE SERVICE**

A celibate life is considered by the *halakha* and the *aggada* as an unblessed state which contravenes a basic tenet of Judaism. Adam did not meet Eve incidentally, but in accordance with the original scheme of creation. God Himself considered a self-denying solitary life of man or woman as bad, declaring that "It is not good that man be alone" (Gen. 2:18). Judaism was opposed to any maiming of the natural life for the sake of some transcendental goal, since holiness arises out of the naturalness of man.

On the other hand, Judaism could not approve of the natural sexual life without subjecting it to a remedial process of purification, as it was too well aware of all the evils intrinsic in an unchaste life, in unharnessed and undisciplined sexual practices, in lewdness and lust. *Halakha* made no concession

# Zimmun For A Sheva Berakhot Meal

*The leader takes a cup of wine in his hand and says:*

*Leader* Gentlemen, let us say grace.

*Others* May the name of the LORD be blessed from now and for ever. *Ps. 113*

*Leader* May the name of the LORD be blessed from now and for ever.

Banish grief and anger.
Let even the mute celebrate in song.
Guide us in the paths of righteousness.
Hear the blessing of the children of Aaron.

*Add the appropriate words in parentheses:*

With your permission, (my father and teacher / my mother and teacher / the Kohanim present / our teacher the Rabbi / the master of this house / the mistress of this house) my masters and teachers, let us bless our God, in whose dwelling place is joy, from whose food we have eaten.

*Others* Blessed be our God in whose dwelling place is joy,
from whose food we have eaten, and by whose goodness we live.

*Leader* Blessed be our God in whose dwelling place is joy,
from whose food we have eaten, and by whose goodness we live.
Blessed be He, and blessed be His name.

*Continue with Birkat HaMazon on page 130, at the end of which say the Sheva Berakhot (on the next page) over a cup of wine.*

---

*kiddushin,* which sanctifies the relationship of man and woman by placing it within the framework of *halakha*. With the *Birkat Eirusin,* we thank God for making Israel holy through the laws of *ḥuppa* and *kiddushin* – first we praise Him for the institution of *nissuin,* which we share with the other nations of the world, and then for choosing us from amongst all the other nations and giving Israel alone the concept of *kiddushin.* (*Mesorah,* vol. 8, p. 50)

זימון לשבע ברכות – ZIMMUN FOR SHEVA BERAKHOT

שֶׁהַשִּׂמְחָה בִמְעוֹנוֹ *In whose dwelling place is joy.* Joy, according to the *halakha,* can be experienced only when the person is in the presence of God. We find

# זימון לסעודת שבע ברכות

*The leader takes a cup of wine in his hand and says:*

*Leader* רַבּוֹתַי, נְבָרֵךְ.

*Others* יְהִי שֵׁם יהוה מְבֹרָךְ מֵעַתָּה וְעַד־עוֹלָם: תהלים קיג

*Leader* יְהִי שֵׁם יהוה מְבֹרָךְ מֵעַתָּה וְעַד־עוֹלָם:

דְּוַי הָסֵר וְגַם חָרוֹן  וְאָז אִלֵּם בְּשִׁיר יָרֹן.
נְחֵנוּ בְּמַעְגְּלֵי צֶדֶק  שְׁעֵה בִּרְכַּת בְּנֵי אַהֲרֹן.

*Add the appropriate words in parentheses:*

בִּרְשׁוּת (אָבִי מוֹרִי / אִמִּי מוֹרָתִי / כֹּהֲנִים / מוֹרֵנוּ הָרַב /
בַּעַל הַבַּיִת הַזֶּה / בַּעֲלַת הַבַּיִת הַזֶּה) מָרָנָן וְרַבָּנָן וְרַבּוֹתַי
נְבָרֵךְ אֱלֹהֵינוּ שֶׁהַשִּׂמְחָה בִּמְעוֹנוֹ וְשֶׁאָכַלְנוּ מִשֶּׁלּוֹ.

*Others* בָּרוּךְ אֱלֹהֵינוּ שֶׁהַשִּׂמְחָה בִּמְעוֹנוֹ, שֶׁאָכַלְנוּ מִשֶּׁלּוֹ וּבְטוּבוֹ חָיִינוּ.

*Leader* בָּרוּךְ אֱלֹהֵינוּ שֶׁהַשִּׂמְחָה בִּמְעוֹנוֹ, שֶׁאָכַלְנוּ מִשֶּׁלּוֹ וּבְטוּבוֹ חָיִינוּ.
בָּרוּךְ הוּא וּבָרוּךְ שְׁמוֹ.

*Continue with* ברכת המזון *on page 131, at the end of which say the* שבע ברכות *(on the next page) over a cup of wine.*

---

*of the canopy and sacred covenant of marriage.* The conclusion of this blessing would seem to be out of order, as *kiddushin,* when the groom betroths his bride by giving her a ring, precedes the step of the *ḥuppa,* which refers to the subsequent *nissuin*. Rav Ḥayyim Soloveitchik explained that the order of the blessing is not in chronological sequence because it refers not to the stages of a particular wedding between two individuals, but to the unique bond between the Almighty and the people of Israel. Maimonides (*Hilkhot Ishut* 1:1) writes that before Sinai, a man would marry a woman simply by taking her into his home; that is, living together as man and wife would itself create the matrimonial relationship between them. This aspect of marriage is represented by the *ḥuppa,* which symbolizes the bride and groom living together in a shared home. However, at Sinai God gave Israel the additional institution of

THE SEVEN BLESSINGS OF MARRIAGE

בָּרוּךְ Blessed are You, Lord our God, King of the Universe, who has created all for His glory.

בָּרוּךְ Blessed are You, Lord our God, King of the Universe, Creator of mankind.

בָּרוּךְ Blessed are You, Lord our God, King of the Universe,
who made humanity in His image, the image of His likeness,
and out of his very self formed a building for eternity.
Blessed are You, Lord,
Creator of mankind.

---

"יוֹצֵר הָאָדָם, Creator of mankind," but then, almost immediately, we repeat this idea with the blessing of "אֲשֶׁר יָצַר אֶת הָאָדָם בְּצַלְמוֹ, who made humanity in His image." We say a short, terse blessing, and then, apparently not satisfied, we not only repeat the blessing, but elaborate on it. What is the need for two separate blessings? The Talmud (*Ketubot* 8a) already discussed this problem and explained that there are two blessings because there were *shtei yetzirot*, two stages or two aspects in the creation of man. In other words, man is not a harmonious, uniform being; there exists a duality – really, a contradiction – within him. First, man is a natural being as is the brute in the field or the beast in the forest. He is a part of the landscape of nature as is the bush or the tree. However, while part of nature, man is extremely skillful, and was endowed with certain qualities and talents which make him the ruler of his environment. The Almighty equipped him with certain talents, particularly his intellect, which allow him to "fill the earth and conquer it" (Gen. 1:28). He has a tremendous power of adaptability that allows him to live both near the North Pole and in tropical countries, and he is uniquely equipped with a cumulative memory upon which he can draw, allowing him to understand past experiences and plan how to act in the future. Man is unique, even as a natural being, and for this aspect of his creation we say the blessing of יוֹצֵר הָאָדָם. However, man is not only planted here on this earth. Spiritual man, unique and singular, belongs to a different dimension of existence. He quests not only for his material success, but for something which he cannot define.

שבע ברכות הנשואין

בָּרוּךְ אַתָּה יהוה אֱלֹהֵינוּ מֶלֶךְ הָעוֹלָם
שֶׁהַכֹּל בָּרָא לִכְבוֹדוֹ.

בָּרוּךְ אַתָּה יהוה אֱלֹהֵינוּ מֶלֶךְ הָעוֹלָם
יוֹצֵר הָאָדָם.

בָּרוּךְ אַתָּה יהוה אֱלֹהֵינוּ מֶלֶךְ הָעוֹלָם
אֲשֶׁר יָצַר אֶת הָאָדָם בְּצַלְמוֹ, בְּצֶלֶם דְּמוּת תַּבְנִיתוֹ
וְהִתְקִין לוֹ מִמֶּנּוּ בִּנְיַן עֲדֵי עַד.
בָּרוּךְ אַתָּה יהוה, יוֹצֵר הָאָדָם.

---

that whenever the Bible commands "you shall rejoice," there is always a qualification, "before the Lord, your God." The feeling of joy and the awareness of the unseen presence of the Almighty are identical. Joy, according to Judaism is not an emotion or a mood. Moods are passing and superficial. A mood can be provoked by any stimulus. When Judaism speaks of joy, for example in the obligation to rejoice on the festivals, it means a deep-seated experience of joy, which expresses itself in a state-of-being, an existential awareness. True joy is the awareness that one's existences has a purpose, that there is self-fulfillment and commitment to a great objective, that there is meaning to life. A person who feels that life is meaningless leads a hand-to-mouth existence, not in the economic sense, but in the metaphysical sense. Such a person can have a lot of fun – he can be drunk, he can dance and sing, he can joke around – but he cannot rejoice in the sense of *simḥa*. It is interesting to note that this experience of joy is attributed to God as well: "Honor and majesty are before Him; strength and gladness are in His place" (I Chron. 16:27). When we recite the *Sheva Berakhot* at a wedding, we similarly state that joy is in His abode. True happiness exists only in God's abode, in His habitation. There can be joy only when one stands in the presence of God and is in communion with his Maker, who provides purpose and meaning to his existence. (*Days of Deliverance*, pp. 98–99)

**יוֹצֵר הָאָדָם** *Creator of mankind.* In the *Sheva Berakhot*, we recite the blessing of

שׂוֹשׂ Bring great happiness and joy to one who was barren [Zion],
as her children return to her in joy.
Blessed are You, LORD,
who gladdens Zion through her children.

שַׂמֵּחַ Bring great joy to these loving friends,
as You gave joy to Your creations in the Garden of Eden.
Blessed are You, LORD,
who gives joy to the bridegroom and bride.

בָּרוּךְ Blessed are You, LORD our God, King of the Universe,
who created joy and gladness, bridegroom and bride,
happiness and jubilation, cheer and delight,
love, fellowship, peace and friendship.
Soon, LORD our God, may there be heard
in the cities of Judah, and in the streets of Jerusalem,
the sounds of joy and gladness,
the sounds of the bridegroom and bride,

---

building for eternity." The essence of marriage is to make permanent and eternal something which is transient and temporal. The marriage community is not complete before it becomes a "*binyan adei ad*," an eternal community, in which husband and wife pass on a *mesorah* and way of life, a hierarchy of values and an ethical code. Marriage can be understood only in metaphysical-theological terms of Adam who was created "*Betzelem demut tavnito*," as a divine and transcendental being. (*Man of Faith in the Modern World*, pp. 58–60)

קוֹל שָׂשׂוֹן וְקוֹל שִׂמְחָה *The sounds of joy and gladness.* It is impossible to be truly joyous while alone; indeed the *halakha* maintains that joy experienced while alone is not joy at all. Maimonides (*Hilkhot Yom Tov* 6:18) writes that whoever closes the doors of his home while he is in a good mood and has cause to rejoice, and does not share his happiness with others, has enjoyed nothing more than "the joy of his belly." There might be excitement and giddiness, but real joy is when one shares such beautiful moments with others. Similarly we find that in multiple places, whenever the Torah speaks about rejoicing,

שׂוֹשׂ תָּשִׂישׂ וְתָגֵל הָעֲקָרָה בְּקִבּוּץ בָּנֶיהָ לְתוֹכָהּ בְּשִׂמְחָה.
בָּרוּךְ אַתָּה יהוה, מְשַׂמֵּחַ צִיּוֹן בְּבָנֶיהָ.

שַׂמֵּחַ תְּשַׂמַּח רֵעִים הָאֲהוּבִים כְּשַׂמֵּחֲךָ יְצִירְךָ בְּגַן עֵדֶן מִקֶּדֶם.
בָּרוּךְ אַתָּה יהוה, מְשַׂמֵּחַ חָתָן וְכַלָּה.

בָּרוּךְ אַתָּה יהוה אֱלֹהֵינוּ מֶלֶךְ הָעוֹלָם
אֲשֶׁר בָּרָא שָׂשׂוֹן וְשִׂמְחָה, חָתָן וְכַלָּה
גִּילָה, רִנָּה, דִּיצָה וְחֶדְוָה
אַהֲבָה וְאַחֲוָה וְשָׁלוֹם וְרֵעוּת.
מְהֵרָה יהוה אֱלֹהֵינוּ יִשָּׁמַע בְּעָרֵי יְהוּדָה וּבְחוּצוֹת יְרוּשָׁלָיִם
קוֹל שָׂשׂוֹן וְקוֹל שִׂמְחָה
קוֹל חָתָן וְקוֹל כַּלָּה

---

Food, clothes, and money do not satisfy him. There is a *ratzon elyon*, a higher will, which cannot be rationalized by natural man, that drives him on a quest to seek God. Here is a different personality which, somehow, looks upon itself as homeless in this world, as somehow rooted in another mysterious world which is strange to us but without which we cannot exist. This is transcendental man, man as a spiritual being, and he deserves his own blessing, "who created man in His image."

Marriage would seem to revolve around procreation and preservation of the species, a natural institution built by natural man. Yet the first blessing, which belongs to natural man, doesn't mention procreation, survival, or the preservation of the species. Only in the second blessing, when we speak about man as a transcendental being, do we refer to marriage and the bond between the male and female. This is because marriage is not a natural institution which is explainable in sociological terms. Procreation is surely a purpose of marriage, and of course, marriage is a source of pleasure, comfort, and joy. However, the main purpose, the *telos* of marriage, is a transcendental one, to transmit something to the next generation and perpetuate a great tradition. "וְהִתְקִין לוֹ מִמֶּנּוּ בִּנְיַן עֲדֵי עַד, and out of his very self formed a

the joyous sounds of bridegrooms
from their wedding canopy
and of young people at their feasts of song.
Blessed are You, Lord,
who makes the bridegroom rejoice with the bride.

בָּרוּךְ Blessed are You, Lord our God, King of the Universe,
who creates the fruit of the vine.

---

of the bride and groom, how they attracted friends, were helpful to them, and aroused love in their hearts. (*Sheva Berakhot*, 1982)

בּוֹרֵא פְּרִי הַגָּפֶן *Who creates the fruit of the vine.* Maimonides distinguishes between the different blessings which are recited *al hakos*, over a cup: With regard to Kiddush, *Birkat HaMazon*, and *Birkat Nissuin* (*Sheva Berakhot*), Maimonides rules that the blessings must be recited over a cup of wine specifically (see *Hil. Shabbat* 29:17, *Hil. Berakhot* 7:15, and *Hil. Ishut* 10:4). This stands in contrast to Havdala and *Birkat Eirusin*, regarding which Maimonides rules that the blessing may be recited over a cup of wine or *ḥamar medinah*, the local beverage (see *Hil. Shabbat ibid.* and *Hil. Ishut* 3:24). This distinction stems from the different functions of these blessings. In the case of Havdala and *Birkat Eirusin*, the blessings do not relate to a meal; all that is necessary is a *kos shel berakha*, a blessing recited over an important beverage. But in the case of Kiddush, *Birkat Nissuin* and *Birkat HaMazon*, the *berakhot* create an elevated meal, a meal sanctified by praise of God; for this function, to create a *se'uda al hayayin*, we require the blessings be made over a cup of wine. This also explains why regarding Kiddush, *Birkat Nissuin* and *Birkat HaMazon*, Maimonides stipulates that the one making the blessing must drink from the wine, in contrast to Havdala and *Birkat Eirusin*. To elevate the entire meal, the one making the blessing must drink of the wine in order to connect the blessing with the meal. (*Shiurim LeZekher Abba Mari*, vol. 2, pp. 128–129; *Harerei Kedem*, vol. 2, pp. 138–139)

קוֹל מִצְהֲלוֹת חֲתָנִים מֵחֻפָּתָם
וּנְעָרִים מִמִּשְׁתֵּה נְגִינָתָם.
בָּרוּךְ אַתָּה יהוה, מְשַׂמֵּחַ הֶחָתָן עִם הַכַּלָּה.

בָּרוּךְ אַתָּה יהוה אֱלֹהֵינוּ מֶלֶךְ הָעוֹלָם
בּוֹרֵא פְּרִי הַגָּפֶן.

---

(e.g., Deut. 12:18; 16:11, 14), it includes not only "you" but "your son, your daughter," and "your servant and your handmaid." Everybody who is in your house should rejoice with you, and if you cannot make them happy, it is apparent that the joy is not genuine. True happiness spreads like an epidemic, catches like a wildfire. It is part of human nature that when we experience something that is cause to celebrate, we want to run home to tell our mother and father, brother and sister, and all of our friends. It is very difficult to suppress joy; it explodes and draws in even those that are not involved.

In particular, when it comes to the celebration of a marriage, we know how much the *halakha* values the joyous excitement and cheerful disposition of wedding guests. Many laws have been constructed whose prime purpose is the planned manifestation of our great joy on such an occasion. The Talmud (*Ketubot* 17a) tells of King Agrippa that he made way for a bride, and the Sages praised him. The Sages praised Agrippa's forgoing of his honor, because joy cannot be contained for long. Joy must explode. The final blessing of the *Sheva Berakhot* describes such spontaneous outbursts of gladness and delight: "The sounds of joy and gladness, the sounds of the bridegroom and bride, the joyous sounds of bridegrooms from their wedding canopy and of young people at their feasts of song." Though it is only one wedding, everybody is enthusiastic, everybody rejoices, makes noise, and sings. However, in order to share his joy with a multitude, a person needs to have many friends. The rejoicing at a wedding depends a great deal upon the friendships that the bride and groom built in the years preceding the wedding. Thus, joy at a wedding also reflects the morality and the charisma

# סדר ברית מילה

## BRIT MILA CEREMONY AND MEAL

# Brit Mila Ceremony

*When the baby is brought in, all stand and say:*

Blessed is he who comes.

*The mohel (in some congregations, all) say (in Israel omit):*

**וַיְדַבֵּר** The LORD spoke to Moses, saying: Pinehas the son of Elazar, *Num. 25*
the son of Aaron the priest, turned back My rage from the children of Israel, when he was zealous for Me among them, and I did not annihilate the children of Israel in My own zeal. And so tell him, that I now give him My covenant for peace.

*The following verses, through "LORD, please, grant us success," are only said in Israel.*

*Mohel:* Happy are those You choose and bring near to dwell in Your courts. *Ps. 65*

*All:* May we be sated with the goodness of Your House, Your holy Temple.

*The father takes the baby in his hands and says quietly:*

**אִם אֶשְׁכָּחֵךְ** If I forget you, O Jerusalem, may my right hand forget *Ps. 137*
its skill. May my tongue cling to the roof of my mouth, if I do not remember you, if I do not set Jerusalem above my highest joy.

*The father says aloud, followed by the congregation:*

Listen, Israel: the LORD is our God, the LORD is One. *Deut. 6*

*The Mohel, followed by the congregation, recites each of the following three phrases:*

The LORD is King, the LORD was King,
the LORD shall be King for ever and all time.
LORD, please, save us. *Ps. 118*
LORD, please, grant us success.

*The baby is placed on Eliyahu's seat, and the Mohel says:*

This is the throne of Elijah the prophet,
may he be remembered for good.

---

singular historical destiny of the Jewish people. The patriarchal covenant means identification with Abraham the Hebrew, Avraham HaIvri, who, as the Rabbis put it, stood on one side of the river as the rest of the world stood on the other. The covenant manifests itself in the Jew's isolation and seclusion, in the fact that the security of the general society doesn't necessarily

# סדר ברית מילה

*When the baby is brought in, all stand and say:*

בָּרוּךְ הַבָּא.

*The* מוהל *(in some congregations, all) say (in* ארץ ישראל *omit):*

וַיְדַבֵּר יהוה אֶל־מֹשֶׁה לֵּאמֹר: פִּינְחָס בֶּן־אֶלְעָזָר בֶּן־אַהֲרֹן הַכֹּהֵן הֵשִׁיב אֶת־חֲמָתִי מֵעַל בְּנֵי־יִשְׂרָאֵל, בְּקַנְאוֹ אֶת־קִנְאָתִי בְּתוֹכָם, וְלֹא־כִלִּיתִי אֶת־בְּנֵי־יִשְׂרָאֵל בְּקִנְאָתִי: לָכֵן אֱמֹר, הִנְנִי נֹתֵן לוֹ אֶת־בְּרִיתִי שָׁלוֹם: במדבר כה

*The following verses, through* אָנָּא יהוה הַצְלִיחָה נָא *are only said in Israel.*

המוהל: אַשְׁרֵי תִּבְחַר וּתְקָרֵב, יִשְׁכֹּן חֲצֵרֶיךָ תהלים סה

הקהל: נִשְׂבְּעָה בְּטוּב בֵּיתֶךָ, קְדֹשׁ הֵיכָלֶךָ:

*The father takes the baby in his hands and says quietly:*

אִם־אֶשְׁכָּחֵךְ יְרוּשָׁלָםִ, תִּשְׁכַּח יְמִינִי: תִּדְבַּק לְשׁוֹנִי לְחִכִּי תהלים קלז
אִם־לֹא אֶזְכְּרֵכִי, אִם־לֹא אַעֲלֶה אֶת־יְרוּשָׁלַםִ עַל רֹאשׁ שִׂמְחָתִי:

*The father says aloud, followed by the* קהל*:*

שְׁמַע יִשְׂרָאֵל, יהוה אֱלֹהֵינוּ, יהוה אֶחָד: דברים ו

*The* מוהל*, followed by the* קהל*, repeats each of the following three phrases:*

יהוה מֶלֶךְ, יהוה מָלָךְ, יהוה יִמְלֹךְ לְעוֹלָם וָעֶד.
אָנָּא יהוה הוֹשִׁיעָה נָּא תהלים קיח
אָנָּא יהוה הַצְלִיחָה נָא:

*The baby is placed on the* כסא של אליהו*, and the* מוהל *says:*

זֶה הַכִּסֵּא שֶׁל אֵלִיָּהוּ הַנָּבִיא זָכוּר לַטּוֹב.

---

**סדר ברית מילה** – BRIT MILA CEREMONY

The covenant of Sinai expresses itself in the undertaking of the six hundred and thirteen *mitzvot*, in the fulfillment of all four sections of the *Shulḥan Arukh*. However, there is another covenant, represented by the *mitzva* of *mila*, which is the covenant of the Patriarchs, the *brit avot*, the unique and

*The Mohel continues:*

לִישׁוּעָתְךָ For Your salvation I wait, O LORD. I await Your deliverance, *Gen. 49 Ps. 119*
LORD, and I observe Your commandments. Elijah, angel of the covenant,
behold: yours is before you. Stand at my right hand and be close to me.
I await Your deliverance, LORD. I rejoice in Your word like one who finds *Ps. 119*
much spoil. Those who love Your Torah have great peace, and there is no
stumbling block before them. Happy are those You choose and bring near *Ps. 65*
to dwell in Your courts.

*All respond:*

May we be sated with the goodness of Your House, Your holy Temple.

*The baby is placed on the knees of the Sandak, and the Mohel says:*

בָּרוּךְ Blessed are You, LORD our God, King of the Universe,
who has made us holy through His commandments,
and has commanded us concerning circumcision.

*Immediately after the circumcision, the father says:*

בָּרוּךְ Blessed are You, LORD our God, King of the Universe,
who has made us holy through His commandments,
and has commanded us to bring him [our son]
into the covenant of Abraham, our father.

*In Israel the father adds (some outside Israel add it as well):*

בָּרוּךְ Blessed are You, LORD our God, King of the Universe,
who has given us life, sustained us, and brought us to this time.

*All respond:*

אָמֵן Amen. Just as he has entered into the covenant,
so may he enter into Torah, marriage and good deeds.

---

aware of this revelation when a famous German rabbi, fully observant, let slip the remark in my then young and naïve presence that he had more in common with a German gentile than he had with an irreligious Polish Jew. "What connection do I have with such a Jew?" he asked. I thought at the time that what he had in common with the non-religious Polish Jew was that in the eyes of the Jew-hater they were both Jews and that our enemies make no distinction between them. But I was young and never had chutzpah, and so I let his words pass with silence. (*The Rav Speaks*, pp. 146–147; *Abraham's Journey*, pp. 165–166)

לְהַכְנִיסוֹ בִּבְרִיתוֹ שֶׁל אַבְרָהָם אָבִינוּ *To bring him [our son] into the covenant of Abraham, our father.* The *mitzva* of *brit mila* consists of two distinct elements.

*The* מוהל *continues:*

לִישׁוּעָתְךָ קִוִּיתִי יהוה: שִׂבַּרְתִּי לִישׁוּעָתְךָ יהוה, וּמִצְוֹתֶיךָ עָשִׂיתִי: בראשית מט תהלים קיט
אֵלִיָּהוּ מַלְאַךְ הַבְּרִית, הִנֵּה שֶׁלְּךָ לְפָנֶיךָ, עֲמֹד עַל יְמִינִי וְסָמְכֵנִי.
שִׂבַּרְתִּי לִישׁוּעָתְךָ יהוה: שָׂשׂ אָנֹכִי עַל־אִמְרָתֶךָ, כְּמוֹצֵא שָׁלָל רָב: תהלים קיט
שָׁלוֹם רָב לְאֹהֲבֵי תוֹרָתֶךָ, וְאֵין־לָמוֹ מִכְשׁוֹל: אַשְׁרֵי תִּבְחַר וּתְקָרֵב, תהלים סה
יִשְׁכֹּן חֲצֵרֶיךָ

*All respond:*

נִשְׂבְּעָה בְּטוּב בֵּיתֶךָ, קְדֹשׁ הֵיכָלֶךָ:

*The baby is placed on the knees of the* סנדק*, and the* מוהל *says:*

בָּרוּךְ אַתָּה יהוה אֱלֹהֵינוּ מֶלֶךְ הָעוֹלָם
אֲשֶׁר קִדְּשָׁנוּ בְּמִצְוֹתָיו וְצִוָּנוּ עַל הַמִּילָה.

*Immediately after the circumcision, the father says:*

בָּרוּךְ אַתָּה יהוה אֱלֹהֵינוּ מֶלֶךְ הָעוֹלָם, אֲשֶׁר קִדְּשָׁנוּ בְּמִצְוֹתָיו
וְצִוָּנוּ לְהַכְנִיסוֹ בִּבְרִיתוֹ שֶׁל אַבְרָהָם אָבִינוּ.

*In* ארץ ישראל *the father adds (some in* חוץ לארץ *add it as well):*

בָּרוּךְ אַתָּה יהוה אֱלֹהֵינוּ מֶלֶךְ הָעוֹלָם
שֶׁהֶחֱיָנוּ וְקִיְּמָנוּ וְהִגִּיעָנוּ לַזְּמַן הַזֶּה.

*All respond:*

אָמֵן. כְּשֵׁם שֶׁנִּכְנַס לַבְּרִית, כֵּן יִכָּנֵס לְתוֹרָה וּלְחֻפָּה וּלְמַעֲשִׂים טוֹבִים.

---

mean security for the Jews. The covenant of Abraham is realized within the Jewish consciousness when others point at him and say "He is a Jew!" In a word, the patriarchal covenant finds expression in the sense of oneness with the entire people of Israel, in one's participation in the lot of all Jews, and in the consciousness of the fact that being Jewish is singular and unique. One who lacks this mentality and does not sense himself as bound to the strange, paradoxical Jewish fate, lacks the sanctity of the patriarchal covenant. One may observe the Torah and *mitzvot* and be fully within the covenant of Sinai, yet at the same time profane the patriarchal sanctity. I personally first became

*After the circumcision has been completed, the Mohel (or another honoree) takes a cup of wine and says:*

בָּרוּךְ Blessed are You, Lord our God, King of the Universe, who creates the fruit of the vine.

בָּרוּךְ Blessed are You, Lord our God, King of the Universe, who made the beloved one [Isaac] holy from the womb, marked the decree of circumcision in his flesh, and gave his descendants the seal and sign of the holy covenant. As a reward for this, the Living God, our Portion, our Rock, did order deliverance from destruction for the beloved of our flesh, for the sake of His covenant that He set in our flesh. Blessed are You, Lord, who establishes the covenant.

אֱלֹהֵינוּ Our God and God of our fathers, preserve this child to his father and mother, and let his name be called in Israel (*baby's name* son of *father's name*). May the father rejoice in the issue of his body, and the mother be glad with the fruit of her womb, as is written, "May *Prov. 23*
your father and mother rejoice, and she who bore you be glad." And it is said, "Then I passed by you and saw you downtrodden in your *Ezek. 16*
blood, and I said to you: In your blood, live; and I said to you: In your blood, live."

---

blessing in the father's place. Ra'avad and others maintain that the entire nation is obligated in both aspects of the *mitzva*, to circumcise the child and to include him in the covenant. However, Maimonides understands that while the entire nation is responsible to circumcise a child whose father ignores his responsibility, they are only obligated to make sure the child is physically circumcised. The father alone has the additional *mitzva* to carry his child into the covenant of Abraham. Finally, Rabbenu Tam (*Pesaḥim* 7a) explains that the second blessing is, in fact, not a typical *birkat hamitzva*, recited before the performance of a *mitzva*, but a *birkat hashevah*, a blessing of praise, which is therefore recited after the event. With the additional blessing, we express our thanksgiving to God for elevating the Jewish people, forging with them an eternal covenant, and giving us the opportunity to escort this baby into the covenantal-*mesorah* community. (*Shiurim LeZekher Abba Mari*, vol. 2, pp. 137–138; *Mesorah*, vol. 6, pp. 9–10)

*After the circumcision has been completed, the* מוהל *(or another honoree) takes a cup of wine and says:*

בָּרוּךְ אַתָּה יהוה אֱלֹהֵינוּ מֶלֶךְ הָעוֹלָם, בּוֹרֵא פְּרִי הַגָּפֶן.

בָּרוּךְ אַתָּה יהוה אֱלֹהֵינוּ מֶלֶךְ הָעוֹלָם, אֲשֶׁר קִדַּשׁ יְדִיד מִבֶּטֶן, וְחֹק בִּשְׁאֵרוֹ שָׂם, וְצֶאֱצָאָיו חָתַם בְּאוֹת בְּרִית קֹדֶשׁ. עַל כֵּן בִּשְׂכַר זֹאת, אֵל חַי חֶלְקֵנוּ צוּרֵנוּ צַוֵּה לְהַצִּיל יְדִידוּת שְׁאֵרֵנוּ מִשַּׁחַת, לְמַעַן בְּרִיתוֹ אֲשֶׁר שָׂם בִּבְשָׂרֵנוּ. בָּרוּךְ אַתָּה יהוה, כּוֹרֵת הַבְּרִית.

אֱלֹהֵינוּ וֵאלֹהֵי אֲבוֹתֵינוּ, קַיֵּם אֶת הַיֶּלֶד הַזֶּה לְאָבִיו וּלְאִמּוֹ, וְיִקָּרֵא שְׁמוֹ בְּיִשְׂרָאֵל (פלוני בֶּן פלוני). יִשְׂמַח הָאָב בְּיוֹצֵא חֲלָצָיו וְתָגֵל אִמּוֹ בִּפְרִי בִטְנָהּ, כַּכָּתוּב: יִשְׂמַח־אָבִיךָ וְאִמֶּךָ, וְתָגֵל יוֹלַדְתֶּךָ: משלי כג
וְנֶאֱמַר: וָאֶעֱבֹר עָלַיִךְ וָאֶרְאֵךְ מִתְבּוֹסֶסֶת בְּדָמָיִךְ, וָאֹמַר לָךְ יחזקאל טז
בְּדָמַיִךְ חֲיִי, וָאֹמַר לָךְ בְּדָמַיִךְ חֲיִי:

There is the basic obligation of the *mila,* the physical act to circumcise the child, but there also exists a separate obligation of *brit,* the responsibility to enter the child into the covenant of Abraham. This obligation is not fulfilled directly by the mechanical act of the circumcision, but rather by the status change of the child, his becoming a *ben brit,* a member of the covenant. This duality is the reason that the Rabbis instituted two separate blessings before performing a circumcision. The first blessing, "who commanded us concerning circumcision," relates to the *mila,* the physical performance, while the second blessing, "who commanded us to bring him [our son] into the covenant of Abraham," is associated with the obligation to enter the child into the covenant. For this reason, the Talmud (*Shabbat* 137b) notes that the first blessing should be recited by the person who is actually performing the circumcision, while the second blessing should be recited by the father. Maimonides (*Hilkhot Mila* 3:1) argues that indeed only the father is eligible to recite this second blessing, and if he is not present then the blessing should be omitted; Ra'avad disagrees and holds that someone else should recite the

וְנֶאֱמַר And it is said, "He remembered His covenant for ever; the word He ordained for a thousand generations; the covenant He made with Abraham and gave on oath to Isaac, confirming it as a statute for Jacob, an everlasting covenant for Israel." And it is said, "And Abraham circumcised his son Isaac at the age of eight days, as God had commanded him." Thank the LORD for He is good; His loving-kindness is for ever. *Ps. 105* *Gen. 21* *Ps. 118*

*All respond:*

Thank the LORD for He is good; His loving-kindness is for ever.

*The Mohel (or honoree) continues:*

May this child (*baby's name* son of *father's name*) become great. Just as he has entered into the covenant, so may he enter into Torah, marriage and good deeds.

*The Sandak also drinks some of the wine; some drops are given to the baby. The cup is then sent to the mother, who also drinks from it.*

---

great because it produces its own light, while the moon is considered small because it can only reflect the light that the sun shares with it. In other words, a *katan* can only receive, absorb, or reflect, while a *gadol* gives, creates and leads. We pray that the baby, this *katan* who is totally dependent upon others and knows only how to take, should develop into a true *gadol*, a person who teaches others, who gives, shares, and shines his light on those around him. (*Halakhic Positions*, vol. 1, pp. 151–152)

תהלים קה וְנֶאֱמַר: זָכַר לְעוֹלָם בְּרִיתוֹ, דָּבָר צִוָּה לְאֶלֶף דּוֹר: אֲשֶׁר כָּרַת אֶת־
אַבְרָהָם, וּשְׁבוּעָתוֹ לְיִשְׂחָק: וַיַּעֲמִידֶהָ לְיַעֲקֹב לְחֹק, לְיִשְׂרָאֵל
בראשית כא בְּרִית עוֹלָם: וְנֶאֱמַר: וַיָּמָל אַבְרָהָם אֶת־יִצְחָק בְּנוֹ בֶּן־שְׁמֹנַת
תהלים קיח יָמִים, כַּאֲשֶׁר צִוָּה אֹתוֹ אֱלֹהִים: הוֹדוּ לַיהוה כִּי־טוֹב, כִּי לְעוֹלָם
חַסְדּוֹ:

*All respond:*

הוֹדוּ לַיהוה כִּי־טוֹב, כִּי לְעוֹלָם חַסְדּוֹ:

*The* מוהל *(or honoree) continues:*

(פלוני בֶּן פלוני) זֶה הַקָּטָן גָּדוֹל יִהְיֶה, כְּשֵׁם שֶׁנִּכְנַס לַבְּרִית, כֵּן יִכָּנֵס לְתוֹרָה וּלְחֻפָּה וּלְמַעֲשִׂים טוֹבִים.

*The* סנדק *also drinks some of the wine; some drops are given to the baby. The cup is then sent to the mother, who also drinks from it.*

---

זֶה הַקָּטָן גָּדוֹל יִהְיֶה *May this child become great.* The literal translation of this phrase is, "May this little one become great." Our prayer, however, is not just in terms of his physical development, but also regarding spiritual growth. We find that the Torah (Gen. 1:16) uses these same adjectives about the creation of the heavenly bodies: the sun is referred to as the luminary that is *gadol,* great, while the moon is the luminary that is *katan,* small. The difference between the two is not just in the intensity of their glow. The sun is called

# Birkat HaMazon at a Brit Mila

*Leader* Gentlemen, let us say grace.

*Others* May the name of the Lord be blessed from now and for ever. *Ps. 113*

*Leader* May the name of the Lord be blessed from now and for ever.

*Leader then others* We give thanks to Your name among the faithful.
Blessed are you to the Lord.

*Leader* With permission of the Almighty, awesome and revered,
a refuge in times of trouble,
Almighty, girded with strength –
majestic on high, the Lord.

*Others* We give thanks to Your name among the faithful.
Blessed are you to the Lord.

*Leader* With permission of the holy Torah,
pure and clear,
given to us as a heritage
by Moses the servant of the Lord.

*Others* We give thanks to Your name among the faithful.
Blessed are you to the Lord.

*Leader* With permission of the priests, the Levites,
I call upon the God of the Hebrews,
declaring His glory to the furthest isles,
and offering blessings to the Lord.

*Others* We give thanks to Your name among the faithful.
Blessed are you to the Lord.

*Leader* With the permission of the rabbis, teachers and friends,
I open my lips with song,
saying from my innermost being:
"Blessed is he that comes in the name of the Lord."

*Others* We give thanks to Your name among the faithful.
Blessed are you to the Lord.

# ברכת המזון לברית מילה

*Leader* רַבּוֹתַי, נְבָרֵךְ.

*Others* יְהִי שֵׁם יהוה מְבֹרָךְ מֵעַתָּה וְעַד־עוֹלָם: תהלים קיג

*Leader* יְהִי שֵׁם יהוה מְבֹרָךְ מֵעַתָּה וְעַד־עוֹלָם:

*Leader then others* נוֹדֶה לְשִׁמְךָ בְּתוֹךְ אֱמוּנַי, בְּרוּכִים אַתֶּם לַיהוה.

*Leader* בִּרְשׁוּת אֵל אָיֹם וְנוֹרָא

מִשְׂגָּב לְעִתּוֹת בַּצָּרָה

אֵל נֶאְזָר בִּגְבוּרָה

אַדִּיר בַּמָּרוֹם יהוה.

*Others* נוֹדֶה לְשִׁמְךָ בְּתוֹךְ אֱמוּנַי, בְּרוּכִים אַתֶּם לַיהוה.

*Leader* בִּרְשׁוּת הַתּוֹרָה הַקְּדוֹשָׁה

טְהוֹרָה הִיא וְגַם פְּרוּשָׁה

צִוָּה לָנוּ מוֹרָשָׁה

מֹשֶׁה עֶבֶד יהוה.

*Others* נוֹדֶה לְשִׁמְךָ בְּתוֹךְ אֱמוּנַי, בְּרוּכִים אַתֶּם לַיהוה.

*Leader* בִּרְשׁוּת הַכֹּהֲנִים וְהַלְוִיִּם

אֶקְרָא לֵאלֹהֵי הָעִבְרִיִּים

אֲהוֹדֶנּוּ בְּכָל אִיִּים

אֲבָרְכָה אֶת יהוה.

*Others* נוֹדֶה לְשִׁמְךָ בְּתוֹךְ אֱמוּנַי, בְּרוּכִים אַתֶּם לַיהוה.

*Leader* בִּרְשׁוּת מָרָנָן וְרַבָּנָן וְרַבּוֹתַי

אֶפְתְּחָה בְּשִׁיר פִּי וּשְׂפָתַי

וְתֹאמַרְנָה עַצְמוֹתַי

בָּרוּךְ הַבָּא בְּשֵׁם יהוה.

*Others* נוֹדֶה לְשִׁמְךָ בְּתוֹךְ אֱמוּנַי, בְּרוּכִים אַתֶּם לַיהוה.

*Leader* With your permission, my masters and teachers,
let us bless (*in a minyan:* our God,) the One
from whose food we have eaten.

*Others* Blessed be (*in a minyan:* our God,) the One
from whose food we have eaten,
and by whose goodness we live.

*Leader* Blessed be (*in a minyan:* our God,) the One
from whose food we have eaten,
and by whose goodness we live.
Blessed be He, and blessed be His name.

*Continue with Birkat HaMazon on page 130 until "in the eyes of God and man" on page 152. Then continue:*

*Someone other than the father says:*

הָרַחֲמָן May the Compassionate One
bless the father and mother of this child.
May they be worthy to raise him,
educate him, and train him in wisdom.
From this eighth day onward may his blood be accepted,
and may the Lord his God be with him always.

*Someone other than the Sandak says:*

הָרַחֲמָן May the Compassionate One bless him [the Sandak]
who assisted in the covenant of circumcision
and rejoiced to do this pious deed.
May God doubly reward him for his deed,
exalting him ever higher.

---

literally and figuratively, are fundamentally the same concept. If a person does not anticipate and struggle, holiness cannot come into being.

This principle also underlies the difference between the current halakhic status of Mount Sinai and Mount Moriah. Even today, Jews are prohibited from walking on Mount Moriah upon which the Temple stood; no power in the world can neutralize the holiness of that place. Yet, there is no prohibition to climb Mount Sinai, upon which the Torah was given. The difference between the two is that the people of Israel did nothing to contribute to the

Leader בִּרְשׁוּת מָרָנָן וְרַבָּנָן וְרַבּוֹתַי
נְבָרֵךְ (במנין: אֱלֹהֵינוּ) שֶׁאָכַלְנוּ מִשֶּׁלּוֹ.

Others בָּרוּךְ (במנין: אֱלֹהֵינוּ) שֶׁאָכַלְנוּ מִשֶּׁלּוֹ וּבְטוּבוֹ חָיִינוּ.

Leader בָּרוּךְ (במנין: אֱלֹהֵינוּ) שֶׁאָכַלְנוּ מִשֶּׁלּוֹ וּבְטוּבוֹ חָיִינוּ.
בָּרוּךְ הוּא וּבָרוּךְ שְׁמוֹ.

*Continue with* ברכת המזון *on page 131 until* בְּעֵינֵי אֱלֹהִים וְאָדָם *on page 153. Then continue:*

*Someone other than the father says:*

הָרַחֲמָן הוּא יְבָרֵךְ אֲבִי הַיֶּלֶד וְאִמּוֹ
וְיִזְכּוּ לְגַדְּלוֹ וּלְחַנְּכוֹ וּלְחַכְּמוֹ
מִיּוֹם הַשְּׁמִינִי וָהָלְאָה יֵרָצֶה דָמוֹ
וִיהִי יהוה אֱלֹהָיו עִמּוֹ.

*Someone other than the* סנדק *says:*

הָרַחֲמָן הוּא יְבָרֵךְ בַּעַל בְּרִית הַמִּילָה
אֲשֶׁר שָׂשׂ לַעֲשׂוֹת צֶדֶק בְּגִילָה
וִישַׁלֵּם פָּעֳלוֹ וּמַשְׂכֻּרְתּוֹ כְּפוּלָה
וְיִתְּנֵהוּ לְמַעְלָה לְמָעְלָה.

---

ברכת המזון לברית מילה – BIRKAT HAMAZON

הָרַחֲמָן ... מִיּוֹם הַשְּׁמִינִי וָהָלְאָה יֵרָצֶה דָמוֹ *From this eighth day onward may his blood be accepted.* The Midrash relates a question the Roman governor Tineius Rufus asked Rabbi Akiva: "If God hates the uncircumcised, why does He create man in an uncircumcised state?" Rabbi Akiva rejoined: "Does the earth yield bread?" (*Tanḥuma, Tazria* 17). In his elliptical response, Rabbi Akiva conveyed that just as God desires that man bring forth bread through his own effort, likewise man can achieve sanctity only through his own endeavor. Rabbi Akiva's response was that sanctity in this world can be created only through initiative, self-sacrifice, pain, effort, and exertion. Without toil and suffering, there is no holiness. The prophet Ezekiel declared "Through your blood shall you live" (Ez. 16:6). Only through the blood of *mila*, the "blood" of personal sacrifice, can man live on a holy plane. Holiness and sacrifice, both

הָרַחֲמָן May the Compassionate One
bless the tender child, circumcised on his eighth day.
May his heart and hands be firm with God,
and may he be worthy to witness the Divine Presence
three times a year.

*Someone other than the Mohel says:*

הָרַחֲמָן May the Compassionate One
bless him who performed the circumcision,
and fulfilled every part of the precept.
The service of the faint-hearted would not be acceptable
if he failed to perform the three essentials of the precept.

הָרַחֲמָן May the Compassionate One
send us His anointed, blameless in life,
through the merit of this child
groomed by the blood of circumcision,
to proclaim good news and consolations
to the unique people scattered
and dispersed among the nations.

הָרַחֲמָן May the Compassionate One
send us the righteous priest, who was taken into hiding,
until a throne, bright as the sun, radiant as a diamond,
is prepared for him;
the prophet who covered his face with his mantle
and wrapped himself in it [when God declared]:
My covenant is with him for life and peace.

*Continue with "May the Compassionate One make us worthy of the Messianic Age" on page 154.*

*On Shabbat, Rosh Ḥodesh or Yom Tov, continue with the appropriate "May the Compassionate One" on page 152.*

---

the holiness that permeates the Temple Mount. It is precisely because the holiness of Mount Moriah is established upon the foundation of Abraham's dedication and self-sacrifice that its sanctity will last forever. (*Derashot HaRav*, pp. 171–173)

הָרַחֲמָן הוּא יְבָרֵךְ רַךְ הַנִּמּוֹל לִשְׁמוֹנָה
וְיִהְיוּ יָדָיו וְלִבּוֹ לָאֵל אֱמוּנָה
וְיִזְכֶּה לִרְאוֹת פְּנֵי הַשְּׁכִינָה
שָׁלֹשׁ פְּעָמִים בַּשָּׁנָה.

*Someone other than the* מוהל *says:*

הָרַחֲמָן הוּא יְבָרֵךְ הַמָּל בְּשַׂר הָעָרְלָה
וּפָרַע וּמָצַץ דְּמֵי הַמִּילָה
אִישׁ הַיָּרֵא וְרַךְ הַלֵּבָב עֲבוֹדָתוֹ פְּסוּלָה
אִם שְׁלָשׁ אֵלֶּה לֹא יַעֲשֶׂה לָהּ.

הָרַחֲמָן הוּא יִשְׁלַח לָנוּ מְשִׁיחוֹ הוֹלֵךְ תָּמִים
בִּזְכוּת חֲתַן לַמּוּלוֹת דָּמִים
לְבַשֵּׂר בְּשׂוֹרוֹת טוֹבוֹת וְנִחוּמִים
לְעַם אֶחָד מְפֻזָּר וּמְפֹרָד בֵּין הָעַמִּים.

הָרַחֲמָן הוּא יִשְׁלַח לָנוּ כֹּהֵן צֶדֶק אֲשֶׁר לֻקַּח לְעֵילֹם
עַד הוּכַן כִּסְאוֹ כַּשֶּׁמֶשׁ וְיַהֲלֹם
וַיָּלֶט פָּנָיו בְּאַדַּרְתּוֹ וַיִּגְלֹם
בְּרִיתִי הָיְתָה אִתּוֹ הַחַיִּים וְהַשָּׁלוֹם.

*Continue with* הָרַחֲמָן הוּא יְזַכֵּנוּ לִימוֹת הַמָּשִׁיחַ *on page 155.*
*On* שבת*,* ראש חודש *or* יום טוב*, continue with the appropriate* הָרַחֲמָן *on page 153.*

---

seminal event of the giving of the Torah; they didn't toil or sacrifice for it. As a result, despite being the site of the greatest divine revelation in human history, none of Mount Sinai's holiness endures. As soon as the revelation was over, the holiness of the mountain vanished as well. However, the history of Mount Moriah is different. Hundreds of years prior to God resting His presence there, our forefather Abraham prepared an altar on that mountain and placed his son Isaac upon it as a sacrifice. Abraham, with all of his anxiety and inner struggle, thus became a partner with God in the endowment of

# סדר פדיון הבן
# REDEMPTION OF THE FIRSTBORN

# Redemption Of The Firstborn

*A firstborn male child must be redeemed on the 31st day of his birth – unless the father is a Kohen or Levi, or the mother is a daughter of a Kohen or a Levi. If the 31st day falls on Shabbat or Yom Tov, the ceremony is postponed to the following weekday.*

*The father, presenting his child to the Kohen, declares:*

זֶה This is my firstborn son, the first issue of his mother's womb.
The Holy One, blessed be He, has commanded us to redeem him, as is said,

> "Those who are to be redeemed, you must redeem from the age of one month, at the fixed price of five shekels of silver by the sacred standard, which is twenty gerahs to the shekel." *Num. 18*

And it is also stated,

> "Consecrate to Me every firstborn; the first of every womb among the people of Israel, whether of man or beast, belongs to Me." *Ex. 13*

---

home life, the sense of irrevocable commitment and devotion that hovers over his intimate circle, realizes that perfect fellowship between and of finite individual beings is an impossibility, and that only in God can he find absolute friendship and understanding, a great offering is brought on the altar of the Creator. Only against this background we may understand the institution of consecration and redemption of the first-born son. Children are the greatest and most precious charge God has entrusted to man's custody without granting any property rights to him. Man, willy-nilly, must acknowledge this irrevocable though bitter truth; he must be ready to lose everything, if losing is what God demands. He must always answer the call summoning him to perform heroically the movement of withdrawal from the most tightly knit and natural community on earth – that of father and son. The ceremony of redemption of the first born son re-enacts the drama of Abraham offering Isaac to the Lord. The presentation of the child to the *Kohen* is symbolic of Abraham's performance when he bound Isaac and placed him on the altar. The father of today, as Abraham of old, acknowledges the absolute ownership of the child by God. He renounces all his illusory rights and urgent claims to this child; he makes the movement of withdrawal from the most important position in man's life – his relatedness to posterity. God wills the consecration of the first-born son because the emotional involvement of the parent

# סדר פדיון הבן

*A firstborn male child must be redeemed on the 31st day of his birth – unless the father is a כהן or לוי, or the mother is a daughter of a כהן or a לוי. If the 31st day falls on שבת or יום טוב, the ceremony is postponed to the following weekday.*

*The father, presenting his child to the כהן, declares:*

**זֶה בְּנִי בְכוֹרִי הוּא פֶּטֶר רֶחֶם לְאִמּוֹ**
**וְהַקָּדוֹשׁ בָּרוּךְ הוּא צִוָּה לִפְדּוֹתוֹ**
**שֶׁנֶּאֱמַר**
**וּפְדוּיָו מִבֶּן־חֹדֶשׁ תִּפְדֶּה, בְּעֶרְכְּךָ כֶּסֶף חֲמֵשֶׁת שְׁקָלִים** במדבר יח
**בְּשֶׁקֶל הַקֹּדֶשׁ, עֶשְׂרִים גֵּרָה הוּא:**
**וְנֶאֱמַר**
**קַדֶּשׁ־לִי כָל־בְּכוֹר פֶּטֶר כָּל־רֶחֶם בִּבְנֵי יִשְׂרָאֵל בָּאָדָם** שמות יג
**וּבַבְּהֵמָה, לִי הוּא:**

---

סדר פדיון הבן – REDEMPTION OF THE FIRSTBORN

The status of man in the world is that of a guardian in whose care the works of God have been placed as a precious charge. He governs the world on behalf of his master, representing Him. Yet he must not try to usurp privileges and prerogatives which are not his. Whatever man earns and enjoys, to whatever he holds fast, it is not his but God's. God's rights of ownership transcend the bound of the world of physical goods and extend into the human existential realm as well. Man does not own himself. He, as a human being consisting of body, mind and soul, belongs to God. Everything was created by God, for God, and everything is dedicated to God. Since there is nothing within the reach of man which he does not have in trust for and from God, there is nothing whose return to God would not be considered a hallowed sacrificial service. Judaism fought relentlessly against the heathen curse of human sacrifice. The primitive brutal cult of perpetuating murder and of extinguishing the physical existence of man as an object in honor of God is pagan and abominable. Yet the offering of the spiritual personality of the human metaphysical existence to God is a great heroic act, in which Judaism believes man finds his unique charismatic fulfillment.

When the husband and father who is passionately in love with his wife and children, enjoying the community awareness of the family, the serenity of a

*The Kohen checks with the mother that this is her firstborn, and then asks if she has miscarried before this child. If her answer is no, he asks the father:*

מַאי Which do you prefer:
to give me your firstborn son, the first birth of his mother,
or to redeem him for five selas
as you are bound to do according to the Torah?

*The father replies:*

חָפֵץ I wish to redeem my son.
I present you with the cost of his redemption
which I am bound to give according to the Torah.

*Holding the redemption money, the father says:*

בָּרוּךְ Blessed are You, LORD our God, King of the Universe,
who has made us holy through His commandments,
and has commanded us concerning the redemption of a son.

בָּרוּךְ Blessed are You, LORD our God, King of the Universe,
who has given us life, sustained us, and brought us to this time.

*The redemption money is given to the Kohen, who then returns the child to his father. The Kohen takes a cup of wine and says:*

בָּרוּךְ Blessed are You, LORD our God, King of the Universe,
who creates the fruit of the vine.

*Placing his right hand on the head of the child, the Kohen blesses him as follows:*

יְשִׂמְךָ May God make you like Ephraim and Manasseh. May the LORD *Gen. 48* *Num. 6*
bless you and protect you. May the LORD make His face shine on
you and be gracious to you. May the LORD turn His face toward you
and grant you peace. The LORD is your Guardian; the LORD is your *Ps. 121*
protection at your right hand. The LORD will guard you against all
harm. He will guard your life. For length of days, years of life, and *Prov. 3*
peace He will increase for you.

---

receiving the child from the *Kohen*, the father must always remain aware that it was only through God's infinite grace that this infant was returned to him in sacred trust. (*Community, Covenant and Commitment*, pp. 296–302)

*The* כהן *checks with the mother that this is her firstborn, and then asks if she has miscarried before this child. If her answer is no, he asks the father:*

מַאי בָּעֵית טְפֵי
לִתֵּן לִי בִּנְךָ בְּכוֹרְךָ שֶׁהוּא פֶּטֶר רֶחֶם לְאִמּוֹ
אוֹ בָּעֵית לִפְדּוֹתוֹ בְּעַד חָמֵשׁ סְלָעִים, כְּדִמְחֻיַּבְתְּ מִדְּאוֹרַיְתָא.

*The father replies:*

חָפֵץ אֲנִי לִפְדּוֹת אֶת בְּנִי
וְהֵילָךְ דְּמֵי פִדְיוֹנוֹ כְּדִמְחֻיַּבְנָא מִדְּאוֹרַיְתָא.

*Holding the redemption money, the father says:*

בָּרוּךְ אַתָּה יהוה אֱלֹהֵינוּ מֶלֶךְ הָעוֹלָם
אֲשֶׁר קִדְּשָׁנוּ בְּמִצְוֹתָיו וְצִוָּנוּ עַל פִּדְיוֹן הַבֵּן.

בָּרוּךְ אַתָּה יהוה אֱלֹהֵינוּ מֶלֶךְ הָעוֹלָם
שֶׁהֶחֱיָנוּ וְקִיְּמָנוּ וְהִגִּיעָנוּ לַזְּמַן הַזֶּה.

*The redemption money is given to the* כהן*, who then returns the child to his father. The* כהן *takes a cup of wine and says:*

בָּרוּךְ אַתָּה יהוה אֱלֹהֵינוּ מֶלֶךְ הָעוֹלָם, בּוֹרֵא פְּרִי הַגָּפֶן.

*Placing his right hand on the head of the child, the* כהן *blesses him as follows:*

יְשִׂמְךָ אֱלֹהִים כְּאֶפְרַיִם וְכִמְנַשֶּׁה: יְבָרֶכְךָ יהוה וְיִשְׁמְרֶךָ: יָאֵר בראשית מח / במדבר ו
יהוה פָּנָיו אֵלֶיךָ וִיחֻנֶּךָּ: יִשָּׂא יהוה פָּנָיו אֵלֶיךָ וְיָשֵׂם לְךָ שָׁלוֹם:
יהוה שֹׁמְרֶךָ, יהוה צִלְּךָ עַל־יַד יְמִינֶךָ: יהוה יִשְׁמָרְךָ מִכָּל־רָע, תהלים קכא
יִשְׁמֹר אֶת־נַפְשֶׁךָ: כִּי אֹרֶךְ יָמִים וּשְׁנוֹת חַיִּים וְשָׁלוֹם יוֹסִיפוּ לָךְ: משלי ג

---

with his first born is of the most intricate and intimate nature. The closer the relation and the more deep-rooted the commitment of the father to the child, the more sublime and hallowed is the sacrifice. When the *Kohen* returns the child to the father and accepts the five shekels, he presents him on behalf of God with a new child; something precious is re-entrusted to him. After

# הנהגות הרב

# HANHAGOT HARAV

# Hanhagot HaRav

▸ CANDLE LIGHTING

1 The Rav recounted that in the communities where he grew up, the practice was to accept Shabbat and light candles thirty minutes before sunset. [See *Tosafot* and *Tosafot Rabbenu Peretz, Beitza* 30a; *Nefesh HaRav*, p. 154]

2 The Rav maintained that all of the women of a household, including unmarried daughters, should light Shabbat candles with a blessing on *Erev Shabbat*. [*MiPeninei HaRav*, p. 75]

3 The Vilna Gaon (*Biur HaGra, Oraḥ Ḥayyim* 529:5) defines the *mitzva* of *kavod* for Shabbat and Yom Tov as acts of preparation done in honor of the day before it commences. Therefore, the Rav explained that even though Yom Tov candles may be lit after the onset of Yom Tov, it is more appropriate to light them before sunset in order to optimally fulfill the *mitzva* of *kevod Yom Tov*, to honor the day by preparing for it before its arrival. [See *Shu"t Peri Yitzḥak* 1:6; *Divrei HaRav*, p. 173]

4 The Rav cited the ruling of his father, Rav Moshe Soloveitchik, that one may fulfill the *mitzva* of Shabbat candles by turning on an electric incandescent light bulb, and that a blessing should be recited on this as well. [*Nefesh HaRav*, p. 155]

5 The Rav maintained that before one lights Shabbat candles, he should first turn off all of the electric lights in the room, then light the Shabbat candles and turn the electric lights back on in honor of Shabbat, and finally recite the blessing over all of the sources of light in the room. [*Nefesh HaRav*, p. 156]

▸ SHALOM ALEIKHEM

6 In accordance with the practice of Rav Ḥayyim Volozhiner, the Rav omitted the stanza "*barekhuni leshalom*" in *Shalom Aleikhem*. One of the fundamental principles of faith is that everyone can communicate directly with God; we do not need to beseech angels as intermediaries to bless us. (See *Keter Rosh*, no. 93.) The Rav also did not recite the stanza "*tzeitkhem leshalom*" (see *Siddur Ya'avetz*). [Rabbi Menachem Genack]

◂ 7 When singing

7 When singing *Shalom Aleikhem*, the Rav, following the version of the text in the siddur of Rabbi Yaakov Emden, would recite "מַלְאֲכֵי עֶלְיוֹן, מֶלֶךְ מַלְכֵי הַמְּלָכִים" (מֶלֶךְ instead of מִמֶּלֶךְ). The phrase thus means, "the angels of the exalted One, the King, King of all kings." [*Divrei HaRav*, p. 168]

▸ KIDDUSH

8 The Rav would stand when reciting the introductory verses and then sit for the *berakha* of Kiddush. [*Nefesh HaRav*, p. 159; *Eretz HaTzvi*, p. 14; *Davening with the Rav*, p. 118]

9 In order to avoid the prohibition of reciting half of a verse, the Rav would say the entire verse of "וַיַּרְא אֱלֹהִים אֶת־כָּל־אֲשֶׁר עָשָׂה וְהִנֵּה־טוֹב מְאֹד וַיְהִי־עֶרֶב וַיְהִי־בֹקֶר יוֹם הַשִּׁשִּׁי" before Kiddush. He would recite the first half of the verse quietly and then begin aloud with the phrase "וַיְהִי־עֶרֶב." [*Nefesh HaRav*, p. 159]

10 The Rav explained that the common practice to eat *mezonot* after Kiddush, in order to fulfill the requirement of *Kiddush bimekom se'uda*, is based on a combination of halakhic opinions: Perhaps the *halakha* follows the opinion of the Geonim that *mezonot* is sufficient, and even according to the Vilna Gaon that bread is necessary, we can rely on the opinion of Ra'avad that the requirement of *Kiddush bimekom se'uda* only applies on Shabbat eve and not to the Kiddush of Shabbat day. Accordingly, the Rav held that a person should not make Kiddush on Shabbat eve over *mezonot*; this is opposed to the opinion of the *Magen Avraham* (274:2) who equates the Kiddush of Shabbat eve and Shabbat day. Similarly, even if a person earlier recited Kiddush and ate *mezonot*, he should recite Kiddush again before his meal in order to fulfill the opinion of the Vilna Gaon. [*Nefesh HaRav*, p. 165; *Eretz HaTzvi*, p. 47]

11 The Rav was personally stringent to follow the opinion of Maimonides (*Hilkhot Shabbat* 29:14) who maintained that wine which had sugar added to it or had been cooked is invalid for Kiddush. [See *Shulḥan Arukh Oraḥ Ḥayyim* 271:8 and commentaries; *Nefesh HaRav*, p. 184]

12 On Shabbat day, the custom of Rav Ḥayyim Soloveitchik was to fulfill Kiddush by saying only the blessing of *borei peri hagafen* without the introductory verses commonly recited beforehand. However, the Rav would recite these verses, in accordance with the practice of his maternal grandfather, Rav Eliyahu Pruzhaner. The Rav would first recite the paragraph of *zakhor* and then the paragraph of *veshamru*, in the order that these sections appear in the Torah. [*MiPeninei HaRav*, p. 87; *Davening with the Rav*, p. 118]

13 The Rav maintained that it is more appropriate for one person to recite

◂ Kiddush for all

Kiddush for all of the participants at a meal than it is for each person to recite Kiddush on his own. While we generally prefer that each person perform his own *mitzva,* here, when everyone listens together as a group to one Kiddush, there is a fulfillment of *berov am hadrat melekh,* honoring God as a multitude, which outweighs the other considerations. [*Divrei HaRav,* p. 168]

14 The Rav did not recite Kiddush in the synagogue on Shabbat eve. In Talmudic times, Kiddush was recited in the synagogue on behalf of the guests who ate their meal there (see *Pesaḥim* 100a). Nowadays, however, meals are not generally served in the synagogue, and to recite Kiddush without an accompanying meal would violate the rule that Kiddush must be recited in the place where one eats his meal. [See *Shulḥan Arukh Oraḥ Ḥayyim* 269:1 with commentaries for further discussion; Notes of R. Isaiah Wohlegemuth]

15 On the second night of Sukkot, the Rav would recite the blessing in the same order as on the first night, namely the blessing of *leisheiv basukka* before the blessing of *sheheḥeyanu,* and would not reverse their order. [*Nefesh HaRav,* p. 219]

### ▸ THE SHABBAT MEALS

16 The Rav did not follow the practice of dipping his challah into salt. [*Divrei HaRav,* p. 169; *Rabbi Menachem Genack*]

17 While every person must eat bread at the Shabbat meals, the Rav maintained that it is not necessary for each person to have a piece of the *leḥem mishneh,* the two whole loaves required at each meal. As long as the person who recites the blessing of *hamotzi* for the other participants eats from the *leḥem mishneh,* all the participants fulfill this requirement. [*Harerei Kedem,* vol. 2, pp. 144–145]

18 The Rav maintained that no food should be placed on the table before the recitation of Kiddush, both at the meal of Shabbat eve as well as at the meal of Shabbat day. Ideally, even the challah should not be brought to the table before Kiddush. If any food was already brought to the table it should be covered just like the bread. [*Nefesh HaRav,* p. 158; *MiPeninei HaRav,* p. 84]

19 The Rav recounted that his father was stringent to not say God's name when singing *zemirot,* but rather to say "Hashem." [See Rama *Oraḥ Ḥayyim* 188:7 and *Biur Halakha* s.v. *ve'ein*; *Nefesh HaRav,* p. 160]

20 While the common custom in Volozhin was not to sing *zemirot,* Rav Ḥayyim Soloveitchik's personal practice was to sing at his Shabbat meals. However,

the Rav, like his father, Rav Moshe Soloveitchik, did not sing *zemirot*. [*MiPeninei HaRav*, p. 79; *Nefesh HaRav*, p. 160]

▸ *BIRKAT HAMAZON*

21 When leading the *zimmun* at a *Sheva Berakhot*, the Rav added the phrase "*birshut hehatan ve'hakallah*, with the permission of the bride and groom." [*Sheva Berakhot*, 1974]

22 The Rav recounted that the common practice in Lithuania was that when a minyan would recite *Birkat HaMazon* together, the participants would not stand when they said the name of God in the *zimmun*. [*Nefesh HaRav*, p. 148]

23 In the third *berakha* of *Birkat HaMazon*, the Rav would say "כִּי אִם לְיָדְךָ הַמְּלֵאָה, הַפְּתוּחָה, הַגְּדוּשָׁה וְהָרְחָבָה, only on Your full, open, *overflowing* and generous hand" instead of "הַקְּדוֹשָׁה, holy." This was also the text used by the Ba'al Shem Tov. [*Nefesh HaRav*, p. 148]

24 In the concluding line of *Ya'aleh VeYavo*, the Rav would omit the word "מֶלֶךְ," saying only "כִּי אֵל חַנּוּן וְרַחוּם אָתָּה." However, on Rosh HaShana the Rav would include the word "מֶלֶךְ." [See Rama, *Orah Hayyim* 188:3 and *Mateh Ephraim*; *Nefesh HaRav*, p. 209.]

25 When reciting *Ya'aleh VeYavo* on a holiday coinciding with Shabbat, the Rav would insert a reference to Shabbat prior to the reference to the particular holiday. For example, he would say "לְחַיִּים וּלְשָׁלוֹם בְּיוֹם הַשַּׁבָּת הַזֶּה וּבְיוֹם רֹאשׁ הַחֹדֶשׁ הַזֶּה." This practice accords with what is implied by the *Shulhan Arukh* (*Orah Hayyim* 487:1) and by the Rama (*ibid.* 487:3), and is indeed found in many Sephardic texts. [*Nefesh HaRav*, p. 183]

26 In the conclusion of the third blessing, the Rav followed the preferred text of the Vilna Gaon and would recite "בּוֹנֵה יְרוּשָׁלָיִם, אָמֵן" without including the word "בְּרַחֲמָיו" (see *Ma'aseh Rav* no. 87). The Rav would explain (see *Beit Yosef Orah Hayyim* 188 in the name of *Kol Bo* and *Orhot Hayyim*) that Jerusalem will be redeemed not by God's mercy but through the fulfillment of justice, as it is written, "Zion will be redeemed through justice" (Is. 1:27). [*Nefesh HaRav*, p. 148]

27 In the fourth blessing, the Rav would say, "הוּא הֵיטִיב לָנוּ, הוּא מֵיטִיב לָנוּ, הוּא יֵיטִיב לָנוּ" including the word "לָנוּ" three times. [See *Shulhan Arukh, Orah Hayyim* 189, and commentaries there; *Nefesh HaRav*, p. 148]

28 The Rav would end his recitation of *Birkat HaMazon* at the words "וּמִכָּל טוּב לְעוֹלָם אַל יְחַסְּרֵנוּ," prior to "הָרַחֲמָן." When eating as a guest in someone else's home, he would recite the הָרַחֲמָן for the בַּעַל הַבַּיִת (and not the prayer "יְהִי רָצוֹן

שֶׁלֹּא יֵבוֹשׁ בַּעַל הַבַּיִת"). It is worth noting that the Rav expressed uncertainty as to whether some of the הָרַחֲמָן prayers may actually be part of the concluding blessing (see Maimonides' *Seder HaTefilla* which includes some of the הָרַחֲמָן prayers at the conclusion of *Birkat HaMazon*). [*Rabbi Menachem Genack*]

29 The Rav maintained that the person who leads the *zimmun* must recite the entire *Birkat HaMazon* aloud so that everyone can hear him. [*Nefesh HaRav*, p. 148; *Eretz HaTzvi*, p. 47; *Shiurim LeZekher Abba Mari*, vol. 2, pp. 98–99]

30 The Rav inferred from Maimonides (*Hilkhot Berakhot* 5:3) that it is not sufficient for the participants at a meal to merely listen to the leader recite the *Birkat HaMazon*. As opposed to other *Berakhot* where it suffices to listen with intent to fulfill the obligation, in order for the group to fulfill the *mitzva* of *zimmun* they must respond *amen* to each blessing. [*Nefesh HaRav*, p. 148; *Eretz HaTzvi* p. 49; *Shiurim LeZekher Abba Mari*, vol. 2, pp. 105–106]

31 The Rav was stringent to recite *Birkat HaMazon* in the same place that he ate the meal and not in another location even within the same room. [See *Sha'ar HaTziyon* 184:3; *Divrei HaRav*, p. 162]

32 The Rav maintained that the cup of wine that was used for *Birkat HaMazon* of *Se'uda Shelishit* that concluded after nightfall should not be used for Havdala; rather, the leader of the *zimmun* should drink that wine after Havdala, which should be recited over a different cup. [*Sheva Berakhot*, 1974]

▸ *BERAKHOT*

33 Based on historical evidence, some have questioned the identification of rye and oats as being two of the five grains for which one says *al hamiḥya*. However, the Rav rejected this opinion and stressed that the *halakha* is determined by the *mesorah* alone. [*MiPeninei HaRav*, p. 69]

34 The Rav maintained that the proper *berakha* for grape juice is *borei peri hagafen*. [*MiPeninei HaRav*, p. 70]

35 Rav Ḥayyim Soloveitchik would not say the blessing of *borei peri ha'etz* on grapes that grew without seeds. [*MiPeninei HaRav*, p. 69]

36 When many people eat *mezonot* together, the Rav maintained that it is not proper for one person to say *al hamiḥya* aloud and for everyone to listen. Rather, each person should say the blessing himself. [*MiPeninei HaRav*, p. 70]

37 The Talmud (*Pesaḥim* 115a) records that a person must wash his hands before eating a food that is wet with water or other liquids. However, there is a

◂ dispute

dispute whether or not this law applies nowadays when we no longer abide by many of the laws of ritual purity. The *Shulḥan Arukh* (*Oraḥ Ḥayyim* 158:4) rules that a person must wash his hands, but should not recite a blessing, and *Magen Avraham* records that many have the custom not to wash at all. The Vilna Gaon, though, maintained that this law is still in full force, and a person must wash and recite the blessing of *al netilat yadayim* before eating a wet food. This was also the common practice in Brisk and the practice of the Rav as well. [*Halakhic Positions,* vol. I, p. 170]

### ▸ HAVDALA

38 The Rav followed the practice of the Vilna Gaon to stand while reciting Havdala. [*Nefesh HaRav,* p. 159; *Eretz HaTzvi,* p. 14]

39 If a person doesn't have wine, he may recite Havdala over *ḥamar medina,* a beverage that is commonly served in that locale. (See *Shulḥan Arukh Oraḥ Ḥayyim* 296:2 and commentaries, and 272:9 regarding Kiddush.) While many assume that coffee or tea would be included in this category, the Rav followed the opinion of Rav Ḥayyim Volozhiner that only alcoholic beverages can be considered *ḥamar medina.* [*MiPeninei HaRav,* p. 87]

### ▸ *SE'UDAT MITZVA* AND *SHEVA BERAKHOT*

40 The Talmud (*Pesaḥim* 113b) records that a person who is able to participate must join the celebration of a *se'udat mitzva,* and if he abstains from the *mitzva* celebration he receives heavenly excommunication. Based on this, the Rav ruled that if a person, due to time constraints, can only attend either the *brit* itself or the meal that follows it, he should attend the celebratory meal. Similarly, the Rav maintained that the primary fulfillment of rejoicing with a bride and groom is at the meal and *Sheva Berakhot* that follow the wedding. Therefore, it is more important to be present at that part of the celebration than at the actual wedding ceremony. [*Halakhic Positions,* vol. IV, p. 162]

41 The Rav maintained that a person may recite one of the blessings of the *Sheva Berakhot* even if he didn't eat anything at the meal. [*Nefesh HaRav,* p. 257]

# רשימות

## RESHIMOT

### THE NATURE OF *BIRKAT HANEHENIN*

There are two different ways to conceptualize the obligation to recite a blessing before eating food. One approach is to view the obligation as fundamentally a *mitzva*, a positive obligation. Alternatively, we could view the blessing as a *matir*, an act that removes the preexisting prohibited status of the food. To illustrate the difference between the two approaches, consider the following question: if one eats without first pronouncing a blessing, has he merely failed to fulfill his obligation to praise God, or has he violated a prohibition and indeed eaten forbidden food?

The Talmud, after rejecting a number of proposals, concludes simply that the source for *birkat hanehenin* is a *sevara*, a supposition based on reason: "it is forbidden to a man to enjoy anything of this world without saying a blessing" (*Berakhot* 35a). This conclusion implies that without the prior recitation of a blessing, all food is prohibited. The blessing is not merely a *mitzva*, but it is the *matir* that removes the preexisting prohibition. This is also clear from the Jerusalem Talmud (*Berakhot* 6:1) which states: "The entire world is like a [holy] vineyard. What is its redemption? A blessing." The world is forbidden until one recites a blessing which is its redemption.

At the same time, the Talmud (*Berakhot* 17b) teaches that a person who is an *onen*, one whose immediate relative has passed away and has yet to be buried, is exempt from reciting blessings. Rashi writes explicitly that the *onen* does not need to say *hamotzi* before he eats. As a general rule, an *onen* is only exempt from fulfilling positive *mitzvot*, but is not permitted to violate any prohibitions. This then would imply that reciting blessings before eating is primarily a *mitzva* and not a *matir*.

To reconcile these sources we must conclude that the prohibition of eating before the recitation of a blessing is not an independent one, but rather flows from the obligation to praise God for the food. Because there is an obligation to praise God, one cannot benefit from the world without discharging this obligation, and thus it is forbidden to eat before reciting a *berakha*. However, in the case of an *onen*, since he is exempt from the obligation to praise God, there exists no resulting prohibition and he may eat without any blessing. (*Shiurei HaRav*, pp. 291–292; *Reshimot Shiurim, Berakhot*, pp. 242–243, 400)

### *BIRKAT HANEHENIN* AND *SHOMEI'A KE'ONEH*

The Mishna (*Berakhot* 42a) states that if several people eat together, each person should recite his own blessing before eating. But if they recline together, thus forming a group, one person should recite the blessing for everyone present.

This *halakha* and the surrounding discussion seem to contradict the principle of "*shomei'a ke'oneh*," which tells us that when one person listens to another's recitation it is as if he himself has uttered those words. In applying *shomei'a ke'oneh*, we do not require that the two parties recline or sit together. The Mishna (*Rosh HaShana* 27b) in fact states that if a person is even walking behind a synagogue and hears the blasts of the shofar or the reading of the *Megilla*, he may listen and fulfill his obligation. No further connection to the group is required; merely hearing the sound of the shofar suffices.

We can only understand the law that requires the group to recline together in order for one member to make blessings for the others if we realize that in this *halakha*, "*shomei'a ke'oneh*" is not the operative principle. Indeed, Rabbeinu Nissim (on R. Alfasi, *Rosh HaShana* 11b s.v. *yaḥid*) cites the Talmud Yerushalmi which says that regarding *keriat shema*, *tefilla*, and *birkat hanehenin*, the rule of *shomei'a ke'oneh* does not apply. With regard to these *mitzvot*, the Rabbis maintained that individuals must recite the blessings on their own, and cannot fulfill their obligation by merely listening to another person's recitation. However, when a group of people eat together they form a *ḥabura*, an integrated group, and *halakha* allows one person to recite a blessing on behalf of the entire collective. The concept of the *ḥabura*, though, differs from the mechanism of *shomei'a ke'oneh*. In applications of *shomei'a ke'oneh*, each individual is obligated in his own private recitation, and by listening intently to another he has fulfilled his individual obligation; the concept of a *ḥabura* means that each individual is not obligated in his own recitation. Instead, as in the case of *zimmun*

◀ (see "The

(see "The *Zimmun*: Eating Together, Blessing God as a Community," p. 17), the *ḥabura* as a whole must pronounce a blessing over their shared eating, and this is accomplished by one representative's recitation of the blessing.

We must note, though, a discrepancy between the blessings before eating and *Birkat HaMazon* after eating. While the *halakha* requires a minimum of three people to form a *ḥabura* for the purpose of *zimmun,* two people suffice for the *ḥabura* necessary for a joint *birkat hamotzi* or other *birkat hanehenin*. We may explain this difference based on the comment of *Tosafot* (*Ḥullin* 106a) that before people begin to eat, there is greater cohesion between them as they are about to share their meal, and thus two people suffice to create a *ḥabura*. However, after a meal has concluded, the participants are readying themselves to leave and go on in their separate directions, and, thus, a larger group of three is necessary to create a communal *ḥabura*. (*Shiurim LeZekher Abba Mari,* vol. 2, p. 102; *Reshimot Shiurim, Berakhot,* pp. 463–465)

### THE PURPOSE OF *NETILAT YADAYIM*

If a person doesn't have water to wash his hands before prayer, the Tamud (*Berakhot* 15a) rules that he may rub his hands on a stone or use any other substance to clean them. While the Talmud states this dispensation regarding prayer, it is unclear if it would apply to the washing required before one eats bread. In fact, it would seem to depend on a fundamental dispute between Maimonides and Ra'avad regarding the reason for *netilat yadayim* before eating bread. Maimonides (*Hilkhot Avot HaTum'ah* 8:8) writes: "King Solomon and his court decreed that a person's hands automatically have a secondary level of ritual impurity... but King Solomon did not make this decree regarding *teruma,* only regarding holy objects [*kodesh*], and a later court extended this decree to *teruma*." Here, Ra'avad adds that "they later decreed that ordinary food [*ḥullin*] also requires *netilat yadayim*." Thus, according to Ra'avad, the obligation to wash one's hands before eating bread is to make them ritually pure (*tahor*) based on the enactment of washing before eating *teruma*. Maimonides, on the other hand, classifies the obligation to wash before ordinary bread not together with the obligation to wash before *teruma,* but together

◂ with the

with the obligation to wash before prayer and *keriat shema*. He writes, "Anyone who washes his hands before eating, before *keriat shema*, or before prayer recites a blessing... for this is a *mitzva* of the Sages whom the Torah commanded us to follow" (*Hilkhot Berakhot* 6:2). Thus, according to Maimonides, washing before food is a Rabbinic enactment whose purpose is cleanliness, comparable to the obligation to wash before prayer. It should follow that Maimonides would allow a person to clean his hands with other materials when water is not available, as the primary purpose of *netilat yadayim* is physical cleanliness. However, according to Ra'avad, the obligation is for the person to ritually purify his hands as he would before consuming *teruma*, and thus a vessel and water would be absolutely necessary.

Moreover, according to Ra'avad, just as a person who eats *teruma* while ritually impure violates a prohibition, one who eats bread without washing his hands also violates a prohibition, in addition to not fulfilling the positive *mitzva*. According to Maimonides, however, the enactment of *netilat yadayim* may only be a positive *mitzva*, without an accompanying prohibition to eat without first washing one's hands. The practical difference between these two possibilities is the case of an *onen*, someone whose immediate relative has died but has not yet been buried, who is exempt from *mitzvot*: If *netilat yadayim* is merely a positive *mitzva*, then the *onen* would be exempt, as he is from all *mitzvot*, but if there is a prohibition to eat without washing, then the *onen* would be required to wash his hands, for he is not permitted to violate any prohibition. Rabbi Akiva Eiger (glosses to *Shulḥan Arukh, Yoreh De'ah* 341) rules that an *onen* must wash his hands, but others disagree (see *Pitḥei Teshuva, ibid.*).

Finally, the *Shulḥan Arukh* (*Oraḥ Ḥayyim* 163:1) rules that if a person is traveling and doesn't have water, and none will be soon available, he may wrap his hands in a handkerchief and eat bread, but he should not recite a blessing over this procedure. We may explain this ruling as follows: *Netilat yadayim* includes both a prohibition to eat without washing one's hands, as well as a positive *mitzva*. If a person doesn't have water he cannot fulfill the positive Rabbinic *mitzva* and thus doesn't recite the blessing, but he is still obligated to wrap his hands so as not to violate the Rabbinic prohibition of eating bread with unwashed hands. (*Reshimot Shiurim, Berakhot*, pp. 202–203)

◂ THE STATUS

## THE STATUS OF *HATOV VEHAMEITIV* IN *BIRKAT HAMAZON*

The Talmud (*Berakhot* 46a) quotes two different opinions about whether *HaTov VehaMeitiv*, the fourth and final blessing of *Birkat HaMazon*, is a *de'oraita* (Biblical) or *derabbanan* (Rabbinic) obligation. While the Talmud concludes that it is only Rabbinic, the entire discussion is quite perplexing because the Talmud explicitly recounts (*Berakhot* 48b) that the Sages of the court of Yavneh enacted the blessing in commemoration of the miracle of Betar. Consequently, how could the Talmud even entertain the possibility that the fourth blessing is a *de'oraita* obligation? In addition, the Talmud's question implies that, while there is a dispute regarding the fourth blessing, all would agree that the first three blessings are indeed *de'oraita*. This would seem to contradict the opinion of Maimonides that one fulfills the *de'oraita* requirement with the first blessing alone. (See the essay "*Birkat HaMazon*: To Bless the Great and Holy Name," p. 7, regarding Maimonides' opinion.)

To resolve the foregoing questions, we must explain that the Talmud never meant to suggest the possibility of a *de'oraita* obligation to recite the fourth blessing; the question instead revolves around how to conceptualize the Rabbinic obligation to recite the fourth blessing. Prior to the Rabbis establishing a set text for *Birkat HaMazon*, a person could fulfill his *de'oraita* obligation with a succinct blessing, or he could offer an elaborate, extended blessing. Although a lengthy blessing was not required, whatever he recited would be part of his fulfillment of the *de'oraita* obligation. Here as well, in a similar vein, the Talmud means to ask whether the Sages of Yavneh established their new blessing as an elaboration and extension of *Birkat HaMazon*, which is incorporated into the *de'oraita* fulfillment, or whether they instituted the last blessing as a Rabbinic addendum that we recite after we conclude the *de'oraita* fulfillment of *Birkat HaMazon*.

Thus, according to Maimonides, even though the second, third, and fourth blessings are all Rabbinic requirements, there is still a fundamental difference between the fourth blessing and those that precede it. Although the second and third blessings are not *de'oraita* obligations, the Sages instituted them as an extended fulfillment of the *de'oraita* obligation. However, when the Sages instituted the fourth blessing, they defined it not as a further fulfillment of the *de'oraita* obligation, but as an independent blessing.

This is the meaning of what Maimonides writes in *Hilkhot Berakhot* (1:16–17): "Anyone who recites *amen* after his own blessing should be denigrated, but someone who recites *amen* after a concluding blessing, for example, after the blessing of *Boneh Yerushalayim,* is praised … And why should one recite *amen* after *Boneh Yerushalayim,* which is followed by the blessing of *HaTov VehaMeitiv*? It is because [*HaTov VehaMeitiv*] was established by the Sages of the Mishna, and is a kind of addendum, but the end of the essential blessings of *Birkat HaMazon* is *Boneh Yerushalayim.*" In other words, the Sages enacted the fourth blessing not as a further expansion of *Birkat HaMazon,* but as a separate addition. This is also why there are different views about whether one must include a reference to *HaTov VehaMeitiv* when reciting the *berakha me'ein shalosh.* Since *HaTov VehaMeitiv* is not an integral part of *Birkat HaMazon,* as are the first three blessings, perhaps it is not included in the condensed version.

Finally, Maimonides writes (*Hilkhot Berakhot* 2:12) that if one forgets to insert the additions for Shabbat and Yom Tov in *Birkat HaMazon,* and he has already begun the fourth blessing, he must repeat the entire *Birkat HaMazon.* Ra'avad disagrees with this ruling based on the *halakha* that a person who forgets a special insertion in the Amida can return to the appropriate point and recite the special insertions even if he has completed the entire Amida, as long as he is still reciting private supplications at the end of his prayer. Regarding *Birkat HaMazon* as well, Ra'avad argues, one may return to the appropriate point and need not return to the beginning. Ra'avad's position is that the permament text of *HaTov VehaMeitiv,* established by the Sages, is no less significant than private suplications, and as such, one should be able to return to the place of the insertion and not have to repeat the entire *Birkat HaMazon.* However, we may explain Maimonides' view as follows: when a person prays, he is halakhically considered to be standing before God, *omed lifnei Hashem,* and as such, even though his additional private suplications are not part of the Amida, they are nevertheless part of his prayer recited "*lifnei Hashem.*" This connects the private suplications to the Amida and allows the person to return to the place of the insertion. However, with regard to *Birkat HaMazon,* the

◂ concept of

concept of *lifnei Hashem,* standing in the presence of God, does not apply and therefore the blessing of *HaTov VehaMeitiv,* defined as an addendum, is not connected to the first three blessings of *Birkat HaMazon.* Hence, Maimonides rules that when a person begins the fourth blessing and forgot a special insertion, he must repeat the entire *Birkat HaMazon* from the beginning. (*Shiurei HaRav,* pp. 279–285; *Reshimot Shiurim, Berakhot,* pp. 491–495, 517–518)

### WHY *AL HANISSIM* IS NOT INCLUDED IN THE *BERAKHA ME'EIN SHALOSH*

The Talmud (*Shabbat* 24a) discusses whether *Al HaNissim* should be recited in *Birkat HaMazon,* and ultimately concludes that it should be recited, in the second blessing. *Tosafot* (*ibid.*) explain that there is no question that *Al HaNissim* is recited during the Amida prayer, because the Amida is generally recited publicly in the synagogue, and therefore it presents a greater opportunity for *pirsumei nisa,* publicizing of the miracle, than *Birkat HaMazon,* which one generally recites privately at home.

Notwithstanding the explanation offered by *Tosafot,* the difference between *Al HaNissim* in prayer and in *Birkat HaMazon* can be explained in an additional way. When a person recites the Amida, he is meant to thank God for all of the blessings in his life, "for Your miracles which are with us every day; and for Your wonders and favors at all times, evening morning and midday." Thus, it is obvious that in the Amida we must give thanks to God for the miracles of Ḥanukka and Purim. The thanksgiving of *Birkat HaMazon,* though, is focused on specific themes; thus the Talmud debates whether the miracles of Ḥanukka and Purim are extraneous to *Birkat HaMazon* and need not be mentioned.

While the Talmud concludes that we do recite *Al HaNissim* in *Birkat HaMazon,* nevertheless, reciting *Al HaNissim* in *Birkat HaMazon* is fundamentally different from the insertion of *Retzei* and *Ya'aleh VeYavo* into *Birkat HaMazon.* The recitations of *Retzei* and *Ya'aleh VeYavo* are based upon the principle enunciated by the Gemara (*Berakhot* 40a): "'Blessed be the Lord day by day' (Ps. 68:20) – offer Him blessings according to the day." This obligation of *hazkarat me'ein hame'ora* (mentioning the day's sanctity) is not relevant to Ḥanukka or Purim, because

◂ it applies

it applies only to days which possess *kedushat hayom*. Rather, we recite *Al HaNissim* because of the obligation of *pirsumei nisa,* publicizing the miracles.

*Retzei* and *Ya'aleh VeYavo,* as fulfillments of the concept of *hazkarat me'ein hame'ora,* are defined as insertions, but are not integrated into the basic text of the *Birkat HaMazon*. However, *Al HaNissim,* when recited, becomes incorporated into the thanksgiving section of *Birkat HaMazon*. In the second blessing, we thank God for the Land of Israel, the Torah, the *brit,* as well as for the miracles of Purim and Ḥanukka on their respective days. This is the reason we include references to Shabbat and Yom Tov in the *berakha me'ein shalosh,* but make no reference to Ḥanukka and Purim in this *berakha*. On Shabbat and Yom Tov, there is an obligation of *hazkarat me'ein hame'ora,* and that applies equally when one recites the *berakha me'ein shalosh*. However, there is no independent obligation to recite *Al HaNissim,* but rather, as we explained, it is one element of the thanksgiving blessing. The *berakha me'ein shalosh* is by definition an abbreviation of *Birkat HaMazon,* and just as it omits specific references to *brit and* Torah which appear in the blessing of *Nodeh Lekha,* it likewise omits specific reference to Ḥanukka and Purim. (*Harerei Kedem,* vol. 1, p. 347; *Eretz HaTzvi,* pp. 49–50; *Reshimot Shiurim, Berakhot,* p. 516)

### OMISSION OF *RETZEI* AND *YA'ALEH VEYAVO*

On Shabbat and Yom Tov, if one forgets to recite *Retzei* or *Ya'aleh VeYavo,* he is obligated to repeat *Birkat HaMazon*. On Rosh Ḥodesh, however, if one forgets *Ya'aleh VeYavo* in *Birkat HaMazon,* he is not required to repeat it. The Talmud (*Berakhot* 49b) explains that since on Shabbat and Yom Tov there is an obligation to partake in *se'udot,* a person is required to repeat *Birkat HaMazon* if he forgets either *Retzei* or *Ya'aleh VeYavo,* respectively, but on Rosh Ḥodesh, when there is no requirement to have a festive meal, if *Ya'aleh VeYavo* is forgotten it does not invalidate the *Birkat HaMazon*. *Tosafot* (*Berakhot* 49b) infer that if one eats a fourth meal on Shabbat, beyond the required three, and forgets *Retzei,* he does not need to repeat *Birkat HaMazon* since the meal was not obligatory.

This *halakha,* that only at an obligatory Shabbat meal is omission of *Retzei* disqualifying, indicates that the fulfillment of *Birkat HaMazon* of

Shabbat does not require inclusion of *Retzei*. Rather, the requirement of *Retzei* is part of the obligation of *se'udat Shabbat*. The Rabbis instituted that we recite *Retzei* on Shabbat and *Ya'aleh VeYavo* on Yom Tov in order to declare that these meals are not ordinary meals, but fulfillments of *oneg Shabbat* and *simḥat Yom Tov*. Thus when one forgets *Retzei*, he has fulfilled the *mitzva* of *Birkat HaMazon*, but he has not properly fulfilled the *mitzva* of *se'udat Shabbat*. To fulfill the *mitzva* of *se'udat Shabbat* (without eating an additional meal) he must repeat *Birkat HaMazon*.

This also explains Rama's ruling (*Oraḥ Ḥayyim* 198) that if three people all forget to recite *Retzei*, each person repeats the *Birkat HaMazon* individually, but they do not repeat the *zimmun* as a group. As explained above, when a person forgets to recite *Retzei*, he does fulfill his obligation of *Birkat HaMazon*; he must repeat the *Birkat HaMazon* only to properly fulfill the *mitzva* of the *se'uda*. The Rabbis instituted the concept of the *zimmun* when three individuals join together to fulfill their obligation of *Birkat HaMazon*, but, in this case, when they are reciting *Birkat HaMazon* only to fulfill their obligation of *se'udat Shabbat*, the institution of *zimmun* doesn't apply. (*Eretz HaTzvi*, p. 46)

### SPECIAL INSERTIONS WHEN A MEAL BEGINS DURING THE DAY AND CONCLUDES AT NIGHT

The *Shulḥan Arukh* (*Oraḥ Ḥayyim* 188:10) rules that if someone begins a meal on Shabbat day and finishes it after nightfall, he should still recite *Retzei* in *Birkat HaMazon*. Similarly, if a person begins a meal on Rosh Ḥodesh, Purim or Ḥanukka, but finishes it after the end of the day, he should nevertheless include the appropriate insertion. The underlying logic of these rulings is that the meal and its *Birkat HaMazon* are defined by the time period when the meal began. However, regarding the parallel situation of one who started eating on Friday afternoon but did not recite *Birkat HaMazon* until Shabbat evening, the *Shulḥan Arukh* (*Oraḥ Ḥayyim* 271:6) writes that he should also recite *Retzei*. Rama (ad loc.) disagrees and argues that in this case as well, we should follow the time of the beginning of the meal: since the meal began before Shabbat, *Retzei* should not be recited.

◂ To resolve

To resolve the inconsistency in the position of the *Shulḥan Arukh,* it is necessary to distinguish between two independent obligations to mention Shabbat and holidays in *Birkat HaMazon.* First, a Shabbat meal, defined as a meal which began on Shabbat, creates an obligation to include *Retzei,* and a Rosh Ḥodesh meal, defined as a meal which began on Rosh Ḥodesh, warrants the inclusion of *Ya'aleh VeYavo.* In addition, there is also an obligation based not on the nature of the meal, but on the time when the person recites *Birkat HaMazon.* The Talmud (*Berakhot* 40a) derives from the verse "Blessed be the LORD day by day" (Ps. 68:20) that there is an obligation to "offer Him blessings according to the day." This obligation is unrelated to the nature of the meal or when it began, but is rather based on the significance of the day when the praise is recited. Thus the *Shulḥan Arukh* maintains that we include *Retzei* both when a meal begins on Shabbat and finishes after nightfall, as well as when a meal begins on Friday and concludes on Shabbat. When one begins a meal on Shabbat, he must recite *Retzei* even after Shabbat has concluded because the meal is defined as a Shabbat meal. And if one begins a meal before Shabbat, such that it is not defined as a Shabbat meal, he nevertheless must include *Retzei* if he recites *Birkat HaMazon* when it is already Shabbat, because the time itself creates an obligation to bless God "according to the day."

This can also illuminate another dispute, regarding the proper procedure for *Birkat HaMazon* when Rosh Ḥodesh falls on *Motza'ei Shabbat* and a person begins a meal on Shabbat which concludes after nightfall. In this case, *Taz* (*Oraḥ Ḥayyim* 188:7) maintains that one must include both *Retzei* and *Ya'aleh VeYavo* because the meal spans both Shabbat and Rosh Ḥodesh. *Magen Avraham* (188:18), however, maintains that to include both the Shabbat and Rosh Ḥodesh insertions is an inherent contradiction. The meal is either a meal of Shabbat or Rosh Ḥodesh, but it cannot be defined as both. However, if there are two distinct sources for the *Birkat HaMazon* insertions, the position of *Taz* is readily understandable. On the one hand, the meal which began on Shabbat is defined as a Shabbat meal which requires the inclusion of *Retzei.* However, since the participants are reciting *Birkat HaMazon* on Rosh Ḥodesh, there is an additional obligation to recite *Ya'aleh VeYavo* based on the time of the recitation of the blessings.

Based on the above analysis, one could argue that the obligation to

◂ include

include the special insertions even when the meal concludes afer nightfall should only apply to Shabbat, Yom Tov, and Purim – days on which there is an obligation to eat a *se'uda*. For this reason, the day's meal is defined as a *se'udat Shabbat* or *se'udat Purim*, and this status continues even after the day is over. However, on Ḥanukka and Rosh Ḥodesh, on which there is no obligation of *se'uda*, seemingly the meal would have no special status to obligate an insertion after the holiday has concluded. In fact, Rama in a responsum (*Teshuvot HaRama*, no. 132) makes this very argument and rules that if a person begins a meal on Rosh Ḥodesh or Ḥanukka, but doesn't finish the meal until the day has passed, he doesn't include any special insertions in his *Birkat HaMazon*. On the other hand, the *Shulḥan Arukh* (188:10) rules explicitly that on all days we follow the time at which the meal began. It seems that the *Shulḥan Arukh* maintains that although there is no obligation to have a meal on Rosh Ḥodesh or Ḥanukka, nevertheless, a meal on those days is defined as a *se'udat Rosh Ḥodesh* or *se'udat Ḥanukka* and therefore has a special status which continues even once the day has concluded. (*Harerei Kedem*, vol. 2, pp. 143–144)

## RECITING *NAḤEM* WHEN ONE MUST EAT ON TISHA B'AV

If a person is required to eat on Tisha B'Av and recite *Birkat HaMazon*, Rama (*Oraḥ Ḥayyim* 557:1) rules that he should include the blessing of *Naḥem* in his *Birkat HaMazon*. The Vilna Gaon (*Biur HaGra* ad loc.) argues that in this case no addition to the regular text is warranted, based on the Talmudic discussion in *Shabbat* 24a. The Talmud explains that we include a special insertion in *Birkat HaMazon* only in honor of days that have a *mussaf* offering, such as Shabbat, Yom Tov, or Rosh Ḥodesh. Even though Ḥanukka and Purim do not have a *mussaf* offereing, the Talmud continues, we include *Al HaNissim* because of the obligation to publicize the miracles of these holidays, *pirsumei nisa*. Since Tisha B'Av lacks both of these characteristics, as it has no *mussaf* offering and no *pirsumei nisa* obligation, the Vilna Gaon argues that no special prayer should be included in *Birkat HaMazon* for someone who must eat on the fast.

To explain the position of Rama, we must once again distinguish between two kinds of additions to *Birkat HaMazon*. (See above, "Why

◂ *Al HaNissim*

*Al HaNissim* is Not Included in the *Berakha Me'ein Shalosh*.") *Retzei* and *Ya'aleh VeYavo* do not relate to the themes of *Birkat HaMazon*, but rather are independent additions that focus on the sanctity of the day. However, *Al HaNissim* and *Naḥem* are changes to the very text of *Birkat HaMazon*: *Al HaNissim* becomes a part of the second blessing of *Nodeh Lekha*, integrated into the thanksgiving section of *Birkat HaMazon*, and *Naḥem* is a different version of the blessing *Boneh Yerushalayim*, appropriate for the day on which we mourn Jerusalem's destruction.

The Talmud's principle that we mention only days that have a *mussaf* offering refers to the independent additions which are based on the sanctity of the holiday, which in turn is determined by the presence of a *mussaf* offering. However, additions which are integrated into *Birkat HaMazon* do not depend on whether there is a *mussaf* offering. Thus, when the Talmud invokes *pirsumei nisa* as the reason for reciting *Al HaNissim* on Ḥanukka and Purim, it means to say that this is not a stand-alone section, but an addition which is integrated into *Birkat HaMazon*. Similarly, Rama maintains that *Naḥem*, like *Al HaNissim*, is not an independent insertion, but a change to the text of *Birkat HaMazon* on Tisha B'Av, and therefore we include it in *Birkat HaMazon* even though the day has no *mussaf* offering. (*Iggerot HaGrid*, pp. 43–44)

### THE DAYTIME KIDDUSH AND USING *MEZONOT* TO FULFILL *KIDDUSH BIMEKOM SE'UDA*

There is a fundamental disagreement between Maimonides and Ra'avad regarding how to define the obligation of the daytime Kiddush. Maimonides (*Hilkhot Shabbat* 29:10) equates the daytime Kiddush to the evening Kiddush and thus rules that just as it is prohibited to eat before reciting Kiddush on Shabbat evening, it is forbidden to eat anything before the daytime Kiddush. Likewise, according to Maimonides, the daytime recitation requires *Kiddush bimekom se'uda*, that Kiddush occur in the place of the meal. However, Ra'avad (*ibid.*) strongly disagrees with these positions and maintains that one cannot extrapolate from the evening Kiddush to its daytime counterpart. The prohibition to eat before Kiddush and the requirement of *Kiddush bimekom se'uda* apply only to the first Kiddush recited at night. We can explain this dispute as follows:

◂ According to

According to Maimonides, there is an obligation of Kiddush during the day just as there is one at night, because the two halves of Shabbat require two acts of sanctification. Ra'avad maintains, however, that the Kiddush at night infuses sanctity into the entirety of Shabbat. The daytime blessing of *borei peri hagafen* cannot be defined as an act of sanctification, because, as he puts it, "the day was already sanctified over wine at its beginning." Rather, according to Ra'avad, the obligation to recite a blessing over wine during the day is in order to establish the meal as being in honor of Shabbat, but since it is not considered a fulfillment of the concept of Kiddush, of infusing sanctity into the day, there is no prohibition to eat beforehand.

The common practice today to eat *mezonot* after the daytime Kiddush, in order to fulfill the requirement of *Kiddush bimekom se'uda,* is based on a combination of this opinion of Ra'avad, that there is no prohibition to eat before the daytime Kiddush, and the view of the Geonim (quoted in *Shulḥan Arukh, Oraḥ Ḥayyim* 273:5) who maintain that bread is not necessary to establish *Kiddush bimekom se'uda.* Although the Vilna Gaon (*Ma'aseh Rav,* no. 122) requires bread in order to establish *Kiddush bimekom se'uda,* we can rely on the lenient opinion of the Geonim that *mezonot* suffice in conjunction with the opinion of Ra'avad that the requirement of *Kiddush bimekom se'uda* does not apply to the Kiddush of Shabbat day at all. According to this analysis, one should not rely on the lenient position of the Geonim that *mezonot* suffice on Shabbat eve; this is in contrast to the opinion of *Magen Avraham* (274:2) who equates in this regard the Kiddush of Shabbat eve with the Kiddush of Shabbat day. (*Shiurim LeZekher Abba Mari,* vol. 2, pp. 162–163; *Eretz HaTzvi,* pp. 46–47)

### *LEḤEM MISHNEH* AT *SE'UDA SHELISHIT*

The first two meals of Shabbat must include *leḥem mishneh,* two whole loaves of bread; however, regarding the third meal, *se'uda shelishit,* there is a dispute. Maimonides rules that there is no difference between the meals and they all require *leḥem mishneh,* while others maintain that one loaf suffices for the final meal, and still others believe that a person can fulfill his obligation with other foods, even fruits or vegetables (see *Tur, Oraḥ Ḥayyim* 291). The opinions that distinguish between the third meal

◂ and the first

and the first two are in fact quite difficult to understand. The Talmud (*Shabbat* 117b) derives the obligation for the three Shabbat meals from the threefold repetition of the word "*hayom*" in the verse (Ex. 16:25), and thus there doesn't seem to be any basis to differentiate between the obligation of any of the Shabbat meals. To explain these opinions we must analyze a different Talmudic passage (*Pesaḥim* 105a) which rules that if a person has only one portion of a specific delicacy, he should reserve it for the daytime meal, because the honor of Shabbat day, *kevod yom*, takes precedence over *kevod layla*, the honor of Shabbat night. We can infer from this *halakha* that the general obligation to honor Shabbat with special foods and other indulgences is subdivided into the two halves of Shabbat. There is one obligation to honor the nighttime, and a second, distinct obligation to honor the daytime. With this understanding, we can explain the opinions that don't require *leḥem mishneh* for *se'uda shelishit*. When the Rabbis instituted the obligation of *leḥem mishneh*, they formulated it not as part of the definition of a Shabbat meal, but as part of the *mitzva* of *oneg Shabbat*, to honor the day with two complete loaves. Therefore, once a person has eaten *leḥem mishneh* at both of his first two Shabbat meals, he has honored both Shabbat night and Shabbat day, fulfilling *kevod yom* and *kevod layla*, and he is not required to have a third set of *leḥem mishneh* at *se'uda shlishit*, as a Shabbat meal, *per se*, does not require *leḥem mishneh*. We can similarly explain the view that bread is not required at all for *se'uda shelishit*. According to this view, Shabbat meals need bread only to fulfill the obligation of *leḥem mishneh*, and thus, once the requirement of *leḥem mishneh* has been fulfilled in the first two meals, the obligation of *se'uda shelishit* can be fulfilled without bread altogether. (*Notes of Rabbi Hershel Schachter*)

## RECITING KIDDUSH AND HAVDALA ON THE CUP OF WINE USED FOR *BIRKAT HAMAZON*

If one begins a meal on Friday, but concludes it after Shabbat has begun, the Talmud (*Pesaḥim* 102b) rules that he should first recite *Birkat HaMazon* on one cup of wine and then recite Kiddush over a second cup. If one would recite both blessings over a single cup of wine, the Talmud explains, it would violate the principle of "*ein osin mitzvot ḥavilot ḥavilot*,"

◂ that we do

that we do not perform *mitzvot* in bundles. In other words, each *mitzva* deserves to be performed discretely, and to pronounce both blessings over a single cup would not give each *mitzva* the due honor that it warrants. Maimonides (*Hilkhot Shabbat* 29:12–13), however, distinguishes between Kiddush and Havdala. A person may not use one cup for both Kiddush and *Birkat HaMazon,* in accordance with the Talmud's ruling, yet if a meal began on Shabbat and concluded after Shabbat, a person may recite *Birkat HaMazon* and Havdala over the same cup of wine. Ra'avad (*ibid.*) disagrees, and maintains that unless a person doesn't have sufficient wine for two cups, he may not recite more than one blessing over a single cup, regardless of whether the blessing is Kiddush or Havdala.

To understand the position of Maimonides, we must explain the fundamental difference between the role of the cup of wine in Kiddush and in Havdala. Havdala is an example of a *kos shel berakha*; that is, the Rabbis instituted that this blessing be recited over a cup of wine to lend importance to the blessing. Fundamentally, however, Havdala does not require a cup of wine. In contrast, the recitation of Kiddush over a cup of wine is not merely a means to add significance to the blessing, but rather is integral to its purpose of establishing the meal as one in honor of Shabbat. The cup of wine connects the blessing of Kiddush to the meal, and elevates the status of the eating. Similarly, reciting blessings and praise over a cup of wine at the conclusion of the meal serves not merely to add significance to the blessings, but to elevate the status of the entire meal. Thus, in the case of *Birkat HaMazon* as well, the cup of wine is required to connect the blessings to the eating. However, Havdala is not connected to a meal and thus the cup of wine for Havdala fulfills only the general function of creating a *kos shel berakha.*

According to Maimonides, when the cup of wine serves only the general function of creating a *kos shel berakha,* there is no problem in using a single cup for more than one blessing. The Talmud's rule against using the same cup for two different blessings applies only to cases in which the cup of wine itself is a fundamental part of the *mitzva,* when it is the *ḥeftza shel mitzva,* the object through which the person performs the *mitzva*. In regards to both Kiddush and *Birkat HaMazon,* the cup of wine is the *ḥeftza shel mitzva* that elevates the status of the meal, and thus, a person may not use one cup to recite both blessings. However, the cup

◂ of wine

of wine used for Havdala is secondary to the blessings and not part of the basic *mitzva*. It is not a *ḥeftza shel mitzva*, and therefore, in the opinion of Maimonides, a person may use the same cup of wine for both Havdala and *Birkat HaMazon*. (*Shiurim LeZekher Abba Mari*, vol. 2, pp. 130–131)

### HAVDALA WHEN TISHA B'AV FALLS ON *MOTZA'EI SHABBAT*

The Talmud (*Pesaḥim* 107a) records a dispute regarding a person who did not recite *Havdala al hakos*, Havdala over a cup of wine, on *Motza'ei Shabbat*: one opinion holds he can recite Havdala only the following day (i.e., until Sunday afternoon), while the other opinion maintains he can recite Havdala through midweek (i.e., until Tuesday afternoon). When Tisha B'Av falls after Shabbat, and all drinking is forbidden until Sunday night, the *Halakhot Gedolot*, quoted by Naḥmanides (*Torat Ha'Adam* in *Kitvei Ramban*, ed. C.D. Chavel, vol. 2, p. 260), argues that Havdala is recited on Sunday night, following the fast – even if in general Havdala is recited only until Sunday afternoon.

Naḥmanides (ad loc.), however, disagrees, arguing that according to this opinion, a person can recite Havdala only on the first day after Shabbat, and the prohibition against drinking on Tisha B'Av cannot transform the second day of the week into the first. Naḥmanides further argues contrary to the *Halakhot Gedolot* that when Tisha B'Av falls on *Motza'ei Shabbat*, even if in general one can recite Havdala until midweek, in this case one cannot recite *Havdala al hakos* at all. Naḥmanides reasons that the primary obligation of Havdala is on *Motza'ei Shabbat*, and the other days are only a secondary opportunity for fulfilling the *mitzva* (*tashlumin*). Therefore, if one is not obligated to recite Havdala on *Motza'ei Shabbat*, he has no obligation to do so on the following days either. Naḥmanides compares the situation of Tisha B'Av on *Motza'ei Shabbat* to a case of *aninut* (in which a person's immediate relative passed away but was not yet buried) on *Motza'ei Shabbat*. Since the *onen* is not obligated to recite Havdala on *Motza'ei Shabbat* because the *aninut* exempts him from all positive *mitzvot*, he remains exempt from reciting Havdala later in the week once the *aninut* has ended.

Initially, Naḥmanides' proof from the case of *aninut* seems compelling,

◂ but upon

but upon reflection, the comparison of Tisha B'Av to *aninut* is extremely perplexing. An *onen* is fundamentally exempt from all positive *mitzvot*. Therefore, since he is not obligated to recite Havdala on *Motza'ei Shabbat*, he is exempt for the entire week. But when Tisha B'Av falls on *Motza'ei Shabbat*, there is no exemption from the obligation to recite Havdala. Instead, there is a practical impediment, in the form of the prohibition to drink, which makes it impossible to fulfill the obligation of *Havdala al hakos*. Seemingly, this mere practical obstacle should not exempt a person from reciting Havdala later in the week.

We can understand Naḥmanides' argument if we view it in light of the function and purpose of *Havdala al hakos*. If we view the purpose of *Havdala al hakos* not as a mark of the end of the prohibition against performing work, but as a mark of the end of the *se'udot* of Shabbat and the beginning of the *se'udot* of the week, Naḥmanides' position becomes much more comprehensible. When Tisha B'Av falls on *Motza'ei Shabbat* and eating and drinking are prohibited, the impediment to fulfilling *Havdala al hakos* is not merely a practical obstacle. Since Tisha B'Av is not a time when a person can eat, Havdala at that time cannot serve as the marker of the beginning of the weekday *se'udot*. Based on this understanding of the purpose of Havdala, Naḥmanides argues that just as an *onen* who is exempt from the obligation of Havdala on *Motza'ei Shabbat* is exempt for the remainder of the week, so too when Tisha B'Av occurs on *Motza'ei Shabbat*, a person is fundamentally exempt from *Havdala al hakos* on *Motza'ei Shabbat*, and is therefore exempt for the entire week.

With this understanding of the purpose of *Havdala al hakos*, we can also explain the position of the *Halakhot Gedolot*. As noted above, the *Halakhot Gedolot* maintains that when Tisha B'Av falls on *Motza'ei Shabbat*, one recites *Havdala al hakos* on Sunday night, even if otherwise Havdala may be recited no later than Sunday afternoon. According to the *Halakhot Gedolot*, Havdala marks the division between Shabbat and its *se'udot*, on the one hand, and the weekday and its meals, on the other. The significance of the first day of the week is not that it is the first weekday after Shabbat, as Naḥmanides maintains, but that it is the first day which has weekday, non-Shabbat meals. Normally, the first day of weekday meals starts on *Motza'ei Shabbat* and ends on Sunday afternoon. When Tisha B'Av falls on *Motza'ei Shabbat*, however, the first day of the week that one

◂ is permitted

is permitted to eat is the following day, i.e., Sunday night/Monday, and therefore Havdala may still be recited on Sunday night/Monday.

The *Shulḥan Arukh* (*Oraḥ Ḥayyim* 556) rules in accordance with the *Halakhot Gedolot* that when Tisha B'Av occurs on *Motza'ei Shabbat, Havdala al hakos* should be recited on Sunday night. However, if someone is ill and must eat on Tisha B'Av, the *Sha'arei Teshuva* (ad loc.) quotes an opinion that the ill person should recite *Havdala al hakos* on *Motza'ei Shabbat,* as he would any other week. Moreover, the *Sha'arei Teshuva* cites the view that if other people who are fasting listen to the recitation of Havdala by the ill person on *Motza'ei Shabbat,* they fulfill their obligation and need not recite *Havdala al hakos* again at the conclusion of the fast. The conceptual basis of this ruling is that when Tisha B'Av falls on *Motza'ei Shabbat,* everyone is fundamentally obligated to recite Havdala on *Motza'ei Shabbat* as they are any other *Motza'ei Shabbat,* and the prohibition to drink wine is only a practical impediment to fulfilling the *mitzva*. Therefore, since even the people who are fasting share the obligation, they can fulfill the *mitzva* of Havdala on *Motza'ei Shabbat* by listening to the recitation of the person who cannot fast. According to the explanation offered above, however, a person who is obligated to fast on *Motza'ei Shabbat* is fundamentally exempt from the obligation of Havdala at that time. If so, someone who is fasting cannot fulfill his obligation by listening to the recitation of Havdala by a person who is ill, because the healthy person is not yet obligated in the *mitzva* of *Havdala al hakos*. Thus, a healthy person who heard Havdala on *Motza'ei Shabbat* would nevertheless have to recite *Havdala al hakos* when the fast concludes. (*Harerei Kedem,* vol. 2, pp. 141–143)

# סימוכין
# REFERENCES

## ENGLISH REFERENCES

Besdin, Abraham R. *Man of Faith in the Modern World: Reflections of the Rav*, Volume 2. Hoboken, NJ: KTAV Publishing House, 1989.

David, Avishai. *Darosh Darash Yosef: Discourses of Rav Yosef Dov HaLevi Soloveitchik on the Weekly Parashah.* Jerusalem: Urim Publications and OU Press, 2011.

Gopin, Mendi. *Davening with the Rav: My Rabbi and My Rebbe.* Jersey City, NJ: KTAV Pulishing House, 2006.

Lustiger, Arnold. *Before Hashem You Shall Be Purified: Rabbi Joseph B. Soloveitchik on the Days of Awe.* Edison, NJ: Ohr Publishing, 1998.

*Derashot HaRav: Selected Lectures of Rabbi Joseph B. Soloveitchik.* Edison, NJ: Ohr Publishing, 2003.

*Koren Mesorat HaRav Siddur*. Jerusalem: Koren Publishers and OU Press, 2011.

Peli, Pinchas H. *On Repentance in the Thought and Oral Discourse of Rabbi Joseph B. Soloveitchik.* Jerusalem: Oroth Publishing House, 1980.

Schreiber, David. *Noraos HaRav*, Volumes 2, 15. 1996, 2005.

Shapiro, David. *Rabbi Joseph B. Soloveitchik on Pesach, Sefirat ha-Omer and Shavu'ot.* Jerusalem: Urim Publications, 2005.

Soloveitchik, Joseph B. *Abraham's Journey.* J. B. Wolowelsky, Ed. Hoboken, NJ: KTAV Publishing House, 2008.

*Community, Covenant and Commitment: Selected Letters and Communications.* N. Helfgot, Ed. Hoboken, NJ: KTAV Publishing House, 2005.

*Days of Deliverance: Essays on Purim and Hannukah.* E. Clark, J. B. Wolowelsky and R. Ziegler, Eds. Hoboken, NJ: KTAV Publishing House, 2007.

*Family Redeemed: Essays on Family Relationships.* D. Shatz and J. B. Wolowelsky, Eds. Hoboken, NJ: KTAV Publishing House, 2000.

*Festival of Freedom: Essays on Pesaḥ and the Haggadah.* J. B. Wolowelsky and R. Ziegler, Eds. Hoboken, NJ: KTAV Publishing House, 2006.

*And From There Shall You Seek.* Translated by Naomi Goldblum. Hoboken, NJ: KTAV Publishing House, 2006.

*Halakhic Man.* Translated by Lawrence Kaplan. Philadelphia, PA: Jewish Publication Society, 1983.

*The Lord is Righteous in All His Ways.* J. J. Schacter, Ed. Hoboken, NJ: KTAV Publishing House, 2006.

*Out of the Whirlwind: Essays on Mourning, Suffering and the Human Condition.* D. Shatz, J. B. Wolowelsky and R. Ziegler, Eds. Hoboken, NJ: KTAV Publishing House, 2003.

*The Rav Speaks: Five Addresses by Rabbi Joseph B. Soloveitchik.* Trans. S. M. Lehrman and A. H. Rabinowitz. New York: Toras HoRav Foundation, 2002.

Wohlgemuth, Isaiah. *A Guide to Jewish Prayer.* Transcribed by A. Reichert. Brookline, MA and Lakewood, NJ: J. Robinson, Israel Book Shop, 2001.

Ziegler, Aharon. *Halakhic Positions of Rabbi Joseph B. Soloveitchik,* Volume I. Lanham, MD: Jason Aronson, 1998.

*Halakhic Positions of Rabbi Joseph B. Soloveitchik,* Volume III. Lanham, MD: Jason Aronson, 2005.

*Halakhic Positions of Rabbi Joseph B. Soloveitchik,* Volume IV. Jersey City, NJ: KTAV, 2007.

## HEBREW REFERENCES

Genack, Menachem. *Shiurei HaRav Al Inyanei Tefilla Ukeriat Shema.* New York, NY: Mesorah, 5770/2010.

*Mesorah,* Volume 5, *Adar* 5751, Volume 6, *Kislev* 5752, and Volume 8, *Nissan* 5753. Union of Orthodox Jewish Congregations of America.

Reichman, Tzvi Yosef. *Reshimot Shiurim – Masekhet Berakhot.* New York, NY 2012.

Schachter, Tzvi. *Eretz HaTzvi.* Yeshiva University Press, New York, NY, 1992.

*Divrei HaRav.* Jerusalem: Mesorah, 5770/2010.

*MiPeninei HaRav.* Jerusalem: Flatbush Beth Hamedrosh, 5761/2001.

*Nefesh HaRav.* Jerusalem: Reishit Yerushalayim, 5754/1994.

Shurkin, Mikhel Zalman. *Harerei Kedem, Mahadura Ḥadasha,* Volumes 1–2. Jerusalem: 5769/2009.

*Harerei Kedem, Shabbat.* Jerusalem: 5773/2013.

Soloveitchik, Joseph B. *Divrei Hagut VeHa'arakha.* Jerusalem: World Zionist Organization, 5742/1982.

*Iggerot HaGrid HaLevi.* Jerusalem: Morasha Foundation, 5761/2001.

*Kovetz Ḥiddushei Torah.* Jerusalem. N.D.

*Shiurim LeZekher Abba Mari,* two volumes. Jerusalem: Akiva Yosef, 5743/1983–5745/1985.

*Yemei Zikaron.* Jerusalem: World Zionist Organization, 5747/1987.

# The Mesorat HaRav Birkon

# ברכון מסורת הרב

KOREN

OUPRESS

THE WINTMAN EDITION

# ברכון מסורת הרב
# THE MESORAT HARAV BIRKON

THREE ESSAYS ON
RABBI JOSEPH B. SOLOVEITCHIK'S
CONCEPTUAL UNDERSTANDING OF
BIRKAT HAMAZON, ZIMMUN, AND KIDDUSH

ADAPTED BY
RABBI DAVID HELLMAN

OU PRESS
KOREN PUBLISHERS JERUSALEM

**Note to the Reader**

For the full text of the Birkon, with commentary by Rabbi Soloveitchik, turn to the other end of this volume.

# *Contents*

## BIRKAT HAMAZON: TO BLESS THE GREAT AND HOLY NAME*

*Birkat HaMazon,* like our entire liturgy, exists on two planes. On the one hand, it is a standardized text instituted by the rabbis that we are obligated to recite after every meal. However, it is much more than a codified formulation; its specific words and language encapsulate ideas, themes, and concepts that we must extract, define, and elucidate. Fundamentally, we must ask, what is the *telos* of *Birkat HaMazon* and what religious experience does it capture? In other words, what is the essence of the *mitzva* that the Torah itself commands? To address these questions we must turn our attention to a few crucial Talmudic passages.

### *The Biblical Obligation*

Before we can appreciate the theological and religious implications of *Birkat HaMazon,* we must clarify the different views regarding its halakhic definition. It is quite clear that the Torah requires some sort of blessing after we eat: "You shall eat and be satisfied and shall bless the LORD your God for the good land which He has given you" (Deut. 8:31). However, when it comes to the *specific* blessings we recite there seem to be two contradictory Talmudic passages regarding their origin and authority. One source, a *beraita* (*Berakhot* 48b), sees allusions to the first three blessings of the *Birkat HaMazon* in the above quoted verse: "Our Rabbis taught: Where is the saying of grace intimated in the Torah? In the

* This essay is based primarily upon a *shiur* delivered by the Rav in Boston in 1961, as well as *Shiurei HaRav al Inyanei Tefilla,* pp. 269–287, and *Reshimot Shiurim, Berakhot,* pp. 516–519. The essay also incorporates material from a *shiur* delivered in 1969.

verse, 'You shall eat and be satisfied and shall bless' – this signifies *Birkat HaZan* [the first blessing]...'For the land' – this signifies *Birkat HaAretz* [the second blessing]. 'The good' – this signifies *Boneh Yerushalayim* [the third blessing]." This source implies that the first three blessings of *Birkat HaMazon* are all Biblical obligations. (The last blessing of *HaTov VehaMeitiv* was established in response to the burial of the victims of the Betar massacre, and is clearly Rabbinic in origin. See Reshimot, p. 209.) Yet, the Talmud (*ibid.*) also quotes Rav Naḥman as stating that these same three blessings were instituted by the courts of three different generations: "Moses established for Israel the blessing of *HaZan* at the time when the manna fell for them; Joshua established for them the blessing of *HaAretz* when they entered the land; David and Solomon established the blessing of *Boneh Yerushalayim*." As opposed to the *beraita*, this second teaching implies that all of the blessings of *Birkat HaMazon* are only of Rabbinic origin.

Looking to the *Rishonim* (medieval authorities), we find two major approaches to harmonizing these sources. Rashba (*Berakhot* 48b) explains that the Biblical obligation requires expressing thanksgiving for the themes of the first three blessings: for sustenance, for the Land of Israel, and for Jerusalem. Every time one eats, he must acknowledge God who provided him with his food, and who gave the people of Israel the Land of Israel and her capital, Jerusalem. However, the Torah did not mandate a set formulation. Instead, each individual could express these motifs in whichever way he chose, using the language he found most fitting. Later, Moses, Joshua, and then David and Solomon instituted set texts for the nation to recite. Thus, the formulation and phrasing are a Rabbinic institution, but the themes and motifs of the first three blessings are all of Biblical origin.

Ritva and *Shita Mekubetzet* (ad loc.), following Rashba's approach, point out a parallel as well as a distinction between *Birkat HaMazon* and the obligation of *tefilla*. Like the commandment of *Birkat HaMazon*, the Biblical obligation to pray also has no required text; originally, one would pray in his own words. Only because of the displacements and chaos of the exile, explains Maimonides (*Hilkhot Tefilla* 1:4), did the Rabbis compose a standardized text of the Amida to facilitate prayer for those who wouldn't otherwise have the tools to express themselves

properly. However, the difference between these two commandments is that the Biblical *mitzva* of *tefilla* does not require reciting any specific praises of God or making any specific requests. A person could recite any prayer to fulfill his obligation. In contrast, the Biblical blessing of *Birkat HaMazon* has a structure that requires the inclusion of three specific themes: that God has granted us sustenance, the Land of Israel, and the city of Jerusalem.

There is, though, another approach which understands that the Biblical commandment of *Birkat HaMazon* involves not three themes, but one simple, core idea. Naḥmanides, in his glosses to Maimonides' *Sefer HaMitzvot* (*Shoresh* 1) discusses several different commandments which are Biblical in nature, but for which the Rabbis codified a standardized text. Discussing *Birkat HaMazon,* Naḥmanides says that although the commandment is clearly Biblical, "its text is not Biblical; rather, the Torah commanded us to recite a blessing after we eat, each person according to his understanding, as in the blessing of Benjamin the Shepherd who recited, 'Blessed is the Merciful One, Master of this bread' (*Berakhot* 40b)." This example of Benjamin the Shepherd proves that one can fulfill the obligation of *Birkat HaMazon* even with this simple blessing. Benjamin the Shepherd was not a scholar. He was a simple Jew who blessed God as best as he could, according to his meager understanding and capabilities. According to Rashba and his school, the Talmud means to say that Benjamin the Shepherd's simple blessing would fulfill the first of the three Biblically-mandated blessings, but it would not have fulfilled the Biblical obligation to mention the Land of Israel and Jerusalem. However, Naḥmanides seems to imply that Benjamin the Shepherd's blessing would fulfill the total Biblical obligation. In other words, according to Naḥmanides, the blessings for the Land of Israel and Jerusalem are Rabbinic in nature.

This opinion of Naḥmanides would also appear to be the position of Maimonides, who opens the first chapter of the *Hilkhot Berakhot* stating simply, "There is a positive commandment to bless after eating food, as it says, 'You shall eat and be satisfied and bless the Lord, your God.'" In discussing the Biblical obligation, Maimonides makes no reference to the Land of Israel or Jerusalem; he mentions those ideas only in Chapter Two of *Hilkhot Berakhot* when he discusses the fixed text of *Birkat HaMazon*

codified by the Rabbis. Like Naḥmanides, according to Maimonides we fulfill the Biblical commandment of *Birkat HaMazon* by reciting any blessing for the food we have eaten, regardless of its specific form or content.

But how can Maimonides and Naḥmanides maintain that there is no Biblical obligation to mention the Land of Israel when the verse states, "וּבֵרַכְתָּ אֶת־יהוה אֱלֹהֶיךָ עַל־הָאָרֶץ הַטֹּבָה אֲשֶׁר נָתַן־לָךְ, You shall bless the Lord your God for this good land that He gave you"? Seemingly, we find in this verse an explicit requirement to mention the Land of Israel. In fact, however, a dispute between the ancient translators on how to translate this verse will resolve this question.

*Targum Onkelos* translates the verse literally, that we are obligated to bless God "עַל אַרְעָא טָבְתָא דִּיהַב לָךְ, for the good land that He gave you." Accordingly, there is a clear Biblical obligation to thank God for the Land of Israel every time we eat, as is the opinion of Rashba and others. However, *Targum Yonatan ben Uziel* translates the relevant phrase as "עַל כָּל פֵּירֵי אַרְעָא מְשַׁבַּחְתָּא דִיהַב לְכוֹן, for the *fruit* of the good land that He gave you." This reading sees the phrase "the good land" as an elliptical reference to the fruit of the land, and thus the Biblical commandment does not include an obligation to thank God for the land itself, but rather only for its fruit, i.e., the produce one has consumed. Thus the dispute between Rashba and his school, on the one hand, and Maimonides and his school, on the other, revolves around how one translates the words "עַל־הָאָרֶץ הַטֹּבָה." The halakhic argument was clearly formulated only in the days of the medieval authorities, but the disagreement regarding how to understand the verse dates back to the ancient Aramaic translators.

## *Remembering God and Recognizing His Mastery*

Returning our focus to Naḥmanides' position, that one can fulfill his Biblical obligation by stating "Blessed is the Merciful One, Master of this bread" – we will recognize that not only does this reduce the number of Biblical themes in *Birkat HaMazon* from three to one, but it also offers a fundamentally different perspective on the *mitzva*. Intuitively, we would assume that *Birkat HaMazon* is a *mitzva* of *hoda'ah,* thanksgiving, of offering our appreciation for the food that we have just enjoyed. Yet Benjamin the Shepherd's formula contains no trace of thanksgiving – his

blessing does not thank God for the food at all. Rather, it is a statement of God's mastery and kingship, that He is the master of this food and that I enjoy it only with His permission. According to Naḥmanides, the Biblical commandment of *Birkat HaMazon* is not an obligation to praise or thank God for the kindness of providing us with food; it is an idea even more basic, a recognition even more fundamental to Judaism's worldview. *Birkat HaMazon* is a declaration of God's lordship over the world, and in particular, His mastery and ownership over the food we have consumed.

Indeed, if we examine the first blessing of *Birkat HaMazon*, we come to the same startling conclusion: it too contains no elements of thanksgiving. In the first blessing we recognize God as the creator and sustainer of the natural world, the one who feeds all living creatures. Only with the second blessing, opening with "We thank you LORD, our God..." does the concept of thanksgiving enter *Birkat HaMazon*. According to Naḥmanides, one fulfills the Biblical obligation of *Birkat HaMazon* even without expressing any sentiments of thanksgiving. The *mitzva* requires recognizing God's sovereignty, and no more. However, according to Rashba and his school, the themes of the first three blessings are all Biblical, and thus *Birkat HaMazon* includes both concepts, recognition of God's mastery over the world, and expression of thanksgiving for sustaining us. *Targum Yonatan ben Uziel* translates the verse as "you shall thank and bless," reflecting these two concepts, and in this regard, he parallels the position of Rashba.

In truth, when we look at the context of the verse, the approach of Naḥmanides is almost explicit in the Bible itself. The Bible commands, "You will eat and be satisfied and bless the LORD your God." However, it continues, "Be careful lest you forget the LORD your God and not guard His commandments... Lest you eat and be satisfied... and your heart will grow haughty and you will forget the LORD your God... and you will think in your heart, my strength and the might of my hand made me all this wealth" (Deut. 8:10–17). The Torah doesn't require man to thank God; rather, the Torah warns man lest he forget God. The purpose of *Birkat HaMazon* is to prevent the arrogance which creeps into a man's heart and causes him to forget that God is the Creator. Fundamentally, *Birkat HaMazon* is not an act of thanksgiving or praise, but an act of remembering God, a fulfillment of the constant command to remember

and be cognizant of our Creator in every aspect of our life. As the Torah concludes the section, "Rather you shall remember the LORD your God who gives you the strength to be successful."

Thus, *Birkat HaMazon* is not simply a particular commandment regarding food and our satiation; it is instead an expression of the belief and commitment that underpins our entire religious life. Indeed, from the standpoint of the psychology of religion, the *telos* of *Birkat HaMazon,* to remember God, is the most important element in one's religious experience. To offer praise before God is easy; to give thanks, one merely has to become sentimental. However, to remember God and ascribe everything to Him, to attribute the whole cosmic process of creation to God, and to know always that He is the Master, the LORD, and the Owner of everything, requires a mental discipline of the highest order, and it is in truth the fundamental religious experience.

### *Birkat HaMazon and All Other Blessings*

Understanding *Birkat HaMazon* in this light – not as an expression of thanksgiving, but as an act of recognizing and remembering God's kingship – also allows us to explain several passages in Maimonides' Code that would otherwise be difficult to understand. In the beginning of *Hilkhot Berakhot,* Maimonides, as usual, begins with the Biblical commandment: "There is a positive commandment from the Torah to bless God after eating." Maimonides then moves on to the Rabbinic obligations: "and there is a Rabbinic obligation to bless before a person enjoys any food … and to bless after anything a person eats or drinks." Maimonides means to say that these Rabbinic obligations are not independent concepts, but extensions of the Biblical idea of *Birkat HaMazon.* However, the blessings that we recite before we eat are not expressions of thanksgiving, as they simply state, "Blessed is the LORD … creator of the fruit of the tree." Moreover, the blessings before we eat couldn't be expressions of thanksgiving, as thanksgiving is only appropriate *after* we have benefited from God's kindness. Rather, the blessings that we recite before we eat are declarations of God's mastery over this world, recognition that the food before us belongs to Him and that we enjoy it only with His permission. If *Birkat HaMazon* would have been an act of thanksgiving, it could not have been the conceptual basis for the Rabbinic blessings that we recite before we

eat. Only because *Birkat HaMazon* is an act of recognizing God's kingship and mastery over our possessions can it serve as the conceptual foundation for all blessings that we recite.

Maimonides continues, "Just as we recite blessings for all physical pleasures, so too we recite blessings before *mitzvot* and only then perform them. The Rabbis instituted many blessings as expressions of praise, thanksgiving, and request in order to constantly remember the Creator." Maimonides groups the blessings that we recite before the performance of *mitzvot* with the blessings that we recite before we eat, and he understands that all blessings are based upon the Biblical blessing of *Birkat HaMazon.* How does *Birkat HaMazon* serve as the conceptual source for the blessings recited before performing a *mitzva*? Based on what we have explained, it is because fundamentally all blessings are statements of God's authority. With *birkot hanehenin* we recognize His dominion over the natural order, and with *birkot hamitzvot* we similarly declare His dominion over the moral order. Just as He is the creator of the physical world and its laws, so too is He the author of the moral norm and the legislator of all religious laws. As Maimonides says explicitly, the common denominator of all blessings is to remember and fear the Creator.

We can now dispel a common misconception. Many believe that to bless God means to praise Him, and in fact, the English translation of *berakha,* benediction, comes from the Latin root words *bene* and *diction,* meaning to speak well of or praise. However, this understanding is simply incorrect. In Genesis we read "God blessed man, saying, 'You shall be fruitful and multiply.'" God didn't praise man; He blessed him: He instilled in him the ability to multiply, a new source of goodness and fortune in his life. So too, Rav Ḥayyim Volozhiner (*Nefesh HaḤayyim* 2:2) and Rav Shneur Zalman of Liadi, the *Ba'al HaTanya (Torah Or, Parashat Ḥayyei Sarah),* both explain that the word "*barukh*" means expansion, and to bless God means to expand God's presence in this world. How can a mortal human being, a frail and finite creature, accomplish such a thing? The answer is that man has the unique ability to recognize and declare God's authority and mastery. By dispelling the mirage of nature's independence and declaring the true Creator, the influence of God's presence thereby increases in this world. Similarly, the *Sefer HaḤinnukh*

(*Mitzva* 430) writes in his discussion of *Birkat HaMazon* that when we say God is "blessed," we declare that all blessing and goodness flow from Him. The prayer that God should be blessed is a wish that all people should recognize God as the source of goodness. All blessings, like *Birkat HaMazon*, are meant to forestall the natural human arrogance that makes man forget God. Blessing God is not an act of thanksgiving, but an act of remembering God, of declaring Him the true master of our world and its fullness, which is the very essence of *Birkat HaMazon*.

### *"His Great and Holy Name"*

Finally, we can understand a cryptic phrase that Maimonides uses in the heading to *Hilkhot Berakhot*, where he writes that the Biblical obligation is "to bless the great (*gadol*) and holy (*kadosh*) name after we eat." What does Maimonides mean when he includes the divine discriptions "great and holy"? Maimonides is known for his precise language, and he should have simply written that we are obligated "to bless the name of God after we eat." Moreover, elsewhere Maimonides attaches different attributes to the name of God. For example, regarding the prohibition to erase the name of God he writes (*Hilkhot Yesodei HaTorah* 6:1) that "anyone who destroys one of the holy and pure names of God is lashed," and similarly, in another context he writes (*Hilkhot Yesodei HaTorah* 2:1) that "there is an imperative to love and fear the honored and exalted God." Maimonides wrote with extraordinary precision, and he was even more careful in his use of divine attributes, as is evident by his discussions in the *Guide for the Perplexed*. If he uses "the great and holy name" to describe God in the context of *Birkat HaMazon*, it is because these two descriptions capture the essence of the commandment. How is this the case?

To understand Maimonides' choice of words, we must first understand what we mean by describing God as "great." We find this divine description in the Bible in the following verse: "For the Lord your God is God of gods, and Lord of lords, a great God, a mighty, and a terrible, who favors no person, and takes no bribe" (Deut. 10:17). In this verse we see that God's greatness flows from His mastery, because He is the master of all other powers. Thus, to recognize God as great is to recognize Him as the authority of our lives, the master of our world. The appellation "holy" means that God is absolutely above and beyond all of creation,

that nothing in this world can be compared to Him. Thus, Maimonides defines the commandment of sanctifying God's name (*Kiddush Hashem*) as demonstrating our absolute commitment to God even to the point of loss of life – to publicize that we recognize no other authority and that no other person or force in the world could intimidate us to violate His will. It follows that when these two appellations are used together, the phrase "the great and holy God" means the God who is the absolute master and authority of all creation, totally unique and beyond all matters and powers of this world. It is in this sense that the prophet Ezekiel uses these descriptions when he writes that God declares that in the end of days, after the war of Gog and Magog, "I will make Myself great and holy, and I will make Myself known in the eyes of many nations, and they will know that I am the LORD." God will be great and holy when the whole world recognizes His dominion, that He is master of the world. The *Tur* (*Oraḥ Ḥayyim* 56) writes that the opening phrase of Kaddish, "Let His name be made great and holy" ("*yitgadel ve'yitkadesh*"), is based on this verse in Ezekiel, and he explains that Kaddish is a prayer for that time when all nations will ultimately recognize the authority and kingship of the one true God.

In defining the Biblical commandment as "to bless the great and holy name after eating," Maimonides underscores that by reciting *Birkat HaMazon* we acknowledge God's mastery of the world, and that He is the provider for the food we have just eaten, or as Benjamin the Shepherd put it, "Blessed is the Merciful One, Master of this bread." The *mitzva* of *Birkat HaMazon* is not to praise or offer thanksgiving, but to remove from our hearts the arrogance of material success that leads man to forget God and to declare "my strength and the might of my hand produced this wealth" (Deut. 8:17). By reciting a blessing after we eat and are full and satiated, we affirm that God is the source of our sustenance, of life, and of existence itself. The purpose of the blessing is to declare, as the whole world will in the end of days, that He is the one true "great and holy God."

## THE *ZIMMUN*: EATING TOGETHER, BLESSING GOD AS A COMMUNITY*

When three people eat together, they are obligated to recite the *zimmun*, a special introduction to *Birkat HaMazon* in which the leader calls the rest of the group to join in blessing "the One from whose food we have eaten." The presence of three people, though, creates not only the forum for an introductory call and response, but also fundamentally alters the nature of the *Birkat HaMazon* itself. The Talmud (*Berakhot* 45a) derives the concept of *zimmun* from the verse, "Declare with me that the LORD is great, and let us exalt His name together" (Ps. 34:4). While the text of the *Birkat HaMazon* doesn't change, the group recites the blessings from a new perspective – not as individuals, but as an assembly gathered "to exalt His name together," a philosophically and experientially different performance. A more sophisticated understanding of the communal nature of the *zimmun* will lead us to an appreciation of the Torah's perspective on eating in general and how man redeems and sanctifies his meals. Through the *zimmun* and the ideals it represents, the Torah transforms eating from a selfish, self-gratifying act into an exalted service that unites man, his fellow, and God.

### *The Definition of Davar ShebiKedusha*

In truth, the introductory call of the *zimmun* can be subsumed under a more basic halakhic concept, that of *devarim shebikedusha*, those passages

* This essay is based on a *yahrzeit* lecture published in *Shiurim LeZekher Abba Mari*, vol. 2, pp. 91–115, a *shiur* delivered in Boston in 1961, *Reshimot Shiurim, Berakhot*, pp. 278–281, and the opening essay in *Festival of Freedom*, especially pp. 4–6, 18–21.

of our liturgy referred to as "holy matters." Thus, before we can understand the *zimmun* we must first understand the concept of *devarim shebikedusha*. The Talmud (*Megilla* 23b) explains that the liturgical concept of the *davar shebikedusha* is based upon the verse "And I will be hallowed amongst the children of Israel" (Lev. 22:32). However, elsewhere (*Sanhedrin* 74a) the Talmud derives from the same verse the obligation of *Kiddush Hashem*, sanctifying God's name, even to the point of giving up one's life to uphold the Torah in public. The Talmud derives both of these concepts from the same verse because at their core they express the same idea. Maimonides (*Sefer HaMitzvot, Aseh* 9) explains that the *mitzva* of *Kiddush Hashem* is to remain firm in our belief and not break from the pressure and threats of others, to demonstrate to the world that we recognize no authority other than God even at the cost of life. It is the ultimate public act of *kabbalat ol malkhut shamayim*, declaring our absolute acceptance of and allegiance to the authority of God. This also clarifies the concept of *davar shebikedusha* in the context of prayer: The *davar shebikedusha* is a communal, public act of *kabbalat ol malkhut shamayim*, accepting the yoke of God's kingship and declaring His mastery.

While a person can accept upon himself the yoke of heaven as an individual, such as by reciting *keriat shema*, there is an added dimension when a group recognizes the kingship of God as a congregation. Only in the context of an assembly of people is the act of *kabbalat ol malkhut shamayim* transformed into a *davar shebikedusha*; this is why we require a *minyan* to recite a *davar shebikedusha* in prayer. In contrast, with regard to praising or thanking God, we find no distinction between the act of an individual and of a group within *halakha*. A person can sing *Hallel* by himself without the presence of a *minyan*. However, when it comes to recognizing God's kingship and accepting the yoke of heaven, the fulfillment is qualitatively greater when a person declares his allegiance to God's exclusive authority publicly, when his commitment is not private but known to all around him. For this reason, the *davar shebikedusha* requires a public forum, and in the context of *tefilla*, this means a *minyan*.

### *The Zimmun and the Ḥabura*

While a *minyan* creates the *davar shebikedusha* in the context of prayer, *zimmun* represents the *davar shebikedusha* in the context of the *Birkat*

*HaMazon. Zimmun* is not an expression of praise, but of a communal recognition of God's mastery. The leader calls out, "Let us bless God," and the others respond, "May God's name be blessed from now and forever." As explained in the previous essay, to bless God does not mean to praise Him, but rather to recognize His kingship and authority, and in so doing, to increase His presence in this world.

The *zimmun* shares another defining element of every *davar shebikedusha*: the dialogue of call and response. In *kedusha, barekhu,* and every other *davar shebikedusha,* the leader calls the others to bless or sanctify God's name, and they respond in turn. This fundamental aspect of a *davar shebikedusha* is based upon the prophet's description of the *kedusha* of the angels: "And one calls out to the other and says 'Holy, holy, holy is the LORD of hosts'" (Is. 6:3). In the blessings before *keriat shema,* we describe the heavenly scene in more detail: The angels "All accept on themselves, one from another, the yoke of of the kingdom of heaven, granting permission to one another to sanctify the One who formed them." The angels first call to each other, they ask of each other to join in their declaration of God's majesty, the other angels respond, and they all pronounce as a unified group that God is holy. Thus, the *zimmun* contains all of the necessary elements of a *davar shebikedusha.* It is a public declaration of God's mastery and kingship, initiated by a leader's call and actualized by the group's unified response.

In one detail, though, the *zimmun* does differ from the *davar shebikedusha* in prayer: We require a full *minyan* to recite *kedusha* or *barekhu,* but to form a *zimmun,* three people suffice. We can explain this discrepancy with a comment of *Tosafot* (*Berakhot* 49b s.v. *amar*) in a slightly different context. A *minyan,* a gathering of ten adult males, is necessary to create a *tzibbur,* an assembly, which provides the public character necessary for a *davar shebikedusha.* However, when it comes to a shared meal, even the conjunction of three people creates a sense of community. *Tosafot* explain that in the synagogue, people come and go, they enter and leave; thus, there is a weaker bond amongst the people, and, therefore, a larger group of ten is necessary to create a sense of *tzibbur.* However, when people eat together, there is a greater cohesiveness; there is a camaraderie and fellowship formed by people who sit down to enjoy a meal as a group. Therefore, in the context of eating, the *halakha* recognizes the

concept of the *ḥabura,* that a group of three can generate a communal blessing modeled after the *davar shebikedusha.*

## *The Collective Birkat HaMazon*

The *zimmun* doesn't end with the introductory call and response; it is not merely a flourish that the group adds before each of its individuals recites the *Birkat HaMazon* privately. Maimonides (*Hilkhot Berakhot* 5:2), in his ever clear and precise fashion, defines the concept of *zimmun* as follows: "What is the blessing of the *zimmun*? ... One of them blesses and says 'Let us bless the One from whose food we have eaten,' and they all respond 'Blessed is the One from whose food we have eaten, and by whose goodness we live'... [The leader] then recites [*Birkat HaMazon*] until he finishes the four blessings, and they respond *amen* after each blessing." There are, in fact, two components to the *zimmun*: first, the introductory call and response, and second, the collective recitation of the blessings. One person says them aloud, and the rest of the company listens quietly and answers *amen.** The practice (according to the original enactment) in which only the leader recites the *Birkat HaMazon* gets to the essence of the concept of *zimmun.* Across all areas of *halakha,* there are two models for the communal fulfillment of a *mitzva. Tefilla* is an example of this duality. In our communal prayers, the entire congregation recites the silent Amida simultaneously – thus, each person fulfills his individual obligation through his own recitation. This is *tefilla betzibbur,* individuals satisfying their private obligation together with others who are doing the same. The communal context is created by the act of many discrete individuals. However, when the *ḥazzan* repeats the Amida aloud, it is a fundamentally different performance. While

* According to the original enactment of *zimmun,* which is its optimal fulfillment, only the leader recites *Birkat HaMazon.* Even if the others at the meal know how to recite the blessings themselves, they do not. The *Shulḥan Arukh* (*Oraḥ Ḥayyim* 183:7), based upon earlier sources, rules that today it is proper for each person at the meal to recite *Birkat HaMazon* quietly along with the leader. However, this is a compromise based on the reality that people will not focus on the leader's recitation. Even today the leader of the *zimmun* should recite the four blessings of *Birkat HaMazon* aloud so that everyone can hear him, as was the original enactment.

only the *ḥazzan* actually recites the prayer, the fulfillment relates to the entire congregation; it is *tefillat* **hatzibbur**, a prayer offered on behalf of the congregation as a whole, the indivisible, metaphysical entity which is more than the collection of individuals. The Rabbis modeled the *ḥazzan*'s repetition on the offering of the communal sacrifices in the Temple. While only one priest slaughtered and sacrificed the animal, he represented the entire congregation of Israel. Similarly, the *ḥazzan* stands in the place of his congregation, and offers one communal prayer on its behalf.

The *zimmun* parallels *tefillat hatzibbur*: it is not the simultaneous recitation of *Birkat HaMazon* by three individuals, but rather, one *Birkat HaMazon* offered on behalf of the integrated *ḥabura*. This is a new concept based on the verse "Let us exalt His name together." The halakhic construct of *zimmun* revolves around the assembly as a whole, what the Rabbis called the *ḥabura*. Moreover, the people sharing the meal not only discharge their obligation as a group, but the obligation itself devolves upon the integrated group and not upon each individual separately. Therefore, the *Shulḥan Arukh* (*Oraḥ Ḥayyim* 197:3) rules that if two people eat bread and a third eats only fruits or vegetables, they must still form a *zimmun*. Even though this group lacks three individuals who are required to recite *Birkat HaMazon*, a *zimmun* is still viable; the *zimmun* doesn't need three separate individuals, but a group who shared a meal. Since a group of three people ate together, and the majority of the group ate bread, it is defined as a *ḥabura* who shared a meal over bread, and they thus can form a *zimmun*.

## *Listening and Responding*

Because the *zimmun* is not composed of the actions of individuals but the unified activity of a group, the method by which participants in the *zimmun* fulfill their obligation differs from other *mitzvot* as well. For example, when a person hears the reading of the *megilla* or the *shofar* blowing performed by another person, it is considered as though the listener performed the *mitzva* on his own, based on the concept of *shomei'a ke'oneh* (literally, "one who listens is considered to be like one who responds"). The concept of *shomei'a ke'oneh* applies to obligations that relate to the individual. Each person must blow the *shofar* or read the *megilla*;

however, he can either perform the *mitzva* himself or fulfill his duty by listening to another. However, as explained above, both the obligation and performance of the *zimmun* do not relate to the individuals separately but to the group as a whole. Therefore, the principle of *shomei'a ke'oneh* is neither necessary nor applicable to the *zimmun*. Instead, every member of the *zimmun* fulfills his obligation by belonging to the *ḥabura*, by participating in the single, communal recitation of the *Birkat HaMazon*. Practically, there is one leader and the others respond, but fundamentally the performance relates to all of them equally, as they are all equal members of the *ḥabura*.

This insight into the mechanism of the *zimmun* has practical applications as well. In cases where we apply *shomei'a ke'oneh*, Maimonides rules that merely listening with intent to the other's blessing suffices and responding *amen* is not required. However, in describing the collective *Birkat HaMazon* Maimonides writes that the leader recites the four blessings aloud and that all those listening "respond *amen* after each blessing." In the *zimmun*, the participants must not only listen to the leader's blessings, but must respond *amen* as well. To join the *ḥabura*, to integrate into the collective recitation, the participant cannot only passively listen, he must actively participate.

Maimonides (*Hilkhot Berakhot* 1:11) distinguishes between merely listening to a blessing and actively responding: "Anyone who hears a blessing from its beginning until its end and has intention to fulfill his obligation fulfills it even though he did not respond *amen*. However, anyone who responds *amen* after the the blessing is as if he himself pronounced the blessing." Although the classical commentaries do not identify the source for Maimonides' ruling that responding *amen* surpasses merely listening to a blessing, it would seem that it is based on the following Talmudic passage (*Shevuot* 36a): "R. Yose b. Ḥanina said: '*Amen*' implies acceptance of words... as it is written (Deut. 27:26), 'Cursed is the one who does not maintain all the words of the Torah to do them. And all the people shall say, *amen*.'" The Talmud derives the power of responding *amen* from the instruction to pronounce the curses and blessings at Mount Gerizim and Mount Ebal. In that case, it was not necessary for each individual to recite the blessings and curses, and the *amen* of the people thus didn't serve as a vehicle of *shomei'a ke'oneh*. Rather, through

the response of *amen*, the people joined the Levites in the communal acceptance of their responsibilities. This was a covenant forged between God and the community of Israel as a whole. Through the declaration of the blessings and curses by the Levites and by the response of the Israelites, the nation accepted God's law as a congregation.

Similarly, whenever there is a halakhic institution that necessitates individuals to act as a congregation and not as a collection of individuals, the response of *amen* is indispensable. This then is why Maimonides writes that the participants in the *zimmun* must not only listen to the leader's *Birkat HaMazon*, but they must respond *amen* after his blessings. Even today, when we all read the *Birkat HaMazon* quietly, the leader must recite his blessings aloud, and the others must respond *amen*. Without this interaction, we are left with a collection of individuals simultaneously reciting the same blessings, not a unified *ḥabura* offering a collective blessing to God in fulfillment of the verse "We shall exalt His name together."

### *A Meal of Ḥessed*

From a philosophical perspective, the institution of the *zimmun* encapsulates the *halakha*'s approach to the meal and eating in general. The fundamental problem which assailed the minds of our sages is that the drive for food and nourishment is a biological one, shared by man and animal alike. There is nothing uniquely human or meaningful in consuming food; it is instinctual, coerced and mechanical. Indeed, many Greek philosophers reached the conclusion that eating is a disgraceful necessity, a sensual, carnal pleasure that satisfies the beast in man. Thus, according to legend, many wise men shied away from eating in public, as they were embarrassed to be seen eating. Judaism is also concerned with this same problem, but it arrives at an entirely different conclusion. While the physical process might be identical, we believe that man can elevate eating into a uniquely human, meaningful act. *Halakha* has formulated many rules around the meal, especially the *Birkat HaMazon* and *zimmun*, and has transformed eating into the halakhic institution of the *se'uda*. It is neither an ordinary meal nor a feast; it is the crucible in which the bread of man is transposed into the bread of God. It expresses the fellowship between God and man and the participation of God in all human pursuits and activities.

When man is engaged in a carnal pursuit such as eating, and his own need presses the most, insisting upon immediate satisfaction, the Torah expects of him attentiveness to the need of the other self. The meal is turned into an occasion for the practice of *ḥessed*. The opening of the Haggada includes the invitation "Let all who are hungry come and eat," but the source of this phrase is not connected to Passover at all. The Talmud (*Ta'anit* 20a) recounts that whenever Rav Huna would eat a meal he would first open the doors to his home and invite anyone in need to join him, using the same phrase. Similarly, in a celebrated passage, Maimonides writes that on holidays we are "obligated to feed the convert, orphan, and widow along with the other downtrodden poor. However, someone who locks the doors to his courtyard and eats and drinks, alone with his children and his wife, and doesn't feed the poor and depressed – this is not the joy of a *mitzva*, but the rejoicing of his belly… and such a rejoicing is a disgrace" (*Hilkhot Yom Tov* 6:18). On holidays, there is a particular responsibility to think of others and share; when we eat a sumptuous meal and rejoice, there is an added duty to invite others. However, fundamentally, this is our perspective every day. Ideally, every meal should include *ḥessed*. Man should not eat alone, for the food does not belong to him; he eats from the hand of God and thus he must share with others. With this perspective, man no longer eats like a beast in the field who knows only of his own appetite. When he shares his food with others, he transforms his meal into a performance of *ḥessed* and finds God in the experience.

### *"You Shall Rejoice Before the Lord, Your God"*

Moreover, the *halakha* also recognizes that a shared meal unites people, fosters friendships, and takes man out of seclusion and loneliness in order to join the "thou." While the beast drags his prey back to his lair to devour it alone, man can choose to eat as part of a community. The host invites the destitute to share his material possessions, but he also invites the lonely and abandoned who crave companionship. He opens up his mind and heart and invites others to join him. The invitation to share a meal expresses the sense of responsibility and sympathy that he feels towards his fellow. He doesn't only think of himself, and he is not driven by his biological impulses alone. He wishes to enjoy the food given to

him by the Almighty with others. Ideally, from such a *se'uda* of *ḥessed* a new community arises, one in which there is no division between host and guest, master and servant, generous philanthropist and embarrassed recipient. Everyone eats together, before the LORD. The meal is transformed into an exalted service, and their shared eating is redeemed. It is not primitive or beastly, but sanctified, a wholly human, even spiritual, experience.

In other words, the Torah doesn't tell man to hide when he eats, but rather to redeem eating by sharing his food as part of a *ḥessed*-thinking community before the LORD. This is the vision that the Torah (Deut. 12: 7, 12) sets forth: "And you shall eat there before the LORD your God… and you shall rejoice before the LORD your God, you, your sons and your daughters, your slaves and your maidservants, and the Levite in your gates for he has no portion or heritage amongst you." To the ancient Greeks the concept of "eating before God" would have been unthinkable. How can man unite with God through such an unrefined, temporal act? Yet, the Torah and *halakha* maintain that man can eat in the presence of the LORD. When man recognizes the *ḥessed* of God who sustains him, his eating ceases to be a mechanical act and becomes a great service in which he stands in reverence and awe before his Maker. When he shares his abundant blessings with his neighbor, the host's act of *ḥessed* merges with the *ḥessed* of God, and the meal becomes a divine-human affair. Finally, the meal pulls man out of his self-centered state of mind and creates a community of equals, a fellowship of the God-committed and God-seekers.

The ceremony of the *zimmun* is the halakhic institution that gives expression to this philosophy, that man can invite others to his table and eat before his LORD. The Torah instructs us to share God's physical and spiritual blessings in order to create a community, but that community doesn't cease when the meal concludes. Before the participants depart and go on their separate ways, the assembly performs one last act together, they turn to bless God. They do so not as individuals, but as a fellowship that doesn't know the distinction of host and guest or rich and poor. In their *ḥessed* community there is a union between God and man and man and his fellow. First, the participants of the meal eat together and share the blessings that God has bestowed upon them, and, second, they conclude

their meal by offering a joint blessing of *Birkat HaMazon*. Their blessing surpasses the blessing that a single person can offer, no matter how heartfelt, for theirs is the blessing of a congregation, a *davar shebikedusha* offered by a *ḥabura*, the ultimate expression of a *ḥessed* fellowship rejoicing before the Lord, their God.

# THE MITZVA OF KIDDUSH: TO SANCTIFY, TO PRAISE, TO REDEEM*

The *mitzva* of Kiddush, all agree, is a Biblical obligation. The Rabbis (*Pesaḥim* 106a; *Mekhilta* on Ex. 20:8) derived this imperative from the fourth of the Ten Commandments: "Remember the day of the Sabbath to sanctify it" (Ex. 20:8). This seemingly straightforward command, though, contains within it a complex, multi-dimensional *mitzva*. Thus, to properly understand Kiddush, as is the case for many *halakhot*, we must isolate each of its distinct components and analyze each one separately. Only when we understand each of its elements and themes independently can we appreciate the *mitzva* as an organic whole and perceive the totality of its beauty and depth.

## *An Act of Sanctification*

First, there is a fundamental question that we must ask regarding the very essence of the *mitzva* of Kiddush. Literally, the word Kiddush means sanctification, implying that with its recitation we sanctify the day of Shabbat itself. According to Maimonides (*Hilkhot Shabbat* 29:1), the *mitzva* is "to sanctify the day of the Sabbath with words, as it says, 'Remember the day of the Sabbath to sanctify it.' This means to remember it by utterance of sanctification and praise." Naḥmanides (Commentary, Ex. 20:8) takes the idea of sanctification further, comparing Kiddush to the sanctification of the *Yovel* year. According to Naḥmanides, just as the court sanctifies the *Yovel* by its declaration of *mekudash*, we sanctify Shabbat as well through the proclamation of Kiddush.

* This essay is based on three *yahrzeit* lectures that analyzed different aspects of Kiddush published in *Shiurim LeZekher Abba Mari*, vol. 2, pp. 116–165.

However, the notion that we sanctify the day of Shabbat through Kiddush would seem to contradict a fundamental distinction between the sanctity of Shabbat and that of Yom Tov. The Jewish people, through its jurisdiction over the calendar, establishes the beginning of each new month, and thus the dates of the holidays. Shabbat, though, exists independently of man's actions; when the sun sets on Friday afternoon, the holiness of Shabbat fills the world even if no one comes to greet it. The source of *kedushat Shabbat* resides not within man, but with God, who by resting on the seventh day of creation sanctified every Shabbat of the future: "And God blessed the seventh day and sanctified it" (Gen. 2:3). For this reason, the Kiddush of Yom Tov concludes with the phrase, "Blessed are You, LORD, who sanctifies Israel and the Festivals," whereas on Shabbat, it concludes, "Blessed are You, LORD, who sanctifies the Sabbath," without mention of Israel. The Talmud (*Pesaḥim* 117b; *Beitza* 17a) explains that unlike the sanctity of Yom Tov, the sanctity of Shabbat stands independently of the Jewish people. How then can Naḥmanides compare the recitation of Kiddush on Shabbat to the declaration of the *Yovel* year, when the sanctification of the *Yovel* year is effected precisely through the human court's declaration, unlike the sanctity of Shabbat?

To resolve this problem, we must conclude that while the holiness of Shabbat indeed exists independently of man, there is also a second element to the sanctity of Shabbat which man endows. This second aspect of *kedushat Shabbat* is implicit in the Torah's list of the yearly cycle of holidays, in which Shabbat is recorded as first in the list of holy times, *mo'adei Hashem* (Lev. 23:3). Shabbat too is one of the *mo'adei Hashem*, and like the other festivals "which you shall declare," it must be sanctified by man. This duality also expresses itself in the disparity between the reasons given for Shabbat in the two versions of the Ten Commandments. In the first version, in Exodus, we read: "For God made the heavens and earth in six days…and He rested on the seventh day" (Ex. 20:10–11). Here, the sanctity of Shabbat flows directly from God, and from His rest on the seventh day of creation. However, in the second rendering of the Ten Commandments, in Deuteronomy, instead of observing Shabbat to commemorate creation, we are bidden to observe the Sabbath to "remember that you were a slave in the Land of Egypt, and the LORD your God

redeemed you" (Deut. 5:14). In this version, Shabbat commemorates the Exodus, as do the rest of the holidays on the Jewish calendar. While the primary holiness of Shabbat is created by God, there is an added element of Shabbat, as one of the *mo'adei Hashem*, which must be instilled by man.

In other words, if man does not actively sanctify the day, if his Shabbat observance is only passive, he cannot experience the totality of its holiness. While the basic level of *kedushat Shabbat* commences on its own with the sun's descent on Shabbat eve, only man's declaration of Kiddush can create the additional element of holiness. Just as the sanctity of the *Yovel* year necessitates the declaration of the court, the day of Shabbat is infused with its full holiness only though the initiative of man. This idea that man contributes to the sanctity of Shabbat is the basis for the concept of *tosefet Shabbat*, that one can begin Shabbat before sunset and create *kedushat Shabbat* before its designated time. If God alone would have the ability to sanctify Shabbat, if man would have no role in investing the day of its holiness, then *tosefet Shabbat* would be impossible. Only because man has a part in the endowment of sanctification does he also have the ability to alter when Shabbat begins and to invest holiness into otherwise mundane time.

Moreover, according to the Talmud (*Berakhot* 33b), there are two components to the *mitzva* of Kiddush, of instilling this added dimension of holiness into the day. First, the central *berakha* of the Amida of Shabbat eve, the *berakha* of *kedushat hayom*, constitutes a Kiddush. Then we again recite Kiddush as a blessing over wine before eating. These two recitations, though, are not a mere duplication, but rather represent two different acts of sanctification, corresponding to the two elements of *kedushat Shabbat*. The recitation of the Kiddush in the Amida ushers in the holiness of the day which generates the prohibition to perform work. It celebrates Shabbat as a day of rest, beginning with the phrase, "May You find favor in our rest," and concluding, "so that Israel... may find rest on it." This first Kiddush is connected to the passive aspect of Shabbat observance, the imperative of *Shamor*, to guard the day by abstaining from prohibited activity. However, the Kiddush that we recite over a cup of wine at our meal relates not to the restrictions of *Shamor*, but to the commandment of *Zakhor*, to actively affirm the sanctity of the day. This is accomplished though the *mitzvot* of *kibud* and *oneg*, honoring and

enjoying Shabbat. This Kiddush ushers in the aspect of the day's sanctity which obligates us to partake in *se'udot* to celebrate the grandeur and beauty of Shabbat.

## *An Expression of Praise*

Kiddush, though, is not only an act of sanctification which infuses a new level of sanctity into the day. Maimonides, we saw, writes that the *mitzva* of Kiddush is to recite words of "sanctification and praise." Similarly, in *Sefer HaMitzvot* (*Aseh* 155), Maimonides writes: "We are commanded to sanctify the Shabbat ... to remember the greatness of the day, its elevated status, and its uniqueness as compared to all other days." There are thus two aspects to Kiddush: first, to invest holiness into the day, and second, to extol the day and its elevated status. Specifically, we declare Shabbat as the day on which God rested, and which, by His rest, He sanctified and blessed for all eternity. As we recite in the *birkot keriat shema* of Shabbat morning: "This is the praise of the seventh day, for on it God rested from all of His work." We praise the day of Shabbat by proclaiming it as the day God chose for an eternal testimony to His creation and His sovereignty.

This aspect of the *mitzva*, the imperative to praise the day of Shabbat, allows us to understand the nature of the Kiddush that we recite on Shabbat day, before the second Shabbat meal, and how it differs from the Kiddush of Shabbat evening. The evening Kiddush, with which one fulfills the Biblical obligation, contains both components of the *mitzva*, sanctifying Shabbat, and extolling the day. However, the daytime Kiddush, which is a Rabbinic enactment, fulfills only the second aspect of the *mitzva*, praising Shabbat. The evening Kiddush invests holiness in the entire day, making another act of sanctification unnecessary and, in fact, impossible. However, while sanctification cannot be performed twice, praise can be recited more than once. Thus, the second recitation of Kiddush fulfills the obligation to declare the unique stature of Shabbat. We do not repeat the blessing of "*mekadesh HaShabbat*" during the daytime Kiddush, because it is not an act of sanctification.

Indeed, the minimum text of the daytime Kiddush is nothing more than the blessing of "*borei peri hagafen*." However, we must ask: how can this simple blessing fulfill the *mitzva* of Kiddush? Rashbam (*Pesaḥim* 106a, s.v. *amar*) cites R. Ahai Gaon, author of the *She'iltot*, who explains

the nature of this Kiddush as follows: "One brings a cup of wine, makes a blessing, and drinks in honor of Shabbat, to distinguish between the attribute of Shabbat and of the weekdays. It is a form of song (*shir*), for we only recite song over wine (*ein omrim shirah ela al hayayin*)." In other words, the blessing of "*borei peri hagafen*," as we explained, is not an act of sanctification, but rather an expression of song, praise for the day and its uniqueness among the days of the week. In this context, "*borei peri hagafen*" is not simply a *birkat hanehenin*, a blessing required before we partake of food, but a declaration in honor of Shabbat. It is praise of the Creator, but also a song for Shabbat, the ongoing testimony to His creation. On Shabbat we feel God's majesty and kingship as Creator more intensely than on any other day. To express these feelings and mark the greatness of the day, we take a cup of wine and pronounce, "Blessed is the LORD, our God, King of the Universe, who creates the fruit of the vine."

### *A Process of Redemption and Elevation*

There is yet still another important dimension to Kiddush, which underlies its relationship to the Shabbat meals. All week long we acknowledge that God is the Creator of everything and thus possesses ownership over the entire world. "The earth is the LORD's and all it contains, the world and all who live in it" (Ps. 24:1). On the basis of this verse, the Talmud (*Berakhot* 35a) declares that one who derives benefit from this world without a blessing has performed an act of "*me'ila*," meaning, theft of an item dedicated to the Temple. In other words, every apple, each loaf of bread, every glass of wine belongs to God, and it is the blessing which serves as the *matir*, the act which allows us to derive benefit from it. As the Talmud Yerushalmi (*Berakhot* 6:1) puts it: "The entire world is like a [holy] vineyard. How is it redeemed? With a blessing." The blessing that we recite before we eat food redeems the item from its consecrated status, which is akin to redeeming an item from the Temple's holdings. The entire week we see God as the Creator of the universe, and thus, as the true owner of everything. To enjoy His world without desecrating it, we must redeem it through a blessing, an affirmation that God is the Creator of all.

On Shabbat, though, we experience the world differently. We perceive God not just as the Creator of the universe, but also as the One who

completed it and brought it to perfection through His rest on Shabbat. The Midrash (*Bereishit Rabba* 10) compares the newly formed world after the first six days of creation to an ornate wedding canopy without a bride. When God rested on the seventh day, He escorted the bride into this world, completing and elevating the rest of creation. Thus on Shabbat, we sense God's kingship and claim over this world more profoundly, for He is both the One who fashioned it during the six days of creation and the One who perfected it on the seventh day. It follows that on Shabbat, the world is doubly consecrated to God: "God blessed the seventh day and declared it holy" (Gen. 2:3). God's property rights are doubled on Shabbat. He owns the world because He created it, and He reacquires the world on Shabbat because the world was finished on that day. Therefore, His property rights on the Sabbath are more strict and rigid than those He exercises on an ordinary day.

During the week, a regular blessing can redeem food from its consecrated status and render its consumption permissible; on Shabbat, however, we need an additional "*matir*" to permit the food, because of its additional sanctity. Kiddush serves as the "*matir*" which gives us license to partake of Shabbat meals. We declare in the Kiddush of Shabbat eve, "in love and favor, He gave us His holy Sabbath as a heritage." With the recitation of Kiddush, God gives us His Shabbat; He allows us to enjoy His creation that was completed on the seventh day.

There is, however, a fundamental difference between the "*matir*" of the regular blessing during the week and the "*matir*" of Kiddush on Shabbat. A simple blessing "redeems" the item, as the Talmud Yerushalmi defines it, allowing it to be used for the human purposes of nourishment and enjoyment. This act of redemption takes the item from the world of the sacred into the world of the mundane. Kiddush on Shabbat, though, does the reverse. By recalling that God blessed and sanctified the day of Shabbat, we do not remove the sanctity of the food, but rather elevate our meal to the status of *se'udat Shabbat*. Our meal becomes a fulfillment of the *mitzva* of *oneg Shabbat*, and is thus no longer a desecration of the food's holiness but, on the contrary, a fulfillment of it. During the week, we can enjoy the world only by removing its holiness; on Shabbat, our food remains consecrated to God, but we may partake of it within the framework of Kiddush and the *se'udat Shabbat*. We recite Kiddush to distinguish between our

mundane eating during the week and the holy meals of Shabbat which fulfill the prophet's call to "declare Shabbat a delight."

This background explains the concept of *Kiddush bimekom se'uda,* the requirement that Kiddush be recited in conjunction with a meal. Part of the essential nature of Kiddush is to usher in the sanctity of the day that creates the obligation of *oneg Shabbat,* and to establish the Shabbat meals as a fulfillment of *oneg Shabbat.* Only through the redemption, the "*matir,*" of Kiddush can we enjoy God's food without desecrating its elevated Shabbat sanctity. While a Shabbat meal without the anchor of Kiddush is not complete, the converse is true as well; a recitation of Kiddush which is not connected to a *se'uda* is itself deficient, as it doesn't fulfill one of its central purposes, to establish a meal as a *se'udat Shabbat.* The requirements of Kiddush and *se'uda* are not distinct obligations; each one needs the other, as they are intertwined in one complementary fulfillment.

The connection to the meal also adds significance to the cup of wine and the *borei peri hagafen* blessing as part of Kiddush. *Magen Avraham* (*Oraḥ Ḥayyim* 296:2) rules that if one hears only the blessing of Havdala (*hamavdil bein kodesh leḥol*), but not the opening blessing of *borei peri hagafen,* he nonetheless has fulfilled his obligation, because hearing the blessing over the wine is not crucial to the fulfillment of Havdala. However, Rav Ḥayyim Soloveitchik ruled that this is only true regarding Havdala, which is an example of a *kos shel berakha,* a blessing recited over a cup of wine to grant it greater significance. For such recitations, the cup of wine and its blessing enhances the *mitzva,* but if someone did not hear the *borei pri hagafen,* it is not crucial. However, in the case of Kiddush, the blessing of *borei peri hagafen* is an integral and indispensable part. If one doesn't hear the *borei peri hagafen,* he has not fulfilled his obligation at all and must recite the entire Kiddush again. Kiddush must establish the meal as a *se'udat Shabbat* and elevate it to a *mitzva.* Without the cup of wine, the recitation alone would not be integrated into the meal. The cup of wine doesn't merely extend significance to the blessing, as in other *kosot shel berakha;* it is the vehicle through which the Kiddush fulfills its function of establishing the Shabbat meal.

Not only is the blessing of *borei peri hagafen* a crucial part of the Kiddush, but drinking the wine is itself part of the *mitzva.* Maimonides (*Hilkhot Shabbat* 27:9) stresses that when one makes Kiddush he must

drink from the cup, a point that he doesn't make, for example, when he describes the laws of Havdala. Similarly, the *Shulḥan Arukh* (*Oraḥ Ḥayyim* 271:14) cites the opinion of the Geonim that though in the case of other blessings one of the listeners may drink the wine, in the case of Kiddush, the one reciting the blessing must drink the cup himself. For other blessings, we require someone to drink the wine merely so that the blessing of *borei peri hagafen* has not been said in vain, but for Kiddush, the requirement to drink the wine is an intrinsic part of the *mitzva*. Drinking the wine connects the blessings to the meal and elevates the meal to be a holy one, in honor of Shabbat, which is one of the purposes of Kiddush.

In sum, the recitation of Kiddush constitutes three distinct fulfillments. First, it is an act of sanctification, infusing into the day an aspect of holiness that would not exist without man's initiative. Second, it is an expression of praise for Shabbat, extolling its uniqueness as the eternal testimony to the Creator who rested on the seventh day. Finally, Kiddush establishes the meal as a *se'udat Shabbat* and sanctifies our eating to be a fulfillment of *oneg Shabbat*, which permits us to partake of and enjoy the food despite its added holiness.